ISBN 978-1-334-25050-7
PIBN 10235578

1 MONTH OF
FREE
READING

at

www.ForgottenBooks.com

By purchasing this book you are
eligible for one month membership to
ForgottenBooks.com, giving you
unlimited access to our entire
collection of over 700,000 titles via
our web site and mobile apps.

To claim your free month visit:

www.forgottenbooks.com/free235578

MEMOIR

OF THE

N SCUDDER, M.D.,

B. WATERBURY, D.D.

BROTHERS, PUBLISHERS.

1870.

MEMOIR

OF THE

Rev. JOHN SCUDDER, M.D.,

THIRTY-SIX YEARS MISSIONARY IN INDIA.

BY

Rev. J. B. WATERBURY, D.D.

NEW YORK:

HARPER & BROTHERS, PUBLISHERS,

FRANKLIN SQUARE.

1870.

PREFACE.

WHEN Dr. Scudder rested from his labors, there was a wish expressed, on the part of those who knew him and appreciated his high qualities as a Christian missionary, that a memoir should be given to the public. After years of delay—owing to providential circumstances—the attempt has been made, with what success the reader will of course decide for himself.

The materials for such a work were abundant; but they were scattered here and there, and some parts of his private journal were entirely lost. It has been the compiler's object to select from a very large correspondence and a somewhat extended diary only those facts which would reveal most forcibly the character of the man, and act with salutary effect on the heart of the reader.

One advantage which this Memoir has over other biographies of missionaries consists in the fact that Dr. Scudder's labors were spread over an immense territory. Like the Apostle Paul, he was ever in motion—a great missionary evangelist—penetrating the interior of heathendom, and preaching the Gospel to princes and to the people.

His skill as a surgeon, too, was the key, in many instances, to his success as a preacher. A man who could open the eyes of the blind inspired a reverence far greater than one who appeared simply as a Christian teacher. His twofold profession gave him great power.

It is hoped that this small tribute to his memory—imperfect in many respects as it must be—will serve to keep alive the remembrance of one whose self-denial and self-consecration in the holiest of causes have never in modern times been exceeded, and but seldom equaled. An example like this can not fail to act favorably on the Christian Church, in keeping alive what missionary spirit now exists, and in deepening the sense of obligation to obey our Lord's last command, " Go ye into all the world, and preach the Gospel to every creature."

J. B. WATERBURY.

CONTENTS.

CHAPTER IV.

CHAPTER V.

CHAPTER VI.

CHAPTER VII.

CHAPTER VIII.

CHAPTER XIV.

CHAPTER XV.

CHAPTER XVI.

A 2

MEMOIR

OF

THE REV. JOHN SCUDDER, M.D.

CHAPTER I.

Childhood.—College .Life.—Studies Medicine.—Acknowledges God.—
Beginning of his Domestic Life.—Twofold Profession.—Church Relations.

THE subject of this memoir was a native of Freehold,
Monmouth County, New Jersey. The date of his birth
was Sept. 3, 1793. His father and mother were Joseph
and Maria Scudder. The father was a lawyer of repute,
a gentleman of the old school, and his mother was a lady
of high culture, winning manners, and exalted piety.
Mrs. Scudder was connected with the Johnstons of Revolutionary memory. Her father was colonel of the First
New Jersey regiment in our Revolutionary War, and fell
at the battle of Long Island while bravely storming a
strong position of the enemy.*

* "His death," says one acquainted with the circumstances, "was sincerely lamented by all who knew him, not only as a great private but public loss, the more so as he fell à sacrifice to obstinacy. General Sullivan
commanded that day, and directed Colonel Johnston to take the position.
Colonel Johnston, having served in the French War under Sir William
Johnston, and understanding his profession well, suggested to Gen. S. the
impracticability of the enterprise. Sullivan, in anger, replied, 'Sir, it is
your place to obey, not to dictate or expostulate.' 'Sir,' retorted Colonel

This son John was dedicated in his infancy to God, and, by his mother's testimony—corroborated in after life by himself—was like Samuel, a child of God from his birth. The mother stated that she never knew when he was converted, "for he seemed always to be possessed with the Christian temper." Such cases are not common, but who will say they are not possible?

CHILDHOOD.

Probably this spiritual born, or twice-born child, discovered little in his early development to distinguish him from other amiable and obedient children. There was always with him a conscientious regard to truth, and an affectionate compliance with the parental wishes. Still it must be supposed that he played and sported, and in every respect acted like other children. It is probable, also, that occasionally he was surprised into delinquencies common to impetuous youth; but when his fault was pointed out to him, he expressed his sorrow and made resolutions of amendment. This would not be inconsistent with the declaration of his mother—"that she scarcely knew when he was converted; he was always good."

One trait, however, characteristic of the man, was developed in the boy—a spirit of benevolence and self-sacrifice. "My brother John," writes his sister, "manifested a very devotional spirit from boyhood upward; also a benevolent gift was in him. He would run about the

Johnston, 'I will convince you that I can and will obey; but it will be at the sacrifice of my own life, and that of all the brave band I have the honor to command.' The prophecy proved but too true; but one man escaped out of all the number. That man was Captain Grey, who related the event to my mother with tears."

streets and highways of Freehold and gather sticks to kindle the fires of the destitute. The little fellow was one day drawing a very heavy rail. A person called out, 'John, what are you going to do with that?' 'I am taking it to Miss Becky, who has no fire.' The person alluded to was poor and infirm.

"There was a man who lived near us addicted to strong drink—a bad man, driving his pious wife from her home at midnight, when she sought her father's house for shelter. John, who frequently went to him, said one day, 'Mr. C., why do they call you "Devil John?"' The wife was terrified, fearing he might hurt the child. She was a strict Episcopalian. My brother said to Mr. C., 'If you will throw away your bottle for forty days, I will keep Lent with your wife.' This agreement was verified—the performance was sure. It was the beginning of better days with this man. He abstained totally, lived years after this, and professed Christ in the Presbyterian Church. My brother sent him a message from India as follows: 'I charge Mr. Conover to meet me in heaven,' which affected the old gentleman very much. He said John had great influence over him."

It might be supposed that a youth of such feelings and habits would scarcely have had any deep views of the heart's corruption, whereas we never knew a Christian who had a more overwhelming sense of his own depravity.

IN COLLEGE.

While in Princeton College, young Scudder was not only attentive to his duties as a scholar, but also as a

Christian. He was watching for opportunities to do good, and striving, in every possible way, to win his fellow-students over to the cause of Christ. The following letter is a noble testimony to his faithfulness. It seems to have been addressed to his father, and comes from one whose praise is in many of the churches.

"Wilmington, November 16, 1855.

"In compliance with your request, my venerable friend, I give you in writing what was a day or two since communicated to you orally, though I am sure it will appear differently; but please take 'the will for the deed.'

"I find, from the date of my diploma, I entered college in the spring of 1813,* some four months before your devoted son graduated. I shall ever regard that short acquaintance with such a youth as having an important influence over my whole course of life.

"It commenced in this wise. While sitting in a neighboring room with some classmates, a tall, pale young man came in. Being introduced to Mr. Scudder, his reply, according to custom, was, 'I'll be happy to see you at No. 47.' While he remained, which was but for a moment, there was a general stillness, and when he had gone one of our company remarked, 'That fellow is so religious one can hardly laugh in his presence.' A secret influence touched the heart of one in that company, and, unconscious of its cause as he then was, the thought instantly arose, 'I had far better keep company with such a person.'

"Returning to my lonely room, for I had not yet become acquainted with half a dozen in the place, this thought followed me—'There, now, you have one of the

* *The Princeton Gen. Catalogue gives the date as that of 1811; + his grad. in medicine*

right kind of associates in this building.' But for a while I had to battle with questions of this sort: Shall I at once stand face to face with a principle of right, or give in to the doctrine of expediency? Shall I associate with one who is viewed as singular, and consent before long to be called a hypocrite, a fanatic, or a social heretic, or shall I consent to be drawn into the ranks of an overwhelming majority?

"At last this conclusion was reached—'I will call on Scudder at once, and tell him why I came so soon.' Here was a starting-point for other things that quickly followed. I found him at his studies, and told him of my wish to form a religious acquaintanceship, though myself without religion. Quickly he rose, and grasped my hand with unlooked-for ardor, saying, 'That's right; stand by that; you'll never regret it.' When the twelve o'clock bell rang, J. S. was at my door, and proposed a walk. Our steps were directed into Craig's Woods, near where the railroad dépôt now is. His speech, I believe, was mainly on the great themes with which his heart was filled. In a retired spot we sat down on a log, and sang together 'When I can read my title clear,' and some other hymns. He then proposed kneeling in social prayer, and there, for the first time, with trepidation I made an awkward attempt at extemporary prayer. That open committal on the side of religious anxiety was a seed of moral reform planted by that beloved brother some forty years ago; but alas! how stunted has been its growth, and meagre its fruits!

"Other interviews of like kind were held in that grove, and soon after in several rooms in college, where social prayer was held in rotation. Through J. Scudder I was

introduced to Storrs, Belden, and Price. These were all
who were then known as religious out of one hundred
and twenty youths. Thus does destiny hang upon moments, and lay coiled in a passing event. Those words
of encouragement, given at a critical time, were like the
kiss of approbation given by his fond mother to little
Benjamin West at the sight of his rude drawing. It inspired hope, it fixed inclination, and stimulated to efforts.
Partly through the force of J. Scudder's persuasive influence, I was soon after induced to apply to the Rev. W.
Schenck, your son-in-law, and to his Session, for admission into his Church, and, with the Rev. T. H. Skinner,
D.D., was received.   Yours respectfully,
                     " Nicholas Patterson."

admitted Princeton Oct. 1811, (v Pr. Gen. Catalogue)

STUDIES MEDICINE.

His heart's desire was toward the sacred ministry, but
his father was opposed to this; and so, from a sense of
filial duty, he chose the profession of medicine, more
akin to the ministry than the legal profession, and fur-
nishing opportunities to do good to the soul while administering to the relief of the body.

Among the highest in the profession of medicine at
that time was the late Dr. David Hosack, of New York.
Young Scudder became his student. Here he formed a
friendship with several young men in the same pursuit,
among whom, as his most intimate associates, were the
late Rev. Dr. Ducachet, of Philadelphia, and Rev. Dr. B.
P. Aydelott, of Cincinnati, who survives him.

Scudder was an enthusiast in whatever he undertook.
He threw his whole soul into his profession, studied hard
under his great teacher, whom he admired, and whose

praises, professionally, he was accustomed to sound in what some would call extravagant language.

He fulfilled his course of study with Dr. Hosack, and graduated at the New York Medical College, having previously acted for a considerable period as resident physician of the Almshouse. His next most pressing consideration was where he should start in his practice. His friend, Dr. Aydelott, suggested the eastern section of the city, and offered to introduce him to a family where he would find an agreeable circle and a comfortable home.

ACKNOWLEDGING GOD IN ALL HIS WAYS.

Young Scudder was accustomed to "acknowledge God in all his ways," believing in the promise that, by so doing, "his paths would be directed." Never was there a person who evinced a more conscientious recognition of Divine Providence in every earthly vicissitude. Of course, in so important a matter as fixing his location as a physician, and establishing his home in a strange family, he made it a matter of earnest prayer. His resolution being taken, he became domiciled in his new abode, and busied himself in looking after practice. It came rapidly, as it usually will to one who is both prepared and expectant, and who is as vigilant to observe as he is ready to avail himself of opportunities. He had a peculiar knack in gaining confidence; and families who once employed him were so fascinated with his skill and his kind manners, that they seldom wished to exchange him for another. He thus anchored himself in the esteem of one family after another, so that soon he began to number his patrons with some degree of satisfaction.

Indeed, he even began to think he must have a family
and house of his own.

Dr. Scudder took a deep interest in the spiritual welfare of the family where he resided. It consisted of a
widow, with four daughters and two sons. Two of the
daughters were married, and two lived at home with
their mother and brothers. With favorable religious
antecedents, they still gave no evidence of the experience
of personal piety. This was a grief to one to whom religion was every thing, and whose meat and drink it was
to do the will of God. So he sets himself, with much
prayer and a careful improvement of opportunities, to
awaken their minds to the importance of that which to
him was " the one thing needful." His success outran
his faith. The eldest daughter at home, in whom, for
various reasons, he felt a peculiar interest, was the first
to show signs of contrition. She was lovely in person,
gentle in spirit, and attractive in her manners. How far
affection preceded faith, or how intimately they were
mingled in his efforts to draw her attention to the great
interests of her soul, we can not say. But we can hardly doubt that a deep personal attachment gave additional
impulse to the prayers and efforts which, under God, led
to her conversion. *That* being accomplished, the crown-
ing grace was added to the charms of nature.

The means resorted to for the accomplishment of this
great end were earnest prayer and occasional conversation. But, in addition to these, the doctor—whether judiciously or not—obtained a promise from her that she
would read a book which he would lend her. That book,

as every one acquainted with it must admit, "is strong meat rather than milk." It was the old Puritan work entitled "Boston's Fourfold State." And this, after all, was the chosen instrumentality. The arrow reached her heart, and she went to Him, who was himself pierced, in order to have it drawn. After sufficient time to test the reality of the change had elapsed, she gave her public testimony to her faith, and began her career for glory and immortality. This young Christian became afterward the wife of Dr. Scudder, shared in his labors and trials, and was to him as a guiding-star in the long pilgrimage of his eventful life. But for her he had often fainted; and it was by her superior judgment that, when he was in perplexity, the way and path of duty rose clear and well defined before him. *Her* name must necessarily be associated with *his*, and will often occur in the progress of this memorial.

Other members of the family engaged his attention with a view to their conversion, and ere long the mother, two of the daughters, and the younger son sat down together at the same communion board. We do not affirm that all these conversions were owing to the zeal and efforts of Dr. Scudder. A concurrence of affecting circumstances worked in unison with his Christian efforts to bring about the religious change in this family. The oldest brother, of noble character and dearly beloved, was drowned in mid ocean about this period. *His* death was as God's voice thundering in their consciences. A revival, also, of great power was going forward in the Church which they attended. These events were accessory, and influential, under God, in bringing this whole family to the foot of the Cross. Yet must we gratefully acknowledge the earnest prayers and faithful labors of Dr. S., who seized on these providences to deepen the religious convictions which the Spirit of God seemed now to have commenced.

10. The younger brother, compiler of these memoirs, then only sixteen, was deeply indebted to Dr. Scudder for his fraternal counsels, his affectionate interest, and his earnest prayers. Taking me by the hand, he warned me of danger, pointed out the path of duty, and acted as my spiritual Mentor in the earlier part of my religious experience. He was as an elder brother to me. We prayed and sang together. We visited together. We stood up in the meetings side by side, and testified of the grace of God. In his visitations to the sick often was I with him. We knelt together at the bedside of the invalid. It was a practical school wherein I learned to feel for the suffering, and to pray for the sick and dying.

It was at the evening prayer-meetings held in the chapel of the Rutgers Street Presbyterian Church—then enjoying the outpouring of the Spirit—that Dr. Scudder was in his element. Here his face shone, and his whole soul seemed to stereotype its strong emotions in his voice and features. His exhortations to the impenitent were as powerful as his encouragement to the young converts was sweet and cheering. He was the life of any meeting which he attended; and his pure brotherly affection flowed like oil on Aaron's garments, or fell gently like the dews on Mount Hermon. His heart overflowed with Christian love, and his charity was as large in regard to the faults of others as his condemnation was severe toward his own errors. The hours of sweet communion enjoyed together can never be forgotten. He was a man

of strong emotions, but they were sanctified emotions.
He was on the mount or in the vale—seldom midway.
If a cloud obscured his spiritual horizon, he must go to
prayer till the breath of heaven chased it away. He
never thought of being happy without the felt presence
of God. If *that* were for a season withdrawn, he was
like a child that had lost the father's hand in a crowded
street. He cried out long and loud for God. "Tell me
where I may find him" was the language of his soul.
And when he *did* find Him, you could hear the shout of
song go up from his closet, out of which when he came
you needed none to tell you that the light of God's countenance had risen upon him. The ups and downs in his
Christian pilgrimage were frequent, but the main tenor
of his experience was that of spiritual joy and sunshine.
Blessed man! who lived *on* God as well as *to* God.

TWOFOLD PROFESSION.

Dr. Scudder was minister and physician both. He
never neglected the physical wants of his patients; but
he kept his eye open, as the occasion offered, to pour in
the oil and wine upon the soul. Did he not, in this, walk
in the steps of his great Master? Yes, many a soul has
he met in heaven to whose conversion the sick-bed, under his prayers and counsels, became a spiritual Bethesda.

Sometimes these visits were of a harrowing nature.
Said he to the writer, at the close of one of the prayer-
meetings, "I want you to go with me and see a sick girl."
He led me up an alley into a poor-looking tenement, and
as we entered the room a deep groan issued from the
sufferer. She was beautiful even amid the paleness of
death. She turned her large black eyes upon me, and

they made me shudder. There was despair in them. Then, closing them, she uttered *such* a groan! It seemed to come from a consciously lost soul. The doctor took her hand, and spoke touchingly of Jesus. But oh! such a look as she gave when that name was uttered. It told us that to *her* that name was agony. "Pray for me, pray for me," she exclaimed; "I am lost—I am lost." So we knelt and prayed, weeping as we did it. In the midst of our prayers she would break forth, "Pray on! pray on!" "Don't stop." "Oh, I am lost—I am lost." Every heart trembled, and every eye was in tears. But we could pray no longer, for the spasms of death came, and, with one awful groan, she expired.

This beautiful young creature came into New York from the country to seek employment. She fell into the snares every where laid for the unwary. She went down fast, and such was her end as we have described.

These visits were not only professional, but merciful; and, in the records of eternity, it may be found that this young Christian physician accomplished no small part of his beneficent deeds ere he set sail for heathendom.

CHURCH RELATIONS.

While in New York Dr. Scudder was deeply concerned to find a preacher under whose ministry he could obtain spiritual food, and so be nourished up into higher degrees of strength in the divine life. He at length found such a one in the person of the Rev. Christian Bork, pastor of the Reformed Dutch Church in Franklin Street. He was an aged man, of German origin, having come to this country as a Hessian soldier during Revolutionary times. His conversion took place under the preaching of the Rev. Dr. Livingstone. He could not get into the barn where the doctor was preaching, but contrived to get within hearing; and the Lord opened his heart to "receive the Word." Soon he entered upon preparation for the ministry, and finally settled in the Dutch Reformed Church in New York. When we heard him, he discovered very little of the foreign accent. He was short and stout, and his silvery hair was combed back upon his head. His aspect in the pulpit was impressive, and his manner of preaching very affectionate and impassioned. As he read the Scriptures he usually added a brief commentary on striking passages, and was remarkable in prayer, giving utterance to the most exalted sentiments of devotion. Having taken his text, he closed the Bible, laid it on the cushion behind him, and proceeded with his discourse. He used no notes. His soul was full of his subject, and his memory for pertinent quotations—chapter and verse—astonished every body who listened to him. He preached entirely to believers, holding that if he could edify *them*, he would leave the sinners in the hands of God. He seldom, if ever, addressed a single word of warning or exhortation to the impenitent.

But how could Dr. S., so intensely concerned for the salvation of others, approve of such a course? He did not. Frequent were the conversations he held with his pastor on this point. But Mr. Bork could not be convinced that it was his duty to call sinners to repentance. If others felt it to be *their* duty, he had no objection. He even encouraged the young physician in his efforts to arouse the slumbering consciences of the young, but ungodly part of his congregation.

As a preacher to Christians and on Christian experience, Mr. Bork was almost unequaled. He knew the depths, and heights, and all the intermediate way. He connected his own experience with the Word of God in a manner to rivet the attention of all who had a heartfelt sympathy with Christ and with Christian doctrine. This trait, to Dr. S., was the charm in Mr. Bork's ministrations.

But such preaching, being of the ultra Calvinistic school, tended, though unconsciously to the preacher, to beget in formal professors the idea of electing grace, even where there was neither grace in the heart nor holiness in the life. Seeing this tendency, Dr. S. endeavored to counteract it by his exhortations and prayers in the weekly meetings. He established, with his pastor's concurrence, a meeting for the young people, which he conducted himself. It was largely attended, and soon signs of awakening became apparent. He was greatly encouraged. But some of the old men of the congregation, who had drifted calmly down on the tide of Antinomianism, took ground in opposition to him, and protested against his course, declaring that he preached the law and not the Gospel. Dr. Scudder, still consulting his pastor, asked his consent to read some of President Edwards's sermons to the young people. Mr. Bork gave his consent; and so, at their next meeting, one of the most pungent of Edwards's sermons was read. Then were souls convicted, and ere long a score or more presented themselves to the pastor, seeking admission to the privilege of Church communion. Thus was God, with this young evangelist, setting his own seal upon his labors. All along, within a year or two, continued acces-

şions took place, and so from one to two hundred con-/
verts were added to the Church.

The following extract of a letter to his mother will
give his views and feelings in expectation of the revival:
"The attention to religion in the Dutch Church to which
I am attached is now becoming very great. God's children are crying day and night for a revival of his work,
and we are on the lookout for his appearing with his almighty energy in the midst of us. My hopes have been
raised for some time past, and I communicated them to
my dear pastor, who would rejoice with joy unspeakable
could he see it the case. We had last Monday set apart
as a day of prayer and supplication for the outpouring
of the Holy Spirit in the midst of us, and it was a day
of great power. Some of God's children found it a most
delightful season; an indication, I hope, that he was ready
to hear the prayers of his people."

Dr. Scudder continued his connection with the Reformed Dutch Church up to the close of life. His heart,
however, was in every evangelical church; and wherever
he saw a Christian he recognized the tie of brotherhood,
irrespective of form and of denomination. Bigotry could
never find a home in such a heart as his.

B

CHAPTER II.

New Phase of Life.—Providential Events.—Preparations and Departure.
—The Farewell.

NEW PHASE OF LIFE.

Dr. Scudder prospered greatly in his profession. His practice, as a physician, was rapidly increasing. His wife, steady at her post, aided him by every means in her power, and soon it became evident that his income would enable him to enlarge his scale of living, which, from a sense of duty, had been kept within the most rigid and self-denying limits.

It was just at this juncture, when worldly prosperity had begun to take the thorns out of his path and pave it with flowers, that a crisis in his life occurred, changing the whole current of his subsequent career.

Visiting professionally a Christian lady, he found in her room a tract or little book entitled " The Conversion of the World, or the Claims of Six Hundred Millions." He borrowed it, read it and re-read it, until it entered the very depths of his soul. It was like a lightning flash from heaven. He heard the call, " Come over and help us !" Falling on his knees, he cried, " Lord, what wilt thou have me to do ?" Silently, but emphatically, something said to him, " Go and preach the Gospel to the heathen." What was he that he could withstand this mandate, which day and night rung in his ear, and rolled through the depths of his soul ? Oh, the prayers and tears which went from him unto God, asking again and again for the path of duty!

Here was a profession growing rapidly upon him. Hundreds had become attached to him as a Christian physician. Here was a tender and beloved wife, who married him with no idea of leaving home and friends to live and die an exile on heathen soil. Here, also, was a first-born child of only two years. Could he plant and rear that little flower where no sunlight of heaven was shining? Wide, also, was the circle of Christian influence which surrounded him in two churches. Such were the pleadings against going to the heathen to labor and die as a missionary of the Cross.

But against all this—and more that might be mentioned, of attachments to home and country—rose the Cross, and a dying Saviour, saying, If I, your Lord and Master, have done and suffered all this to save these poor benighted ones, will you hesitate to carry them the glad tidings by which alone they can be saved? This was heaven's logic to a man of deep religious emotions, of conscientious regard for duty, and of intense love to Jesus and to souls. It prevailed. On his knees he said, "Lord Jesus, I go, as thou hast commanded, to preach the Gospel to every creature."

Ever ready to watch the intimations of Providence in all the changes of life, he said to himself, I have one to consult whose interests are blended with my own, and whose happiness may be seriously affected by my decision. I will lay the subject before *her* mind as it lies before mine. If she say nay, I shall regard it as settling the question of duty. With much prayer he proceeds in the case. His beloved is informed of his decision, and

the grounds of it. She is told that if she can not heart-
ily concur, for the present at least, his work is at home,
and not among the heathen. It is hard to throw such a
mountain weight of responsibility on a young and tender wife. But she is a Christian. She has given her all
to Christ. She is adequate to the crisis. "Where thou
goest I will go," was the language of her marriage vow.
She discovers that his mind is made up—that to say no
will send a permanent pang of disappointment into his
soul. Hard as the struggle is, she makes up her mind
on the same principle that he made up his. Much prayer
is offered, and many natural tears shed; and then, from
love to Christ and a sense of duty, she decides for the
life of a missionary. That purpose never gave way. It
never even faltered. She calmly went about the needful preparations for this new and important change of
life.

So soon as this decision was known, there was a general feeling of sadness among those who had become attached to the doctor and his wife; and one would think,
to see their tears and hear their regrets, that a sort of
funereal aspect darkened all the future of these two missionaries. One man came to his door to ascertain the
fact, and, when assured that they were really going,
burst into tears. Others railed at him as almost insane.
Worldly men could not explain it. From *their* stand-
point, it seemed so absurd to give up a lucrative practice,
and all the advantages of civilized life, to live and die
among pagans! Even Christians would say, "Why, doctor, let the young, unmarried men go! Can't you make
yourself more useful at home?" To all of which he had
one answer—*Duty*. I feel under sacred obligations to

the Master to go. I go from love to Christ and to souls. The very self-denial of the work allures me. It is my happiness to go.

CONCURRENCE OF PROVIDENTIAL EVENTS.

Just at the time when Dr. S. had determined, if a door should open, he would go to the heathen, the American Board of Missions at Boston needed a pious physician for India, and advertised in some of the religious papers for one who should combine the qualifications of missionary and physician. At once the doctor offered himself, and opened a correspondence on the subject.

In a letter to the Secretary of the Board, among other things he says: "I am comfortably and pleasantly situated, and have a practice which yields me far more than is necessary to defray the expenses of life; but I hope I am willing to forsake all for Christ; yea, father and mother, and brother and sister, the comforts and enjoyments of the world, and go to 'the help of the Lord against the mighty.' Should the Board think proper to accept me, I feel disposed to act in whatever manner they may deem proper. If it would contribute most to the glory of God, I am perfectly willing to go immediately, as I could complete my theological studies there, at the same time that I would be acquiring a knowledge of their language, and thus much time would be saved. Mrs. Scudder feels willing to go on the mission. I trust, if I go, the Lord will make her, and the little lamb he has given her, when it arrives to years of discretion, eminently useful in his service."

PREPARATIONS AND DEPARTURE.

Short was the period between the acceptance by the
Board and the embarkation. All is busy preparation.
Friends offer their services; and, by a combined energy,
which the circumstances tended to develop, they were
ready at the appointed time.

They had a faithful colored servant named Amy, who,
from strong personal attachment, pleaded with them to
take her along. They endeavored to convince her that
she was wholly ignorant of the trials and perils which
she would have to go through in case she accompanied
them. But her answer was, "If little Maria can meet
them, so can I." Such were her tears and importunities,
that Dr. Scudder said to himself and to his wife, there
must be some Providence in this. So he wrote to Boston and laid the case before the Board, stating the valuable services she could render on the passage, and the
still more valuable help she would be to them after they
reached their destination. Though out of their usual
course, the Board acceded to their request; and "the
faithful Amy," as she was called, was incorporated into
the mission.

THE FAREWELL.

Fulton Street dock was a scene of great excitement
on the day this missionary family sailed for Boston.
The large acquaintance which both the doctor and his
wife had made, embracing the principal members of two
churches, and many others in the various walks of life,
filled the dock and the deck of the steamer, and caused
a wonderment in all the passers-by. It was a different

thing in that day from what it is *now* to embark as a missionary to distant India with a view of never returning, but of living and dying among the heathen. Some looked upon it as being buried alive—a sort of perpetual suttee life. They could not comprehend it; and perhaps it was a mistake which the Board made in impressing somewhat strongly the idea of no return. Yet it worked favorably in one respect; there was very little likelihood, with this living sacrifice before them, that any but the true disciples of a self-denying Saviour would offer themselves to the service. Besides, men could not but feel, as they contemplated the sacrifice, that there was a moral heroism in the consecration. They who saw Dr. Scudder on that day, so jubilant, with a face radiant as if some sudden joy had taken possession of him, were obliged to acknowledge the triumphant power of a Christian's faith.

JAMES BRAINERD TAYLOR.

One young man who beheld that scene never forgot it. It sunk deep into his soul. " What is it," said he, " that lifts this missionary into the precincts of heaven ? What makes him so joyful when leaving country, home, relations, and the refinements of social life, to live on burning plains, and amid the disgusting depravity of pagans ? Surely he is possessed with the spirit and temper of his Master." This young man was James Brainerd Taylor. From that moment he devoted his all to Christ, and thenceforth went " from strength to strength," until —alas ! how soon—he left us for glory.

" I this morning," writes he, in his spiritual diary, " witnessed a scene highly interesting to the heart of a Christian. I saw a missionary and his wife take their departure from this port for India, to declare among the heathen the unsearchable riches of Christ. It may be said of them that they have left all and followed their Saviour. They counted not the blessings of home and friends, or even their own lives, dear unto themselves, that they might win Christ and win others to him.

"I had the pleasure of being introduced to Dr. and Mrs. Scudder. He appeared cheerful. Mrs. Scudder was bathed in tears, but yet rejoicing. They were surrounded by many acquaintances and friends; and we can with difficulty imagine their feelings when, just about to leave home, and country, and all the blessings of Christian society, they heard one and another say, 'My friend, my sister, farewell forever!' I shall never forget Dr. Scudder's looks or his words. His eye kindled, and his cheek glowed with the ardor of Christian benevolence. As the vessel moved off, waving his hand, with a benignant smile on his countenance, he said, 'Only give me your prayers, and that is all I ask.'"

This sight decided James Brainerd Taylor to leave his mercantile business, and prepare to follow the noble example set before him.

"On seeing Dr. Scudder take his last leave of his friends and the people on shore with a true missionary spirit, I felt a tenderness toward the poor heathen to whom he was going which caused my eyes to overflow. I thought that I would be willing to change my situation for his. On returning home I could not attend to business. I retired for prayer, and found the exercise sweet. My mind was impressed with the necessity for more ministers of the Gospel, and many reasons presented themselves why I should devote my life to the good of my fellow-men in that situation."

CHAPTER III.

THE DEPARTURE.

The missionary band designated for Ceylon consisted of Messrs. Winslow, Spaulding, Woodward, and Scudder, with their wives. They embarked June 8th, 1819,
in the brig Indus, Captain Wills, bound to Calcutta. Every thing was favorable. The season was beautiful, and
the voyage promised to be auspicious. It was especially
a kind Providence that gave them a captain whose heart
beat in strong sympathy with their own. He was a true
Christian. He not only provided every thing within his
power for their temporal comfort, but put the whole ship
at their disposal as a floating Bethel. They held religious meetings both in the cabin and in the forecastle.

"Our accommodations," writes one of the missionary
band, "are as good as we could expect, and our spiritual
privileges great. The brethren have had a meeting to
make some arrangement for religious exercises and for
intellectual improvement. It is agreed that there be
public worship in the cabin Sunday mornings, and afternoons on deck: morning and evening prayers, a public
conference on Thursday evening, and prayer-meeting
the first Monday in the month. In our rooms we are to
have a missionary meeting every Friday afternoon, a
prayer-meeting on Saturday evening, besides meetings

at other times, as circumstances may render expedient. Every afternoon we are to meet immediately after dinner for discussion on theological subjects.

"The brethren have conversed and prayed with the seamen, and find them attentive. The sisters presented to each of them a Bible. It is very common to see one reading aloud, while a number surround him with eyes and ears open, as though they would seize every word."

Soon the seamen showed signs of heartfelt interest; and some of them began to ask, "What shall we do to be saved?" The Spirit of God was manifestly hovering over them, and the whole ship seemed pervaded with an atmosphere of solemnity. So marked a revival on shipboard had seldom been experienced; nor will it be uninteresting to give a detailed account of it in Dr. Scudder's own words. It is found in a communication to his mother, written on shipboard just before his arrival at Calcutta.

REVIVAL ON BOARD THE INDUS.

"DEAREST OF MOTHERS,—As it will no doubt afford you much gratification to be made acquainted with the glorious work of grace which God began, carried on, and completed on board the brig Indus, I will proceed to give you some account of it. Soon after we left our native land, we began to direct the attention of the seamen to the great importance of religion. As they were destitute of the Bible, each of them was presented with one. Numbers of tracts also were distributed among them. They soon began to attend to divine things, as was evidenced by reading their Bibles, tracts, and such books as were put into their hands. Several of them, no doubt, were convinced very soon that they were sinners, and we have reason to believe that their convictions never wore off until they terminated in a genuine conversion. On the 20th of July one of the seamen fell overboard, and it was a providential circumstance that he was not lost. On the evening of this day, two of the brethren, with myself, went forward to the windlass deck, and endeavored to impress upon their minds the necessity of being in a state of constant preparation for death. One of them, who has since become a most eminent trophy of victorious grace, began to think somewhat seriously upon divine things, and came to the resolution that he would 'knock off some of his sins' (to use his own expression), 'and be better.' He now began to pray and use the other means of grace, but his heart remained like the adamant. The conversations we had at different times with him afforded us no satisfaction whatever of that change of heart, without which no man can see God and live, until the latter part of August, when we trust his name was enrolled among the followers of the Lamb. The twenty-second day of this month of release to his soul from the captivity of sin and Satan will be a day long to be remembered by him. On the evening of the 20th I held some conversation with him on such subjects as were of most importance, and endeavored to examine him and find what his state was, but I was no better satisfied of a change in him than before. I asked him if he had yet seen any loveliness in the character of the Lord Jesus. His answer clearly evinced that he had not seen this King of Zion in his beauty. After I left him, he has since told us what his reflections were. 'I keep thinking to myself,' said he, 'who is Jesus Christ? and

what has he done that I should care any thing about
him?' The next evening he labored under very deep
distress concerning the state of his soul. When he retired to rest he found that sleep had departed from him.
He passed a wretched night. It appears that he has
been a complete infidel, thinking that the Scriptures
were only a book to keep people in order. While at
the helm, before the watch he was in went below, the
Spirit of God came upon him, and swept away all his
doubts respecting revealed truth as with the besom of
destruction. The time was now at hand when he was
to be born into the kingdom of Christ. On Sunday
morning, in his early watch, his mind was so agitated
that he wept like a child. In this state he continued until about six o'clock, when the Sun of Righteousness
arose with healing under his wings, and scattered that
thick darkness in which he was so deeply involved, and
he began to entertain a hope. I did not see him until
Monday evening to converse with him. Brother Spaulding, who had been teaching him navigation, went, as usual, on Monday afternoon, to hear him recite. He said
'he had not gotten a lesson;' adding, 'I have been reading my Bible this forenoon, and conclude that I shall
give up navigation a spell.' In the evening Brother
Spaulding and myself visited the seamen in the forecastle, and experienced sweetly that it was good to be
there. Never shall we forget this pleasant evening. 'I
have been wanting to see you,' said Brown to me, 'to
converse with you.' He wished to tell us of the change
in his views and feelings. Some remarks were made by
Brother Spaulding upon the prodigal son, and his return
to his father's house. He then compared his case of the

returning sinner to that of the prodigal very particularly. After he had finished, Brown said with a smile, 'If
you had not said one fifteenth part so much I should
have believed it, for my heart kept saying all the time
that it was all true.' He was most violently opposed to
us when we first left Boston, and delighted to ridicule
us, regretting very much that he should so long be shut
up with the 'holy brotherhood,' as he styled us. He said
'that if a man rips out a civil oath to ease his conscience,
he will receive a maul at the elbow with it,' and added
that we shall forever be tormented with these men. But
his views were now very different. The things which before he hated, now he loved. Jesus became precious to
him, the chiefest among ten thousand, and altogether
lovely. I will just remark that, like all other men by
nature, he (though a most openly wicked sinner) was
building upon that sandy foundation which has ruined
so many millions of souls, hoping to be saved by his good
works. He thought that he should do well enough at
last, as he was not as bad as some other men were, and
that when he bought his grog he paid for it. But when
the veil was removed from his eyes, and he was convinced of his deep depravity, of his lost and undone state
except through the blood of Christ, and of his utter in-
ability to do any thing to recommend him to the favor
of God, he saw clearly what a refuge of lies all his boast-
ed morality was. Time will not permit me to be more
particular. Suffice it to say that, from all appearances,
he is one of the most genuine converts I have ever seen.
Truly he adorns the doctrine of God his Saviour, and has
been useful among his shipmates. It would affect your
heart to hear with what fervor he prayed before us for

those whose hearts remained a long time callous to every
feeling.   Never have I seen a person grow so fast in
grace and in the knowledge of our Lord and Saviour Jesus Christ; and I sincerely believe that it is his meat and
drink to do the will of him who gave himself for him.

"The next person whom I shall mention as having
a hope that Jesus is precious to him is a lad of about
seventeen years of age.   His name is Learned.   When
he left one of his companions in Boston, he was told to
take care that he was not converted by the missionaries.
He said that he would risk that.   Little did he think that
a more powerful arm than that of man was about to slay
all his enmity of heart and opposition to divine things.
He at first ridiculed us, but at last began to think that
religion was worth attending to.   When he found how
narrow the path to eternal life was, he left off reading his
Bible, and had recourse to other books to see if there
were 'no cheaper way of getting to heaven.'   It pleased
God to direct his attention to Baxter's Saints' Rest, which
had been put in his hands, but he soon found that he
had looked into the wrong book to obtain comfort; he
therefore had again recourse to his Bible, which is now
to him more precious than rubies.   We often conversed
with him, and he appeared to be convinced that he was
a sinner, and that there was no salvation for him except
through Christ.   But he never felt his utter depravity
until about the middle of September.   The life of John
Newton was blessed to him.   A few days afterward I
had some conversation with him, when he mentioned
that before this period he had not felt himself a sinner.
He knew that he was a sinner, but did not feel it; and,
he added, there is a great difference between knowing

and feeling himself a sinner. I asked him how the Redeemer appeared to him since he felt himself a sinner. He answered, a great deal more lovely. He felt that it would be perfectly just in God to condemn him forever; that his own righteousness could not save him; and that, if he ever were saved, it would be a display of divine mercy. He said that he had given himself up into the hands of God to do as he pleased with him. He now groaned under sin, longed for deliverance therefrom, and felt willing to give up all for Christ. The things he formerly loved now he hated, and what he formerly hated now he loved. It is unnecessary that I should be more particular. I will just observe that he fell overboard on the 5th of October; and that hope which he had previously entertained enabled him to look upon death with composure, and feel willing to take his departure from time into eternity. He sustained no injury. He is now rejoicing in God his Saviour.

"This glorious work appeared to be gradually going on until the latter part of September, when the Holy Ghost came, as it were, with a rushing mighty wind, and bowed the most stubborn sinners before him. In less than one week I believe there was not a thoughtless sinner on board. Those who had heretofore turned a deaf ear to all our warnings and entreaties were now humbled in the dust. All of them are now entertaining the hope that they have passed from death unto life. As there never was an instance, as far as I can recollect, of such a wonderful work on board of any vessel, it will be necessary that I should enter somewhat minutely into a description of it. You may rest assured that there has been no enthusiasm, no wild-fire in this work. It has

been carried on in great silence, with the still small voice
of the Spirit. The Lord has shown that he can work
without us. Five of the persons who were convicted
this week were convicted when alone. I have been in
revivals of religion at home, but never did I see such
manifestations of divine power. I stood still, as it were,
wondered, admired, and adored. We could say surely
the Lord was in this place, and we knew it.

"The first mate, Mr. Day, an amiable young man, formerly a ridiculer of all serious things, and who long endeavored to believe in the doctrine of universal salvation,
while on the martingale, under the bowsprit end, on the
Sabbath, in the act of having the harpoon raised to strike
a fish, was struck under the most deep and pungent conviction. He soon laid aside his harpoon. All his past
sins were set in array before him, and horror and darkness overwhelmed his soul. The Lord was pleased soon
to lift the light of his countenance upon him, and before
the week was out he was one of the happiest men on
board. He who never wept before, now wept like a
child. He was so humbled in the dust before God that
he felt below the dog we have on board. On Saturday
his cup of happiness was full. He declared to me that
he never enjoyed one hundredth part so much happiness.
He observed that he felt as if he could go and preach the
divine Redeemer to his former companions. It is unnecessary to be more particular. During this same memorable week, the second mate and clerk, who had been
warned and prayed with in vain by us, were also humbled in the dust. It is astonishing to see with what ease
the most stubborn sinner is bowed down when the Holy
Ghost visits him. It appears that both of these young

men have taken very great delight in ridiculing us. When the former came from home, his mother told him that she was glad he was going out with the missionaries, and hoped that it might be the best voyage he ever made. He laughed at her, and told her that they would serve to make him a little fun now and then, as they were psalm-singing fellows. His convictions were remarkably deep. When aloft among the rigging the Spirit of God came upon him. I never saw a person under deeper distress for so great a length of time. Truly it was with him a time of lamentation and mourning. The night of the 30th of September will never be forgotten by him. He saw that God would be just in sending him to hell; that he was lost and undone; and that there was no salvation for him out of Christ. After continuing a little time in this wretched situation, the Lord was pleased to visit him with his great salvation, and before the week was ended he also was enabled to rejoice in God his Saviour. The clerk also became unusually affected. There were some darling sins, however, which at first he was unwilling to give up. The Holy Spirit soon convinced him that they must be given up. The next day, after a solemn interview with him the preceding night, when I told him of the absolute necessity of parting with every sin before we could come acceptably to God, he was, I hope, convinced of his dreadful situation, and deeply humbled for sin. He now felt willing to give all up and come to Christ. He also, before the week ended, was rejoicing in the hope that Jesus had become precious to him. The second mate longed for an opportunity to be ridiculed as he had ridiculed us, and thought he would rather part with his neck than pursue his old course of sin. On Thursday evening, the boy, a lad of fourteen years, who had been very thoughtless, after having been conversed with, became deeply alarmed about the condition his soul was in. He was told that it was to be feared 'that God had given him up.' These words dwelt with great weight upon his mind. He went to bed, but could not sleep; several times he got up, and went to the steward to tell him what distress he was in. About ten o'clock I observed him standing near my state-room. I conversed with him, and found him under deep distress of mind. He saw that there was no salvation for him except through the blood of Christ, and I hope he has found him precious to his soul. He enjoys a sweet peace which the world knows nothing of; and, though he was despairing of God's mercy, or, rather, was fearful that he was too great a sinner to be pardoned, he now thinks, and, I hope, knows that the blood of Christ cleanseth from all sin.

"The cook, a black man, one of the vilest and most hardened wretches on board, and who entirely disregarded all the thunderings of the law, and every thing else which was said to him, was also humbled in the dust. He entirely disregarded every thing of a serious nature, and was one of the most notorious swearers on board. He would very seldom attend at any of our religious meetings. The time was now come that his stubbornness should be overcome. He heard two of the seamen talking about the operations of the Holy Spirit. He, in a light way, said to them, 'May God grant that the Spirit of God may light upon every soul on board this night.' This he did to make a little fun, as usual. He awaked in the night in agony. The Holy Spirit did light upon

him, and he was in very deep distress on account of his
sins, wondering that God had not cut him off, and sent
him to hell long before. He continued in this state for
some time, when the divine Redeemer became precious
to him, and caused him to rejoice in him. He declared
that he felt as happy as he did the morning he left the
prison in which he was for some time confined in France,
adding that it was a bitter cold morning, but I was so
overjoyed I did not feel the cold. All around him see
plainly that he has been with Jesus. From a cross, mo-
rose creature, he has become clothed with meekness and
pleasantness. I have repeatedly found much sweet delight in conversing with him, and now find that he es-
teems that Jesus as altogether lovely, and continues to
run in the way of his commandments.

"On Saturday morning it pleased God to visit another
of the vilest and most hardened sinners on board. His
name is Parker. When we first came on board he became somewhat serious, and in a storm we had near the
Cape of Good Hope he became so much alarmed that he
resolved, if God would spare his life, he would do better;
but his heart became more and more hardened. He even
went so far as to say that he would take all the pleasure
he could get in this world, and that if he went to hell he
would bear it as well as others. He became a violent
opponent of every thing of a serious nature, denied the
truth of the Scriptures, and began to curse and swear at
a most dreadful rate. On Friday evening, at a very solemn meeting, Captain Wills addressed the seamen in a
very impressive manner, and afterward addressed him
particularly. But it was all in vain. He conversed
with him alone afterward, but without making the least

impression. After he had done, Parker went away curs-
ing him for it, and has since declared that he blasphemed
enough to damn a thousand souls. The time of his opposition and wickedness was, however, drawing to a close.
The Holy Spirit was about to convince him that his stubborn neck should bow to his yoke. On Saturday morning I went into the forecastle to read a part of Baxter's
Call to the Unconverted to him. Brown and myself
prayed repeatedly with him. While I was there the
brethren were in the cabin praying for a blessing upon
the means used for his being brought into the fold of
Christ, and I trust their prayers were heard. He was
humbled in the dust before God, convinced of his wretched situation—that he was lost and undone, and that there
was no salvation for him except through the Lord Jesus
Christ. He continued a little time in deep distress, finding that sin, though it had been sweet, now was like the
poison of asps. After viewing what God had done for
others, he had a hope that God would yet have mercy
upon him. He was willing to give up all for Christ, and
be his. The Lord at length appeared for him, removed
his burden, and he truly became a happy soul. Now he
saw very plainly that Jesus, whom he had heretofore despised, was altogether lovely. He truly is a brand plucked
from the burning.

"Mr. Sparrowhawk was awakened at this time also.
This man sailed to India in the same vessel with Mr.
Newell, and we can not but adore Him who has directed
him to embark with us. We have often conversed with
him before, but without any effect. He was particularly addressed one evening in the forecastle. The consequence was that he damned the person who addressed

him. He continued hardened until this ever-to-be-re-membered time of God's merciful visitation. While at the helm the Holy Spirit was graciously pleased to visit him. He was convinced of his lost, undone state, and that there was no salvation for him by any thing he could do. I never saw a man more completely stripped of self-righteousness. He said he tried to become better, but he found that he only got worse. After continuing for some length of time in deep distress, the Divine Re-deemer became altogether lovely to him. He truly is a happy man.

"Mr. Pitts, a very profane swearer, was also brought to bow his neck to the yoke of Christ. He had been a little serious before, but was not willing to give up all his sins. He thought that God was merciful, and that, as he had forsaken some sins, he should do well enough at last. When the Holy Spirit came to him, he was con-vinced that this would not do. Conviction was fastened very deeply upon his mind, and he became very much distressed on account of his sad condition. He men-tioned to Brother Winslow that one night he tried, when alone, to pray, but kept choking up. For two hours he was distressed in this way. He found he could not pray until he went to his knees and gave himself away to God. He was asked by Captain Wills one night if he loved God. He answered, 'I love him in every shape I can think of.' He also asked him if, when going to church in Calcutta, how he would bear it if he were ridiculed for it. He said he did not care if fifty thousand ridi-culed him.

"The steward, who had turned a deaf ear to every call of the Gospel, had also to yield to the operations of the

Holy Spirit. He became deeply affected with his lost condition—that he was lost without he had an interest in Christ, and that his good works could never save him. He formerly believed the Lord Jesus to be an impostor, and imagined that he should be saved by his own works. After continuing for a season in distress, he was comforted. He said that Jesus was to him altogether lovely, and the chiefest among ten thousand. He longed to return home, that he might tell what God had done for his soul. Some time ago he was longing for the time to come when we should be landed at Ceylon, as he was tired of so much praying and singing. This also was the case with others of them. They disliked being disturbed of their rest for the sake of attending to the things of religion. But never was there a greater alteration than when they began to hope that Jesus was precious to them. I believe it will be a sorrowful day when we are called to part from each other.

"The carpenter was also convicted while engaged in performing his duty in some part of the vessel. He had before been a hardened sinner. As we had reason to fear that his seriousness was not of a proper nature, and that he was yet in his sins, Brother Winslow went forward into the forecastle and conversed with him, while the rest of us remained in the cabin to pray for a blessing upon his labors. From the answers he gave to the questions which were put to him, fears were entertained that he was yet, notwithstanding all his seriousness, a proud, unhumbled sinner. However, the Lord's time was near when he must be humbled. While he was in his state-room at prayer upon his knees, the following texts came into his mind, and were so impressed upon him that he had to arise and search for them. The first was in Prov. x., 4 : ' The sluggard will not plow by reason of the cold, therefore shall he beg in harvest and have nothing.' The second in Acts, xiii., 10 : 'And said, O full of all subtilty and all mischief, thou child of the devil, thou enemy of all righteousness, wilt thou not cease to pervert the right ways of the Lord ?' He found them applicable to his case, returned again to his state-room, when the following words came into his mind : 'Believe on the Lord Jesus Christ, and thou shalt be saved.' He again had recourse to prayer, and found that he could give himself away to be the Lord's. He is now rejoicing in the hope that Jesus has become precious to him.

" I might proceed to give you some account of the views and policy of the others ; but enough has been said, I trust, to evince that the work which has been begun and carried on among these dear seamen bears the mark of divine influence. We fear that some of the Lord's own chosen people may fear that the goodness of some of them will be as the morning cloud and early dew, which pass away. Had we declared smooth things to them, we might fear so ourselves ; but when we have held up to their constant view that they were lost and undone in themselves, and under sentence of eternal death ; that their own righteousness could not save them, and that nothing one hair's breadth this side of repentance and belief in the Lord Jesus Christ could in the least avail them, we have reason to hope that God has been pleased to begin that work which shall never cease until they are all safely brought to glory. We do not profess to be judges of the heart, but this much we can say, wonderful is the change. None but Christ, none but Christ for them. Who could change such monsters of iniquity from hatred to love? from being profane swearers to humble adorers of the Lamb, but the Holy Ghost? Surely man could not. The most alarming sermons were delivered and read to them, but all in vain; and when we, as it were, had given many of them up, the Lord came down with his almighty power, after we had labored with them for more than three months in vain, proving to us that he could easily turn them, as the rivers of water are turned. May the great Head of the Church grant that they may prove, by their future walk and conversation, that they have been with Jesus.

"What an encouragement, my dear mother, is here afforded for us to go forward and labor in the vineyard of our Lord. How long it will be before we reach Ceylon we know not. I am not at all sorry that we were obliged to pass it. We should not like to have left our young converts so soon, as they are to remain a considerable length of time in a very wicked place. Though we were a great many leagues—perhaps fifty or sixty—from Ceylon, when we passed it we could sensibly smell the perfume which came from it and sweetened the air. In going to Calcutta we shall have the opportunity of seeing Dr. Carey and the other missionaries there, who have been so very useful in their Master's service. I have kept no journal since I left home in consequence of having other business on hand. Harriet has kept one. I have been unwell, but am better. It is a solemn office, my dear mother, to be a missionary of the Cross. Oh, then, pray ardently for me and my dear Harriet, that we may prove faithful unto death, and at last obtain the crown of glory. Remember the first Monday evening of each month. The people of God meet in every part of the world upon this evening to pray for the success of missions, and it will be pleasing for us to reflect that you are praying at the same moment at the throne of grace that we are. It is true, we do not meet at the same moment, as there is above ten hours' difference between your Monday evening and ours; but this is nothing in the view of God, with whom it is always an eternal now."

In a later communication Dr. Scudder expresses his deep regret and sorrow to find that some of these sailor converts did not hold out, but fell back into their old habits under the power of temptation at Calcutta. But others were steadfast unto the end. The proportion of backsliders was not, perhaps, widely different from what is seen in revivals of religion on shore. Ministers have often occasion to mourn over the "stony-ground hearers;" and even an apostle had to say to some, "Ye did run well, but ye have returned to the beggarly elements of your bondage."

This work of the Spirit was brought about by prayer, combined with faithful and affectionate appeals to the heart and conscience. God answered prayer in making his word "quick and powerful."

ARRIVAL AT CALCUTTA.

Insulated for months on the lonely deep, how grateful was the sight of land, and how many pleasing and painful thoughts rushed through the mind! Regrets at leaving their beloved captain, whose Christian conduct had endeared him to all of them, nor less painful emotions in parting with the new converts, chastened their joy at beholding those luxuriant shores, " where every prospect

C

pleases." To one who has never visited the Orient, the scenery, so soft and beautiful, possesses a charm indescribable. Perhaps it can not be better depicted than by Mr. Winslow, one of the mission band :

"Ascending the River Hoogly toward Calcutta, the scenery presented on each side of the river, though uniform, is pleasant, indeed almost enchanting, to those who for four months have seen little else than sky and water, especially if they have never been in a tropical climate before. ''Tis the land of the sun.' The brightness and transparency of the atmosphere; the luxuriance and freshness of the vegetation; the entirely novel character of every tree, shrub, plant, and flower; the bamboo huts of the natives, scattered along the river banks, or under the shade of palm-trees, and contrasted here and there with some more respectable mansion of brick, or a stone temple, lifting its white dome amid the green foliage of a cocoa-nut grove, or under the spreading banian, all attract and yet bewilder the fancy."

In contrast with this flowery land, however, appears the dark shadow of paganism — the din of discordant music in honor of their gods, impersonated under the most hideous aspects, and suggesting the vilest forms of sensuality. "Soon after the ship anchored," says one of the missionaries, "we saw on the shore directly opposite to us great multitudes approaching the water, with a horrid din of music, carrying their gods, to throw them into the stream. We could discern nothing of their appearance but that they were the size of a common man, and about the waist were painted black. They were held over the water some minutes, while the noise of various musical instruments continued, and then plunged in, to float down with the current. This drowning of the gods is an important ceremony among the Hindoos."

Captain Wills hired a mansion in Calcutta for the accommodation of himself and the missionaries, with large rooms, and dining-hall opening into a wide veranda or portico. These houses are such as are occupied by merchants and other temporary residents in the place. By this arrangement the mission bands were kept together, and were enabled to receive calls from the English and other missionaries at Calcutta. Having received many attentions from Dr. Carey and other good men, residents of Calcutta and Serampore, they seized the first favorable opportunity to set sail for Ceylon, the field of their future labors.

One of their severest trials at this juncture was to bid farewell to their ship's company, with whom for so long a time they had been associated in circumstances to create the deepest spiritual interest and attachment. "To Captain Wills," said one of them, "we shall always feel that we owe more than we can ever repay. May God reward him! He feels much at the prospect of our leaving him so soon, and we shall find it very trying to part with him and the other officers and seamen. The officers give increasing evidence of being born again. At the recollection of what God has done, we are encouraged to devote ourselves more entirely to our work."

On account of the severe illness of Mrs. Woodward, Dr. Scudder and family remained at Calcutta, while the other members of the mission took passage for Ceylon in the ship *Dick*, Captain Harrison, of London.

FIRST DEATH.

The arrow that seemed destined to lay Mrs. Woodward low took effect on another. "That little lamb," as the doctor was accustomed to call his Maria, was suddenly taken to the bosom of the Good Shepherd. It was their first trial, and went deep into their parental affections. She was a lovely creature—too lovely, some would say, for this rough and thorny world. They received the cup as from the hand of their heavenly Father, and drank it in the same spirit which *He* evinced who said, "Not my will, but thine, be done."

Writing to his mother on the subject, Dr. Scudder says, "Oh, my dear mother, how shall I take up my pen to mark upon paper the dark shadow of death! My dear little babe is no more. She has left us forever. She was attacked with dysentery on the 22d of October, and, after three days of suffering, passed into eternity. This is a heart-rending trial; but we *can* say, and we *do* say, the will of the Lord be done. We do not wish her back here in this poor wretched world. My dear Harriet bears it remarkably well. Oh, my mother, had she, the dearest object of my affections, been called away, how dark and disconsolate would I have been! Pray much for us; we need divine support more than you are aware."

She was buried in the Episcopal church-yard in Calcutta. Thus was planted, amid parental tears and sorrows, in this dark, distant land, this precious dust, to await the signal of the archangel's trump to spring forth to new life and more than angelic beauty.

DEATH OF A SECOND CHILD.

Three months after the first flower had faded and gone, the blight of death fell upon another. To use the language of its father, "After breathing the tainted air but one week, it closed its eyes upon us forever, and took its flight to join her beloved sister. This is a severe trial, but we do not repine. We have here no continuing city, no place of rest, and therefore we feel resigned to the will of our heavenly Father, who has housed our tender plants before the storms of sorrow, which we feel, have beaten upon them. We, however, must have the feelings of nature. We must say that our trials have been heart-rending. O that God would sanctify them to us, and make us more meet for that inheritance above, which, through grace, we hope to have when our bodies are consigned to the dust of the earth. Perhaps our dear parents may be ready to say that we are sorry, and repent of our coming to this heathen land; that if we had remained at home we should have been less afflicted. You may rest assured we do not repent of our coming. No; we rejoice, and thank the great Head of the Church for putting it into our hearts to leave America and come and live among this people. I would not exchange situations for a world. No; blessed be God, I hope to be the unworthy instrument of bringing souls to the dear Redeemer." The date of this second child's death was February 25, 1820, Jaffna.

CHAPTER IV.

Ceylon.—Begins preaching at Panditeripo.—Great Temple at Nellore.—
Removes to Panditeripo.—Licensed to Preach.

CEYLON.

This island is one of the richest gems of the tropics.
It is bordered in some parts with fragrant groves of
cinnamon, and in others with the graceful palmyra, with
its "tufted crown of fan leaves" always green. At the
north, particularly in Jaffna, vast groves of the cocoa-nut
are seen, while the beautiful green rice-fields carpet the
soil and relieve the eye, dazzled by the intense glare of
the sun.   From this belt, fringed with tropical verdure,
rise in the centre the lofty hills of Kandy, with magnifi-
cent forests of perpetual green.

This island contains 24,664 square miles; and, according to the census of 1831, has a population of about a
million.   The mass of the population is composed of the
Cingalese, inhabiting the interior and southern parts;
and the Tamulians, who are mostly in the northern and
eastern districts; the former being Buddhists, speaking
Cingalese, the latter Brahminists or Hindoos, using the
Tamul language.   The scene of missionary labor assigned to Dr. Scudder and his associates lay in the Jaffna
district, at the extreme north of the island.   Here the
deserted churches, once occupied by the Portuguese Roman Catholic missionaries, offered eligible positions for
the brethren to commence their evangelical work.   These

churches, built usually of stone, were in a dilapidated condition, but by a small expense could be made convenient and comfortable places of worship.

At one of these stations, Panditeripo, in the district of Jaffna, Dr. and Mrs. Scudder planted themselves, and proceeded at once to repair the decayed premises and commence their work. This was in July, 1820. Dr. Scudder's account of his new residence and the surrounding circumstances, as given to his parents, is as follows:

"MY DEAR PARENTS,—I am now sitting under a bungalow, which is the name of the huts in this country, and would cheerfully employ a few moments in writing to you. The brethren have sent me to a new station called Panditeripo, about four miles from Tillipally, and have committed to my care many immortal souls. I am to be admitted into the ministry at the next meeting of my brethren, and thus become a minister of the everlasting Gospel. I have been in the habit of preaching for some time in the church, but do not feel so reconciled to do it as I should do if I were admitted in the way appointed by our churches at home. I assure you, my dear father and mother, that I have much pleasure in my work of laboring among the heathen, and should be very sorry again to return to my native land. True it is I long to see you, but this can never again be the case; oh no, we must dispense with this pleasure until we meet in the great day of account. God grant that we may then meet to part no more forever. It is a pleasing work to labor here. It is a blessed employment to build up the kingdom of our divine Immanuel. I am very busily engaged in building, and as I am in a bungalow much exposed, my dear Harriet is not with me. I have no one around me but natives who are doing my work. I have been visited by several persons to-day of those who may be properly called respectable men. There are some among them of great genius, and if they had equal advantages with the young men in our country they no doubt would be an honor to any nation.

"How do my dear parents do? More than a year has elapsed since I left America, but not a word from you. How are my brothers and sisters? Perhaps some of them are no more. Oh how fleeting are our days! Should I judge from what has taken place in my own family, I should expect some of you were no more. My two beloved children have been removed by death, as you have been apprized, but our mercies are great and many. We have not been afflicted as we deserve, and we must say that the Lord deals kindly with us. I have heard, by the way of England, that New York has been visited by the yellow fever. No doubt thousands have fallen a sacrifice to it, and, had I been there, in all probability I should have been numbered with them. I hope the Lord had a better work for me to do than to remain in America. I have patients in abundance. Through the means of medicine I hope to do much good, as many hear the Gospel by this means who, in all probability, would never hear it in any other way.

"You can have some idea of my bungalow from the following sketch. It stands before a large stone house in ruins, and very near to one end of the church, which was built probably two hundred years ago by the Catholics. In this district there were thirty churches, built by the Portuguese; but they have all been deserted, and most of them are much injured by exposure, and particularly by the banian-tree, which enters unseen the firmest walls, and splits them to pieces or tears them down. The bungalows are generally covered with olas, the leaves of the palmyra-tree, a description of which I some time since sent in a joint letter to our mother in New York and New Jersey. We have no wood either for floors or for coverings to the houses. The English in Jaffnapatam have their houses covered with tile, and floors made of stone or chunam (lime). The climate of this island is rather pleasant than otherwise. It is sometimes very warm, but as we are continually fanned by the wind it is not generally oppressive. The inhabitants are frequently very poor. The better sort live upon rice and curry—a very hot dish, made of Cayenne pepper and other spices, with plantains, etc. Many of them will not touch animal food. We are in the midst of rice-fields at this place. In the rainy season we shall frequently have vast fields of water. The rice, or paddy, as it is called, requires much water, and will not grow without it. This causes the natives to throw up banks, about a foot or two high, around their fields, which generally are not an acre in size, to keep the water standing.

"We have a great variety of delicious fruit — pine-apples, oranges, mangoes (a most excellent substitute for the finest pine-apples), plantains—a very rich fruit—the custard-apple, so called from its resemblance to a custard, and others unnecessary to mention. The almond, bread-fruit, and tamarind trees all grow here. We have excellent poultry. We also have beef and pork, kid and lamb. There are many shepherds here who have large flocks. If you read the description given in the Old Testament of Eastern customs, you will have a good idea

of many of the customs of this people. They are remarkably fond of jewels, and generally the richer sort
adorn themselves with them. As to their morals, they
are every thing that is bad. They are completely depravity itself. This is now the time of their festivals.
I went on Sabbath night near one of their temples, and
began to preach to them, but found it would not answer.
Such a tumult was raised that, had I not desisted, death
might have been the consequence. I saw one of their
religious ceremonies. A wooden horse, painted red and
ornamented, was first brought out, or, rather, had been
brought out before I arrived there. By his side was a
large cat, painted, and a swan. Upon these the god
whom they trust in and worship, with his two wives,
were placed, and then paraded round among the rabble.
Surely they are a degraded people beyond description ;
and were it not for the hope that the day was approaching when the heathen shall be given 'to our Lord for
his inheritance, and the uttermost parts of the earth for
his possession,' my heart would sink within me."

BEGINS PREACHING AT PANDITERIPO.

The premises at Panditeripo. having been repaired—at
least so as to render them habitable—the doctor commenced his long-coveted work of preaching the Gospel
to the heathen. To give the reader a just impression of
the man and the missionary, we will insert a part of the
journal kept by him, and transmitted to Dr. Worcester.

BEGINS PREACHING.

" *Monday, July* 10*th.* Yesterday morning preached at
Panditeripo for the first time. There were thirty men,

besides a number of children, present. After service I
went to Tillipally, and united with the brethren in the observance of the Lord's Supper. In the afternoon preached by the wayside to numbers who were flocking to one
of their celebrated temples. This is the time of the year
when the great adversary of souls endeavors to strength-
en his kingdom; but we trust the day is not far distant
when this people will bow their knees to Jesus and own
him Lord of all. One of the Brahmins whom I addressed appeared exceedingly enraged, saying, 'There is but
one God; if you speak of Jesus Christ, your religion is a
lie.'"

GREAT TEMPLE AT NELLORE.

"Visited the great heathen temple at Nellore, and
witnessed some of the abominations of heathenism. The
idol had been carried from place to place before the temple during the former part of the evening, but, as it was
late before we reached the place, we saw nothing of the
procession. But we saw enough to sicken the heart,
enough to make us retire and weep for the slain of the
daughter of this people. Behind the idols were a number of poor deluded creatures prostrate on the ground,
who had a short time before been rolling after the cars
as they moved fom place to place. But one of the most
disgusting sights presented to our view was a number of
dancing-girls performing some of the ceremonies of their
religion. An opinion is prevalent among many that the
heathen are fit subjects for the kingdom of heaven, even
though they never embrace the Gospel. But the Word
of God allows us to indulge no such opinion. It de-
clares to us that whoremongers, idolaters, liars, thieves,

and the workers of every abomination, have no part in the kingdom of heaven. The degradation of the people is so great that no language we can use will convey an adequate idea of it. From our unhappy experience we are constantly learning that they have all gone out of the way, that there is not one among them that doeth good, no, not one."

REMOVES TO PANDITERIPO.

"*Saturday, July 22d.* The room which is designed eventually for a medicine - room being finished, Mrs. Scudder removed from Tillipally to this place this afternoon. We have much reason to remember the kindness of Mr. and Mrs. Poor to us, and we take our leave of that station with the full assurance that the great Head of the Church will continue to bless them in that work to which they are so devotedly engaged. We feel our situation to be peculiarly solemn when we remember that a whole parish of immortal souls is committed to our charge, and that if we be unfaithful their blood will be required at our hands. This consideration, we trust, will induce the followers of the divine Redeemer to be earnest in their intercessions at the throne of grace for us."

LICENSED TO PREACH.

"*Tuesday, August 8th.* This day, after having undergone such examinations upon theology as the brethren thought proper, I was licensed to preach the Gospel.

"*August 9th.* Went in company with Mr. Poor to Point Pedro to meet Mr. Garrett. We were much delighted to hear that the cause of the Redeemer continued to flourish in our native schools, but were exceedingly

distressed to hear that so many of the crew of the Indus
had backslidden. We do hope that more than six will
be found in the great day of account at the right hand
of the Saviour. Be this, however, as it may, we know
that the Lord doeth all things well, and, though this be a
most trying event, we shall have reason throughout eternity to adore him, if even these prove faithful unto death.
We trust from among this number one will arise who
will hereafter lift up his voice like a trumpet in proclaiming the unsearchable riches of Christ to the Gentile
world."

PREACHING IN PUBLIC AND FROM HOUSE TO HOUSE.

"*Saturday, August* 12*th*. This morning we had between sixty and seventy at morning prayers. A number
of them were sick. We think it a large congregation
when we can assemble so many, independent of the boys
in our schools. If we should sit down at our ease at
home, and preach but two or three times a week, we
should see but few people. This renders it absolutely
necessary for the missionary of the Cross to go out into
the highways and hedges, to visit from house to house,
warning and exhorting the people to flee from the wrath
to come. To labor in this manner is often a trying duty,
owing in part to the awful stupidity of the people, to the
relaxed state of our bodies from the heat of the climate,
and doubtless much more to that deadness and dullness
in divine things under which we have to groan from day
to day; but we believe if we do not thus labor we are unfit
for our high and holy calling. We believe we are in the
places of more faithful men; and, what is beyond con-
ception dreadful, the blood of this people will be found

in the skirts of our garments in the day when•we must render an account of our stewardship."

PRESCRIBING FOR THE SICK.

"I prescribe for the sick at an early hour every morning, and have prayers and conversation with them before I administer to their wants. I find it an excellent time to compare their present situation with what it will be in eternity, if they reject the only sacrifice for sin. I hope that proper support will be given to the hospital, and medicines largely furnished, that I may not be prevented from recommending the Saviour to many who come from a distance, and who otherwise would, perhaps, never hear his precious name. Many females come for medical advice, and thus are obliged, at least once, to attend the house of prayer."*

SUPERSTITIOUS FEARS.

"*Saturday, September 2d.* One of the rooms of the house being nearly finished, we removed into it this afternoon. This morning some of the people in the hospital were much terrified in consequence of having heard a noise in the night. This noise was occasioned by my endeavors to drive away a rat which was eating the olas of the roof. They supposed that the devil was really here. I mention this as one of the instances of the su-

* I have lately begun to give out tracts to those who can read who come for medical advice. By this means the Gospel will reach many places where the voice of the missionary is never heard. As I have no printed tracts, I am obliged to use those which are written upon the ola; and in general they are preferable, as many people can read the written characters who are much at a loss when they attempt to read the printed characters. I can prepare them written at a very cheap rate. They do not cost more than 8 or 9 cents a dozen.

perstition of this people. They are much afraid of the devil, and, as they believe that he resides in the banian-trees, they erect temples under them in which they worship him. There are two temples of this description near me.

"*Sunday, September 3d.* Preached at the school bungalow and hospital in the morning, and at the villages of Vardealadipoo and Surlepurum in the afternoon. The man at whose house I had appointed the last meeting died yesterday. I had but one opportunity to recommend the Saviour to his acceptance. It is a solemn consideration that many who are in this parish must die before I can possibly proclaim to them the only name by which they can be saved."

HEATHEN CHILDREN IN PRAYER.

"This morning, after service, when I had returned to my study, I heard the voice of one of the heathen children in prayer. I went near the bungalow, and truly my soul was delighted when I learned that at this time of the day they were assembled for the solemn service of God. If those who support these children could have witnessed this scene, they would have lifted up their voices to praise God that he ever put it into their hearts to support them."

THEY SEEK AFTER A SIGN.

" *Tuesday, September 5th.* This morning I adopted a plan which I hope will be attended with the divine blessing. I design to call aside one person daily, and converse and pray with him. The man with whom I conversed this morning was apparently affected. He appeared to feel the force of truth.   In the afternoon proclaimed the name of Jesus in the highways.   The people were atten- tive.   One man, who followed me from place to place, repeatedly asked me how he could know that Jesus Christ would forgive his sins.   He wished me to show some sign to prove it.   I told him that if he would believe in Him, • and forsake his sins, he could then know that his sins would be pardoned."

APPEAL FOR THE SUPPORT OF CHILDREN.

" *Wednesday, September 8th.* Turned away three Cath- olic children who wished to come and live with us. We had hoped and felt assured that, when intelligence should reach us from America, many names would ap- pear on the missionary page as the supporters of chil- dren under our care.   Alas! how are we disappointed! Is it thus that the followers of the Redeemer repay him for his kindness to them, for his bloody sweat in the garden, and for his agony upon the cross, that, when so many heathen children might be plucked from idolatry, and, in all human probability, from eternal burnings, they are unwilling to give the small sum of twelve dollars an- nually for so great an object?   It is a most mournful consideration that so little is done for the cause of mis- sions.   The heathen are going down to hell by millions every year, and yet many who profess to love the Saviour, and obey the great command to do to others as they would wish others to do to them, do not contribute a farthing of the substance God has given them for their salvation. At this very moment, while I am writing, the spirits of some of them are going to the judgment bar to hear their awful doom, and then sink to hell.   What excuse can

Christians offer, in the great day of account, that the
Word of Life has not before been sent to them? Alas!
when they find that it will be impossible for them to
clear themselves from their blood, they will stand speech-
less before God. Oh! who can for a moment think of
the woes of the second death without shuddering. If
death come to our own doors, and snatch one of our
friends from us in an unprepared state, our souls are
torn with anguish, and we refuse to be comforted when
we remember that the gnawing worm has begun to prey
upon his vitals, and will torment him day and night forever. But no concern is manifested though hundreds of
millions of souls equally precious take up their dismal
abode there. Can it be that the present state of things
is to continue? Are Christians who have sworn allegi-
ance to the Saviour at his table to live in violation of
one of his positive commands, and still be permitted to
come to his table? When a heathen is brought to the
knowledge of the truth, how must he be astonished when
he learns that Christians have neglected the heathen world
so long! With wonder he asks the question, Why has not
the Gospel, in compliance with the divine command, been
sent to every nation and people under heaven? But he
asks in vain; there is no one who can answer him. It is
certainly the duty of every one to contribute of his substance to send the Word of Life to the heathen, and yet
there are thousands who, if called upon to do it, can plead
their poverty as an excuse, while at the same time they
can paint their houses with vermilion and deck them
with every unnecessary ornament. This robbing the
Saviour of his due must not, can not continue."

PREACHING IN THE FIELDS.

"*Sunday, September* 10*th.* This being the busy season with the natives, I went into the fields this afternoon to preach. Met with several Catholics at work. I took occasion to warn them of the consequences of breaking the Sabbath. I asked one of them if he thought he treated the Lord Jesus in a proper manner after what he had done; but, notwithstanding I told him that if he persisted, the loss of his soul might be the consequence, no impression could be made upon him. He said he knew it was wrong, but he would go to his priest, confess his sin, and be forgiven. He continued his work. We have much reason to fear that the Catholics in this district will be the last who are brought into the kingdom of God."

THE BRAHMIN AND HIS SON.

"*Thursday, September* 14*th.* I have this morning been conversing with a Brahmin and his son. The son appeared to be a man of intelligence. I asked him how he expected to have his sins pardoned. He answered by praying to their gods. I, however, soon convinced him that sin could not be forgiven in this way. He then said that he must go to hell, and be punished according to his deserts, adding that, as washermen beat the clothes upon large stones until the dirt comes out, so it will be with the soul—after suffering according to its deserts, it will then go to heaven. After our conversation was ended, I performed a painful surgical operation upon him, and endeavored to point out to him how awful would be the misery of those who rejected the Lord Jesus, and at last perished. This people, like all others who have never been humbled at the foot of the Cross, depend upon their own doings for salvation. Generally they tell us that charity, good works, offerings to their temples, washing in some sacred waters, and praying to their gods, will insure them an entrance into heaven. We can confound the simple ones among them very easily by asking them if the performance of these acts would be considered by the government as an equivalent for the crime of breaking one of its laws. They unhesitatingly tell us 'No.' If we tell them that God is as strict as a government, and that *his* justice requires the punishment of the wicked, and again ask them how they can obtain salvation, they tell us, 'We do not know.' We then point out to them the necessity of an atonement for sin.

"Many deny altogether that they have sinned. They imagine if a man has never committed murder, or done some other great crime, he has not sinned. This renders it necessary for us constantly to open to their view the law of God in its length and breadth, teaching them that it extends as well to the thoughts as to the actions of men. Many have the hardihood, notwithstanding, to declare that they have never sinned in word or deed."

"*Sunday, September* 17th. Had a large congregation this morning. Between 150 and 200 persons were present. Preached in the afternoon at Vardealadipoo, and afterward at one of the native houses in a neighboring village to about seventy persons. After service we were treated with rice-cakes, oranges, and cocoa-nut water. In consequence of having so large a congregation, I appointed meeting them again on the ensuing Sabbath afternoon.

"*Wednesday, September* 20*th.* The odigar (the second officer of the parish) of a neighboring village died this morning very suddenly. I went in the afternoon to the house of his son, and preached to a large number of people who were collected to attend him to the house appointed for all the living. He was a Catholic, and had attended my preaching.

"*Saturday, September* 23*d.* Went to Matherkel, a large village about a mile from the church. I have just been building a bungalow at that place, and expect to commence a school there on Monday next. Preached to about 130 people.

"*Sunday, September* 24*th.* Preached on the parable of the sower to about 200 persons. Forty women were present. Administered medicine to fifty persons.

"*October* 4*th.* I have appointed one evening in the week for the schoolmasters to meet at this place, to bring in the report of the number of boys who daily attend the schools. I design to question them regularly upon portions of the Scriptures which I have given them to learn."

PREACHING FOR THE FIRST TIME IN TAMUL.

"*Sunday, October* 8*th.* This morning preached in Tamul at this place for the first time. I hope I was better understood than on Sabbath last at Batticotta. After service went to Batticotta to visit Mr. Richards, who is much more unwell than he has been for some time past. In the afternoon preached at Matherkel to nearly one hundred persons. Preached also at another part of the village to a large number of people who had collected together to attend a cock-fight. Above one hundred of them were Catholics. When I found that so many Catholics were present, I felt (somewhat like the apostle of old) my spirit rising within me to see their abominations. I felt much the want of a better knowledge of this language, that I might cry aloud and spare not. Our addresses, through our interpreters, must necessarily lose much of the effect. Soon after I left them they began to indulge themselves in their wickedness, paying no attention to what I had said to them.

" *Tuesday, October* 17*th.* It is an object of earnest desire as much as possible to gain the affections of this people, but we see so much depravity manifested by them that it is sometimes difficult to display a becoming mildness toward them. We have much more hope of being useful if we can make them believe that our motives for coming among them are to do them good, and that we seek their happiness by our intercourse with them. I have this morning been conversing and praying with two Brahmins, whom I affectionately entreated to throw down the weapons of their rebellion, and submit to the Saviour. I told them that their rejection or reception of the Gospel would be of no consequence to myself, but that the consequences on their part would be dreadful if they should reject it. I told the one who came for medical advice that it gave me much pleasure to cure his sickness, because I wished him to be happy in this world, and because I wished him to be happy in the world to come. I recommended the Saviour to him. May the Lord apply what has been spoken."

SABBATH DESECRATION.—FORCE OF EXAMPLE.

"In the afternoon preached at Makiarpertly for the first time on the Sabbath. It being two miles distant from the church, I rode there in a palankeen. Found but few people. I was told that they had gone to their fields. This circumstance induced me to address those present on the nature of the Sabbath. After the service the question was asked, 'Why does he ride in a palankeen on the Sabbath?' It was the first time I had ever gone out in a palankeen on the Sabbath to preach, and my present feelings induce me to believe that I shall not do so again very soon. After I returned from Makiarpertly I preached at Matherkel, and, though I had to wade through the water to go there, I found it much more comfortable to suffer this inconvenience than to suffer from the reflection that the natives believe my conduct and conversation disagree, and that I break that Sabbath which I enjoin them to keep. This people can not, or will not distinguish between works of necessity and mercy, and we wish, as much as possible, to avoid every occasion of offense."

DEATH OF A MALABAR.

"*Friday, November* 17*th.* Last night a young Malabar from the coast died in the hospital. I have reason to hope, from the evidence he gave of a change of heart, that he has gone to the house not made with hands, eternal in the heavens. He was a Protestant by descent. His attention was particularly directed to divine things a short time before he came here."

SIGHT TO THE BLIND.

"*November* 23*d*. Operated for cataract this morning. 6 This is the third case in which I have succeeded in giving sight to the blind.

"*Sunday, November* 26*th*. This afternoon Mrs. Scudder accompanied me to Vardealadipoo. Besides men and boys, sixty or seventy females were present at our meeting."

MONTHLY CONCERT.—CHRISTIAN DAVID.

"*Monday, December* 4*th*. This day we held the monthly concert of prayer at this place for the first time. Our monthly meetings have become very interesting, and a spirit of prayer seems to prevail among us. We are united in the strongest of bonds to our brethren of other denominations. Christian David preached here this morning to about two hundred and fifty persons. All the schools were assembled; three Brahmins were present. This man possesses a remarkable faculty of gaining the attention of the people. While we were praying for the enlargement of our Lord's kingdom, he went to Matherkel and preached to the people."

CONVERSATION WITH A BRAHMIN.

"*December* 7*th*. This morning had an interesting conversation with a Brahmin, who came for medical advice. After treatment I gave him nine chapters of Genesis, the Sermon on the Mount, and a small pamphlet containing the discourses of our Lord.

"Last night adopted the plan I formerly pursued at Tillipally, in calling a boy aside every evening to converse and pray with him. I have abundant reason to labor with these children when I remember that from among those who have been under religious instruction in this mission for three or four years past, there have been some already, we hope, born into the kingdom of God."

ONE YEAR'S LABORS.

"*December* 11*th*. This day one year ago we reached the place to which our eyes had long been directed, and where, we hope, it will be our unspeakable privilege to labor (unless called by Providence to some other part of the heathen world) until we finish our course and enter our rest. We have much reason to be thankful that our health has generally been very good. We have suffered but little except from the debilitating effects of the climate. Though I have seen but little fruit of my labors except in my boarding-school, where some little good has been done, yet it is a most pleasing circumstance that I have been enabled to employ a considerable portion of my time in tearing up the fallow ground, and in preaching the Gospel to thousands of perishing souls."

EVANGELIZATION.

"*Friday, December* 22*d*. Island of Caradive. I arrived here this morning at eleven o'clock. Began immediately to deliver the message of God to the people. Sent two of the boys whom I took with me to read the plan of salvation from house to house. Valuntalay is the name of the village where we now are.

VISITS THE SCHOOLS.

"It is a melancholy consideration that upon the whole of this island, where there are several thousands of immortal souls perishing for lack of knowledge, there is not perhaps one, with the exception of myself and one of the boys with me, who is looking to Jesus as the only hope of escape from the wrath to come. In looking at the devastations sin has made, the pathetic exclamation has been forcibly brought to my mind, ' O thou Adam, what hast thou done ?' The fields here appear white to the harvest, but there is no one to put in the sickle.

"*Saturday, December* 23d. I slept last night under the veranda of a native house, and was kindly entertained by the man who lived there. He supplied me with cocoa-nut water and milk, but would receive no compensation for them. After breakfast I continued my visits from house to house, until I came to the large open plain where the old Catholic church, in ruins, is standing. I was desirous to visit the schools on this island, hoping that I might, by offering a small compensation to the school-masters, be enabled to introduce some Scripture extracts, and induce them to make their boys commit to memory the plan of salvation, which was unfolded particularly in a tract entitled ' The Way to be Happy,' which I had lately prepared and had caused to be written upon the ola. But I found that little could be effected. I visited two schools. One was composed of four or five, the other of five scholars. I visited a third place, where I was told a school was kept; the schoolmaster and his two boys were absent. I endeavored to give away some Scripture extracts at the first school, but the schoolmas-

D

ter would not receive them. In the second I left five pamphlets. This, I believe, was not with the approbation of the schoolmaster. He was a Brahmin. As I had no pamphlets when I first visited the second school, I returned there a short time afterward. But my appearance before had created so much fear in the minds of the boys that they all ran away before I returned. It is probable that they had never before seen a white person. Many of the people were much afraid of me, and even the beasts, seeing so strange an animal as myself, fled from me."

DISTRUST OF THE HEATHEN.

"I found great difficulty in getting rid of my tracts. Many people who could probably read denied it. I, however, distributed eighteen or nineteen among them; and nearly as many Scripture extracts. I regret that I did not allow my boys to distribute tracts, as the people would have received them from them with less fear. The printed seemed much more desirable to them than the written. I trust, when I next visit them, that their fears will have subsided. I met with very few insults. While at the house of one of the Brahmins whom I had previously addressed, he said, very pleasantly, but with a great deal of self-confidence, 'Why do you pain your legs so much by walking for the purpose of talking to us? We will not come to your religion.' And truly it will be so, if the Holy Ghost do not apply the Word spoken. We daily have to learn the truth of what the apostle has told us, 'That Paul may plant and Apollos water, but God must give the increase.'

"In this island there are no Catholics, which is peculiarly favorable for the spread of the Gospel among them. It would be an excellent situation for a native preacher, but, alas! we have none to send them. It is a matter of devout thankfulness to Almighty God that he has placed under our care a number of boys, many of whom, we believe, will be extensively useful hereafter in building up the kingdom of Christ among this poor, perishing people. Two of them were very diligent in reading to the people and in questioning them."

NEED OF PRAYER FOR MISSIONARIES.

"In this vast and extensive valley of dry bones we require much faith and grace to persevere in well-doing. If any class of ministers ever needed the prayers of God's people, the missionary pre-eminently needs them. When we see all our labor apparently lost, unbelief, to our great shame be it spoken, notwithstanding all the great and precious promises, is sometimes apt to creep in, and we are almost ready to fear that we shall labor in vain, and spend our strength for naught and in vain. We have much reason to be thankful that our own souls are refreshed while watering the vineyard of our divine Master. We reached home a little after six o'clock this evening, and hope ere long that I may again be permitted to bear the Bread of Life with renewed vigor to this starving and perishing people."

SCHOOLS FOR GIRLS.

"*Sunday, December* 24*th.* I have, for some time past, been making efforts to establish schools for girls, but little has yet been done. I am glad, however, to state that one girl is now attached to the school at Surlepurum.

She was present at our service there this afternoon. We have many difficulties to encounter when we attempt to make innovations; but we do not forget the motto of the celebrated apostle to the Indians: 'Prayers and pains, through faith in Christ Jesus, will do any thing.'

"*Wednesday, December 27th.* This afternoon I found three girls at the school in Surlepurum. One was absent. It is certainly a matter of thankfulness to the great Head of the Church that he should thus smile upon the attempts of his unworthy servant. To his name be all the praise."

IMPORTANT SURGICAL OPERATION.

"*Wednesday, January 10th.* This morning I removed a tumor from the side of a man which measured more than one foot in circumference. It was the largest I ever took out."

FOLLY OF HEATHENISH RITES.

"*Sunday, January 14th.* This morning had an uncommonly interesting meeting with the people. Friday last being a great day with many of the natives, on which they offered rice to the sun, I took particular occasion to address them on the folly of such conduct, and endeavored to point out to them the dishonor done to God by rendering worship to any created object. I asked one why the people did so. The answer was, 'For want of wit.' I asked another, Why did you go lately to your temple to worship idols? 'I did it through ignorance.' This was a falsehood, as he had often been told of the folly of such conduct. I asked another why he offered rice to the sun. He said, 'The sun is a witness of God,

therefore we offer him rice.' Another said that they
worshiped the sun because they could not see God;
and said, 'Suppose my child was sick, if I should come
here to tell you of it, and if I could not see you, but see
the young man (meaning the one studying medicine
with me), I would tell him.'

"The catechetical form of preaching is very necessary
among the heathen. They are, in general, so stupid that,
unless we keep their attention awake by asking them questions, they will know nothing of what we say. When I
first began to preach to them I followed that course pursued in Christian churches at home, but not half the effect was produced which I trust now is. When I keep
calling out constantly to the people and our school-boys
to answer me questions, or give me reasons why they
pursue that course of folly which is characteristic of their
worship, they can not avoid paying attention. By asking them questions and reasons for their worship, I also
become acquainted with those refuges of lies to which
they trust, and hope I am enabled frequently to convince
the judgment of their fallacy. This plan Christian David adopts."

LABORS OF THE MISSIONARY'S WIFE.

"I accompanied the doctor this afternoon from house
to house to converse with the people. We found them
very willing to hear; but their minds are darkened, and
they understand not the things that belong to their peace.
One observation a woman made (while talking with her)
is very true of most of them. She said, 'It is all very
good,' but 'as soon as you are gone *I forget all about it*.'
This woman has heard the Gospel almost every Sabbath

since we have been here.   Very many of them say, 'How
shall we get any thing to eat if we spend our time coming to your church?'   They are very ready to confess
that their idols have eyes, but they see not, etc.; but they
say, 'Our ancestors worshiped idols, and why should not
we?'

"*November 3d.* Have to-day been conversing with the
Catholic woman.   I have been very plain with her, and
endeavored to convince her of the vanity of calling upon
the Virgin Mary and saints when she prays, and I entreated her to look to none but Jesus.   She asked me, If
a sinner went to hell, whether, after a few years, he could
go to heaven?   She said their Scriptures told them they
could.

"*November 23d.* We have received a letter from you,
my beloved Mother W., and have great reason to be
grateful, and to bow ourselves before our heavenly Father, and return thanks to you and to our dear family.
I do indeed feel grateful to our God for giving you, my
mother, a quiet mind concerning us.   Although our Father's hand has been heavy upon us, we must not, and we
will not be unmindful of his mercies.   He has preserved
our lives.   He has furnished us with all that has been
needful for our comfort.   He has placed us in the midst
of kind and affectionate friends, who share in our joys
and sorrows, and, I trust, has given us some fervent desire
to see souls brought into his kingdom.   When I receive
letters it seems as if America were drawing nearer to
Ceylon, and my imagination almost brings me into the
company of my dear mother, sisters, and brothers.

"*December 1st.* In consequence of heavy rains and the
cholera prevailing, our congregations have been small for

some time. The number is now increasing. The doctor preaches in Tamul every Sabbath, and the people at times appear attentive. A few women attend every Sabbath, and ten girls are generally present. After the service I am in the habit of calling the females into our hall, and endeavor, in my feeble way, to give them some instruction. But oh! they are in a wretched state of ignorance and superstition.

"*December* 5*th.* On Monday attended the monthly concert of prayer at Manepy. These meetings are very precious and pleasant. All the missionaries in this district, with their wives, attend. In the morning each missionary relates every thing of an interesting nature that has occurred at his station during the past month. In the afternoon one missionary who has been previously appointed delivers an address, and the other missionaries make their remarks upon what has been said. The rest of the day is spent in prayer and singing."

Alluding to Mrs. Scudder's work, Dr. S. says: "Mrs. Scudder is well. She has her hands full of business. She provides for the children, and takes care of almost the whole of the domestic concerns, which are neither few nor small. She has ten females under her care. These she teaches to sew in the afternoons. In the morning she begins to hear the boys recite in English, which is no small labor. She hears three different classes. She sometimes visits the people. My labors are, as you might expect, various, such as preaching, visiting the people from house to house, instructing them in the things belonging to their everlasting peace, visiting schools, taking tours at a distance from home, distributing tracts, attending to the sick, laboring with those un-

der my care, etc. Pray much for both of us that we
may be enabled to discharge the various duties which
have been laid upon us. Our work is an arduous one,
and we need much divine influence to enable us to persevere with diligence."

CHAPTER V.

Worshiping Books.—Has the Sun a Soul?—Thank-offering of a Heathen.—Roman Catholics.—A Bud blighted, etc.

SECOND. JOURNAL FROM PANDITERIPO.

The plan of operations by the missionaries of Ceylon was both simple and effective. A station was selected —central, if possible—and, while cultivating that, they extended their preaching tours to the neighboring towns and districts. These settlements, densely populated, afforded accessible fields for preaching the Gospel, and for the distribution of books and tracts. Generally the missionaries were accompanied by their pupils—at least by such as were reliable—and sometimes by an interpreter.

At Panditeripo there were schools for girls and boys, mostly under the care of Mrs. Scudder while the doctor was engaged in hospital service or on preaching tours. This brought a heavy burden on Mrs. S., which—considering her increasing domestic affairs—could never have been borne but for the presence and assistance of the faithful colored Amy. It was a favoring providence that gave this woman to the Scudder family, especially as the natives, in that capacity, were both lazy and unreliable. She, in fact, became, through mental culture and growing piety, a companion to Mrs. S., while still she never presumed to consider herself in any other light than as a Christian servant.

When the doctor moved off, surrounded by his dusky .

pupils, on these preaching tours, with the expectation of being absent for a week or more, the whole care of the mission at home came upon Mrs. Scudder, and bravely did she meet the responsibility. This may be seen by the few extracts which will be given from her journal. In her were combined the most amiable feminine traits and the heroism of the martyr. Her judgment was quick to discern, and her hand prompt to execute whatever of duty lay before her. Cheerfully did she bid her husband "God speed" as he started on his outside mission, and when he returned she met him with the affectionate welcome ; and then they sat down together, and mutually related the experience of God's goodness.

Dr. Scudder's twofold work as physician to the body and soul, while it gave him the greater influence, imposed upon him unusual labors. He carried along with him medicines and surgical instruments, that he might be ready to meet every case of bodily distress, believing that in this way God opened avenues to the soul. Many an illustration of this occurred ; and some who had been healed, like the grateful leper of Scripture, "returned to give glory to God."

It is not our intention to tax the reader's patience with long journals or varied correspondence. We shall select only, here and there, from these abundant materials, what may be necessary to afford a just impression of these faithful missionaries. The second journal of Dr. and Mrs. Scudder from Panditeripo, a few extracts from which we give, will show more clearly the nature of their work than any outside observer could furnish.

WORSHIPING BOOKS.—HAS THE SUN A SOUL?

"*Friday, January* 5*th.* This afternoon, while laboring among the people, a man told me that I worshiped books. I never heard of this before. This opinion has probably obtained in consequence of seeing books used in courts of justice or by us in our preaching. My interpreter has informed me that a number of ignorant people believe it. Some of this people do worship their books.

"27*th.* This morning I was asked about the sun's having a soul. It was said it must have a soul because it moved. I asked them if a feather had life because it was moved about by the wind. 'No.' I then told them that the world and sun were moved by the agency of God just as the wind moves a feather. This simple manner of reasoning has the desired effect.

"This afternoon visited from house to house. The same man who told me on Friday afternoon that I worshiped books again met me. During our conversation he asked me to show him what color and shape God was. Before I attempted to answer him, I asked him the color and shape of the wind. A number of persons afterward followed me."

THANK OFFERING OF A HEATHEN.

"*Friday, February* 2*d.* This afternoon, while among the people, I went to a heathen temple, and had some conversation with a man who was recovering from a very severe illness. He attributed his relief to his gods. He said that, when very ill, he, with his wife, came there and cried to their gods, and his disease was removed. He had promised that, if he recovered, he would make an offering at the temple.   While I was there the offerings arrived.   I conversed freely with him, but found him exceedingly obstinate.   He had no doubt but that his gods had relieved him, and this was an additional argument with him to trust in them (very natural, and what a rebuke to many in Christian lands!)."

ROMAN CATHOLICS.

"*March* 1*st*.   Have labored almost entirely among the Catholics during the last month, and have had much reason to persevere.   Have been preparing a tract especially for them.   In it I have endeavored to point out the ingratitude of their continuing in sin after what the Son of God had done and suffered to save them.   My boys have been sent out to read it to the people.   It was well received.   Some of the Catholics sent me their 'salam.' "

A BUD BLIGHTED.

"*March* 14*th*.   This morning Mrs. Scudder was made the happy mother of a living child.   We have much reason for thankfulness, as we have been called to part with two children since we left our native land.   Had a visit from Sir Richard Ottley.

"19*th*.   Last evening we committed the beloved child which had so lately been given us to the dust.   It was taken ill on Monday night, and died the following evening.   Mr. Woodward baptized it on Saturday afternoon. We named it Brainerd, after the celebrated missionary to the Indians, in hope that, if God spared its life, we might hereafter hold up to his view the example of that excellent man.   Thus, in less than eighteen months, we have been called to part with three children; enough, it would be supposed, to teach us that this is not our place of rest. May our loss be made up by spiritual children from among this heathen people!"

PREACHING TOUR.

"*Point Pedro, January 9th.* On Tuesday evening last, in company with Mr. Koch, three of my boys (Griffin, Willis, and Gautier), my interpreter and his cook, together with four coolies, I set out for this place. We reached Copay, four or five miles distant from Odooville, about nine or ten o'clock, and, being fatigued, we stopped several hours to rest in an uninhabited house of that place. In the afternoon we divided into three companies, and went out among the people to sow the seed of the Word. We distributed forty tracts and nine books (Scripture extracts) among them. In the evening went to Potoer, about five miles farther. We arrived about eight o'clock. While walking by moonlight, it was a sweet reflection that I was engaged in a work which had the approbation of my God. Oh, how thankful should I feel to the great Head of the Church for allowing me to labor among these heathen! Truly I envy not those who dwell in palaces—I envy not those who are settled in parishes at home. It shall be my joy to spend and to be spent among the heathen.

"On Wednesday morning we continued our visits from house to house; distributed forty-two tracts and twenty books. I performed the operation for cataract upon an old man above seventy years of age, and succeeded in restoring his sight to him."

WHITE ANTS AND ROBBERS.

"In the evening we went to a parish, 'Ocdoepittie.'
Mr. Koch and myself slept under a large piece of coarse
muslin, the corners of which we tied to the trees. I took
possession of a part of the veranda at first, but, being
disturbed by the white ants, I thought proper to change
my quarters. On Friday morning we went from place
to place to visit the people. I stopped at a bazar and
addressed a number of them, but not one of them would
receive either a tract or a book. Passed on to the next
parish (Kattoweller), but did not reach it till nearly elev-
en o'clock. Owing to the intense heat of the sun, we can
not travel in the middle of the day without great danger. We therefore rested five or six hours. In the afternoon visited the people, and distributed a number of
tracts and books. In the evening I removed my lodgings through fear of the robbers, and went to the house
of the Vedar, about a mile distant. We were treated
very kindly, and were accommodated with an open house
which was built for some religious purpose.

"This morning we reached the Wesleyan Mission
House, and were kindly received by Rev. J. Batt. We
distributed the remainder of our books, in all one hundred and twenty, and about thirty tracts. One hundred
additional books have arrived for me from my kind
friend Mr. Mooyaart."

A BRAHMIN.

"This morning a Brahmin with whom I conversed
told me that his religion was true, because they could

foretell future events. The events alluded to were the foretelling eclipses.

"*June* 10*th*. Though separated from the people to whom I statedly preach, the Lord can carry on his work without me. Have visited the sick families, and proclaimed the Saviour's name to those who were present. Though our labors often appear to be in vain, it is a pleasing reflection that we are preparing the way for the coming of the Son of Man. While the day lasts, it seems to be of great importance that we who are the missionaries of the Cross should labor with activity, as upon our exertions perhaps may depend the salvation of thousands who are yet unborn. If we prove unfaithful in one instance, it may affect hundreds who are to live hereafter. Oh that this reflection might induce me to be always engaged for God, and be faithful to my solemn trust!

"This morning, after having conversed with a man, he said he would endeavor to conduct himself according to what I had said. Observing that there was some resemblance between the religion I professed and the Catholic religion, he told me that one of the heathen was about to turn Catholic, because when he was sick he was taken to the Catholic Church and recovered; hence he thought the Catholic faith must be true. The Catholics are very superstitious. At Jaffnapatam there is a priest by the name of Lopez, who died a number of years ago. A part of his dust remains, which the Catholics imagine possesses great virtues. Occasionally his tomb is opened, and sick persons are favored with a little of it to take internally. When they do not recover after this, I know not to what the failure is attributed."

POWER OF PRAYER.

" Prayer is one of the most powerful engines which can be used in destroying the kingdom of the god of this world. Without it we shall labor in vain. Without it missionary societies will send forth heralds of the Cross in vain. One great reason, perhaps, why so few heathen are gathered into the fold of Christ is because the people of God are so seldom in their closets pleading for God's blessing on our labors. Christians may perhaps think that because they have made great exertions in sending missionaries to the heathen, that thousands of conversions will take place. But God, who seeth not as man seeth, will disappoint their expectations unless their exertions are accompanied with earnest prayer for his blessing.

" *June* 11*th.* Set off from Point Pedro, and came to Timmorache district, where the voice of the Gospel minister is seldom heard. In consequence of having so few tracts, Mr. Koch, my interpreter, and myself have been busily engaged to-day in writing " the plan of salvation" on the blank leaf of the Scripture extracts, with which I am now, through the kindness of Mr. Mooyaart and Mr. Batt, well supplied. On my way here, stopped to address a number of women on their way to the bazar. Failed to win and hold their attention. Gautier, one of my boys, stopped at another place and addressed the women. They were quite attentive to what he said. He possesses a great faculty in communicating religious truths.

" *Tuesday, June* 12*th.* We passed on to another parish (Eledoematual); distributed seventeen books and twelve tracts. Most of the people whom I saw this morning were willing to hear what I had to say. We were treated very kindly by the government schoolmaster. These schoolmasters hold a high rank among the natives.

"This morning I passed through much sandy country. A comparison often made by divines was brought to my mind. 'If from this vast body of sand one grain were separated every thousand years, the eternal misery of thousands of these heathen will only just be begining.' Christians, you who have been privileged with the Gospel, I thought then that I would plead with you for the heathen. Think it not beneath a missionary of the Cross if he requests that when you are called upon to contribute largely of your substance to send the Gospel to the heathen, that, before you refuse to contribute, you will think of the innumerable grains of sand on the hill-side or the sea-shore, and remember that if one of these grains were to drop every thousand years, the woes, the miseries, the horrors of the heathen, if lost, will only be beginning. Then let conscience speak, and it will tell you that you must not refuse to do all in your power to save them from eternal burnings. Help us for Jesus' sake. Send us the means to put the Scriptures and tracts into the hands of this people."

WILD BEASTS.

"Having distributed twenty-seven books and fourteen tracts, we set out at five o'clock for Mogomale. We passed through a dreary jungle inhabited by wild beasts, elephants, tigers, wolves, and other animals. We passed unmolested. They had a commission from our divine convoy not to make an attack upon us. The sand in the jungle was exceedingly heavy, and we arrived at the

house of the Maniagar very tired. If I could have traveled without shoes I should have been less fatigued. This,
however, I could not do, as both of my heels are blister-
ed. There are very few people in this dreary parish.

"*June* 13*th.* After having made it a subject of prayer,
I concluded not to go to the two adjoining parishes. I
therefore set off for Catchay, where I arrived after ten
o'clock, after a very unpleasant walk, the greater part of
the way through jungle and sand. The wild animals
most to be dreaded in these jungles are the elephants.
They sometimes prove destructive to life. They possess
so great strength as to push down cocoa-nut and palmyra
trees. We passed some trees yesterday which they had
probably pushed down. We dined under a large tree
near the place where an old church formerly stood. In
the afternoon we set off for Chavicherry, where we arrived between five and six o'clock. To-morrow I intend
to cross over into the Wanny district. I have received a
fresh supply of tracts from home."

CHAVICHERRY.

"*June* 14*th.* At Chavicherry there is a very large bazar. This morning Mr. Koch and the boys distributed
more than fifty books and fifty tracts among the people
who were attending it. All who wished to receive books
could not be supplied, it being necessary to reserve some
for Ponnoreen. It would be a matter for devout thankfulness if their desire to receive these books proceeded
from a right source. But not so. The Lord, however,
can bless the Word to their everlasting good.

" To-day I have suffered much from the heat, and have ·
been much burned by the scorching sun. Ate nothing

after breakfast until evening, with the exception of a little fruit.   Among other palatable things, I ate a piece of peacock for my supper.

"*June* 15*th.* This morning I set out to visit the people before breakfast.   This was imprudent, as in this exhausting climate the powers of the constitution are soon broken down without food.   Tracts and books were distributed.   Continued our walk.   Four Catholic tracts were distributed, the first 'we have given away.   My boys are all complaining with headache.   As circumstances seem to favor it, if Providence permit, I am determined to sail this evening for the Jaffna district.

"*June* 16*th.* After distributing the remainder of our books and forty tracts, we set sail from Ponnoreen about six o'clock last evening, and reached Chavicherry between eight and nine.   This morning early we left the house of C. Vanderlynd, magistrate at Chavicherry, and walked some distance before breakfast.   Found some heathen busily engaged in building a car for their idols.   I endeavored to convince them of the sin and folly of making any representations of God.   They could plead no excuse—only custom."

HAUNTED HOUSE.—REACHES HOME.

"On our arrival at Norvekolie we were admitted to the house of the Vedar.   But, before it was time to retire to rest, we were conducted to a house which the owner had some time before left, one woman having died there, and another, having been bitten by a dog, had been taken with symptoms of hydrophobia.   They hence imagined that the house was possessed by the devil, and they would no longer reside there.   We spent the morning and evening of the Sabbath in sowing the seed of the Word in the villages and the fields. My tracts for the heathen being gone, we distributed about twenty which had been written for the Catholics.

"*Tuesday, June* 19*th.* I reached home last evening, and rejoice in the goodness of God in restoring me in good health to my family. The whole number of Scripture extracts distributed in this tour were three hundred and thirty-two, together with about five hundred and fifty tracts. The Word of Life is now in the hands of many persons hitherto benighted. What is to be the result is known only to Infinite Wisdom. Thus far I feel confident that I have labored in vain, unless God shall give his blessing. This people are so completely sunk in sin that it requires no less an effort to turn them than to raise one from the dead. I rejoice, however, in the work; and so pleasant has it been, that I am sure I shall be induced, ere long, to visit other uncultivated fields. I think it of great importance that we have tracts to distribute when we thus itinerate and preach the Gospel. The people in general will read them, and what they read they will remember better than our conversations with them. I should be very glad if any would contribute something to have tracts written for distribution. I can procure from twelve to fifteen thousand written for one hundred Spanish dollars. The printed tracts are also very desirable, and large funds are needed to print that variety which we should be glad to circulate.

"At Norvekolie a Catholic requested me to give him a Testament. I told him his priest would not allow him to read it. He, however, said differently. I was obliged to tell him I had no Testament which I could spare. I

promised that if he would go to Panditeripo I would
give him some Scripture extracts."

"During my journey I was treated very kindly by
most of the natives. With two exceptions, they would
receive no compensation for the little comforts with
which we were supplied.

"*Tuesday, June 1st.* This morning I set apart as a
special season for prayer and thanksgiving. The young
man who accompanied me returned this morning from
Jaffnapatam. He was very active during the whole time
I was from home, and probably did more work than myself. My boys also were very active. With their assistance, nearly as much was done in one day as I should
have accomplished, if alone, in three.

"*July 13th.* To-day Mrs. Scudder went to Matherkel to
visit the Catholic females. Fifty assembled at the Vedar's house to see her."

"I started with Mr. Koch and the boys, Gautier, Willis, and Brittian, on another tour, to visit the islands Caradive and Unaturai."

"Mr. Koch spent a very pleasant afternoon among the
Catholics. They seemed very anxious to hear what he
had to say. Many followed him, the greater part of
whom were women, from one corner of the street to another, in groups of from forty to fifty, and seemed attentive to his instructions. All to whom he gave tracts and

books received them thankfully, and promised to read them with attention.

"On Monday morning we continued our visits from house to house, distributing tracts and books among the people. Little did I imagine that I would meet with so much success among Catholics in distributing the Word of Life, or I should have made greater preparations. I took above eighty Catholic tracts with me, the greater part of which were then distributed.

"I went to one of the Catholic churches. It was a large building. I went far back behind the curtain where the images were kept. Some people and children following me, I addressed them before their altar. Within the church I saw the car upon which the image of the Virgin Mary is placed when they parade it through the streets. In front of the church they have a long pole erected, upon which a color, with the image of St. Anthony upon it, was flying. Three persons inquired for the New Testament.

"On Monday evening, through the kindness of Mr. Mooyaart, I received twenty-four additional Scripture extracts, some containing the parables, and others the discourses of our Lord. Having taken some congee (rice and water, with cocoa-nut milk), I crossed over the ferry to Caradive. The people on this island are nearly all heathen. It being the sowing season, I went out into the fields and conversed with the people. I was detained out later than I should have been in consequence of the Coolie disobeying my orders. Previous to my arrival near the centre of the island, the cow-house was made ready for my reception.

"In the afternoon I continued my visits among the

people. I arrived before sunset at the house of my old friend (the brother of the Odigar) at Valentalay, much fatigued. His was the first native house in which I ever slept. In this climate I am soon fatigued and overcome by the heat of the weather; but eternity will be long enough to rest in. If I may at last reach that blessed shore, it is of little consequence through how many trials I may be called to pass.

"About fifteen books and fifty tracts were distributed during the morning and afternoon. On Wednesday morning went to the beach and addressed the fishermen there. Had a portion of the Scriptures read to them. We gave away the last of our twenty-four books while at the house where we tarried through the night.

"*Thursday*, 28*th*. Reached home last evening a little after sunset. Nearly thirty tracts were distributed at Caradive and on the way home."

NEW TRACTS REQUIRED.

"I feel the importance of having a tract written on the subject of the new birth, to have read to the Catholics. I have lately finished a tract on the nature and duties of the Sabbath. The boys began to read it in Chillallu last week. A variety of subjects should be presented to this people, for the purpose of endeavoring, through divine assistance, to awaken them from their deplorably wretched state of spiritual death."

TRACTS PREPARED.

"I have prepared five new tracts—one on the ingratitude of sin; the other on the new birth, designed especially for Catholics. The fourth and fifth are dialogues.

One contains a description of the work of grace in the South Sea Islands. The second dialogue points out particularly the character of the Lord Jesus; the insufficiency of any atonement being made by us; and the all-sufficiency of that which has been made by the Son of God.

"Jesus Christ and him crucified is the only doctrine that ever was or ever will be blessed to the conversion of souls; and we may hope that in proportion as tracts embody these precious truths, such will be their success. Convince a man that he is a sinner, and that he can make no atonement by his own works, and we have hope of winning him to trust in Christ alone for salvation. As we expect much good by the distribution of tracts here, we hope to receive many for translation from our native land. Mr. Winslow has also lately written to Mr. Pearce, in Calcutta, for copies of the different tracts circulated in their mission."

PRAYER BY CHRISTIANS AT HOME.

"In this mission we have set apart Wednesday evening for the purpose of pleading at our respective stations for the outpouring of the Holy Spirit upon our missionary stations, and upon those in Bombay. At one of these meetings the Lord commenced a work in one soul which, I trust, will be carried on to the day of Jesus Christ. We shall hail the commencement of any such meeting in our native land. And if persons could not meet together, we should rejoice if they would retire to their closets, and plead at the same time with us. Brethren, pray for us—yes, for us, that we may be kept from falling; that we may be active and diligent laborers while the day lasts; and that we may see the work of the Lord commence with great power among us. Pray that the streams which make glad the city of God may visit this parched and thirsty land. And may the blessing of God the Father, God the Son, and God the Holy Ghost, rest upon every one who bows the knee to Him, and pleads that the kingdom of our Lord Jesus Christ may come!"

E

CHAPTER VI.

Sacramental Season.—New-Year's Thanksgiving.—Encouragement.—A
Child dead.—Absence and Return, etc.

MRS. SCUDDER'S JOURNAL.

THIS journal was somewhat of a family affair, having
been kept for the relatives at home, that they might be
informed of the most interesting incidents of her missionary life. Without drawing aside the veil of domestic
privacy, extracts may be given interesting to the general
reader as well as to those for whom the diary was especially penned.

SACRAMENTAL SEASON.

"Yesterday our dear friends, Mr. and Mrs. Winslow,
united with us in commemorating the death of our Lord
and Saviour. One of the girls in our school professed
her faith in Christ, and was admitted a member of our
little Church. I know you will rejoice to hear of this.
But oh, you can not feel as we feel, who are in the midst
of these benighted wanderers, when we behold one, here
and there, brought into the fold of Christ.

"This girl is fourteen years of age. Her name is Ju-
liana Prime, by birth a Catholic. Pray for her, that she
may be kept faithful unto death."

NEW-YEAR'S THANKSGIVING.

"*January* 1st. This day has been spent in returning thanks to our kind and bountiful Benefactor for the mercies granted to our mission and our several families through the past year. The doctor and myself felt a desire to have our missionary band together at Panditeripo. We have this day been favored with the company of most of them, and have had a pleasant season.

"We gave our boys and girls a feast, with liberty to invite the boarding children of the other schools. It has been at Panditeripo a happy new-year. The doctor preached from the words, ' This year thou shalt die.'

"As the brethren wished to settle their annual accounts, they concluded to spend the night here. You will perhaps wonder how I provided accommodations for them all. I will tell you." She then describes an ingenious arrangement by which all were provided with a sleeping place. In the morning they departed joyfully to their respective stations.

ENCOURAGEMENT.

" I will tell you something for your encouragement to pray for the child bearing the name of my honored father. He is awakened to a concern for his soul, and is anxiously inquiring ' what he shall do to be saved.' It has now been about two weeks since he professed to feel himself a sinner, and we do hope he may be guided to Jesus as his deliverer ' from the wrath to come.' He is a lovely boy. When his father brought him, requesting us to take him, we had our stated number in the school. But I told the doctor I felt as if I could not let the child return with his father; that we must try and see what we could do ourselves for his support, until the Lord should open some other door. We accordingly received him. He has been with us about one year. Oh, pray that he may be raised up to be a preacher of the everlasting Gospel to his poor idolatrous countrymen!"

A CHILD DEAD.

"Mrs. Meigs's child has been summoned from this vale of tears. The disease which speedily terminated her life was the lockjaw. She was in her sixth year, and a very intelligent child. As our dear Mrs. M. possesses the tenderest feelings, I expected and feared she would almost sink under this affliction; but not so. She met me, saying, 'The Lord reigns;' 'It is well;' and after a few minutes she embraced me, saying, 'I now know, my dear sister, the deep waters you have passed through.' My own feelings were sensibly awakened at this, but I trust I found it 'good to go to the house of mourning.'"

ABSENCE AND RETURN.

"The doctor was absent about eighteen days. He returned home in health, and received a most hearty welcome from us all. I suffered considerable anxiety on his account during his absence, and my heart was melted with gratitude upon his safe return. But I am often left alone with the care of about forty persons. I sometimes recall the feelings I once possessed. Before I left America I thought that in a heathen land I could not endure the absence of my husband for a single day."

A BACKSLIDER.

"We have been weeping over one whom we hoped was a spiritual child. She has grievously sinned, and thus brought reproach upon our little Church. Susanna Anthony has fallen into a sin common among this people. But on this subject I will be silent. May she return to Christ! In all these trials we have one unfailing source of comfort—Jesus reigns, and will overrule all events, however deplorable in their nature, for his glory. She is now suspended from the Church. I hope the discipline will do her good, and be instrumental in bringing her back to Christ, and make her more watchful in future, that she may not again enter into temptation."

A DOMESTIC PICTURE.

"You ask many questions which I wish I could answer, so as to give you a just idea of our situation. I wish I could show you the house, the furniture, the garden, the school-children, and our own little mischievous H. I should then rejoice to take the rounds with you to our different stations, and introduce you to each of our dear missionary friends and *their* little ones. J. asks us, among other questions, what we eat, drink, and wear. At our breakfast and dinner we are never without our rice and curry (chicken and rice cooked with spices). In addition to that, our breakfast consists of coffee, with rice cakes. At dinner we have fowls sometimes prepared in one way and sometimes in another. As to vegetables, we generally provide ourselves with yams, sweet potatoes, onions, and greens. A variety of meats are to be had, but, for cheapness' sake, we generally take our fowl and fish.

We sometimes get a little pork and salt beef from Bengal. Our good friend Mrs. Mooyaart occasionally sends us a fine piece of cheese, sausages, and any little variety which she herself has. We had the other evening a dish of Indian pudding and milk, of which the doctor told me I must not fail to tell you. The fruits of the country we have in abundance, but I do not think any of them are to be compared with your strawberries, apples, and peaches.

" Our clothing consists chiefly of white cloth, made on the coast, and brought here for sale. It is similar to our long-cloth at home. There are colored ginghams made in Jaffna, but they do not stand washing. Every piece of European gingham or calico which I brought from home I value highly.

" The doctor's daily suits are white vests, when he will wear any, white jacket, and nankin pantaloons, which are preferable to white. I have received a very beautiful English straw bonnet as a present, a few days since, from our good friend Mrs. Mooyaart."

HARMONY.

" The Lord has kept us, and not suffered us to fall out by the way. Our friends, who have been in this field longer than we have, are dear to us, without one exception. We are, including all the band, united in harmony and love."

THE FAITHFUL AMY.

" I am much fatigued with the labors of the day, which have been more than usual in consequence of Amy's being sick. She complains daily of headache,

growing more and more severe. Wednesday she was
for several hours deprived of her reason. This, as you
may suppose, I felt to be a great affliction. Though now
better, I fear she will never enjoy good health in this
climate. Highly as we value her services, should Providence open some door for her return to America, I think
we shall feel it our duty to permit her to return. She
is to us a treasure which we shall be grieved to part
with; but it is a sacrifice which, perhaps, we must be
called to make."

SEA-BATHING.

"Last night the doctor took his train of boys to the
sea with him to bathe. His health is now not firm, and
salt-water bathing may do him good. I followed with
little Henry. At the bathing-place there is, in good
weather, no surf, and the water for some distance out is
shoal. I have been down repeatedly with the girls. The
children are very fond of bathing; and it is a very necessary thing in this wasting climate. I have heard the
doctor say he would like to be in Greenland for a little
season. Perhaps it might have a restorative power on
his constitution, the natural vigor of which, under this
debilitating climate, he seems somewhat to have lost. A
tour which he took two years ago injured him very much,
and from the effects of the fatigue which he then under-
went he seems never to have recovered. He is now
taking iron and bitters, and rides every morning on
horseback. Next Wednesday he will be thirty years old
—just the age, as he says, when our Saviour commenced
his ministry."

CONVERSION OF A BOY.

"Another month has gone. We hope it is a month long to be remembered by one of the dear boys. His name is Amadasinghum. He has been here a little more than two months. It appears that he came here from a desire to learn about this religion. He had heard the Batticotta boys read about it, and says he became convinced that there was but one God. He did not rest till he came to us, and three weeks ago yesterday he was, I hope, met by the Holy Spirit. We can not now tell what will be the result. He may soon forget it all. Thus much we can say, he appears to be engaged in religion, and none appears so desirable to him as Christ. He often comes to the doctor to converse upon divine things. May the Lord give us still more evidence that a good work has been begun in him!"

PRAYER FOR REVIVAL.

"Our friends from the different stations came here for the purpose of uniting with us in pleading with the Lord to open the windows of heaven and pour us out a blessing. 'Our mouths were opened wide' to ask greater things than we had yet seen, and I believe we can all say, Verily the Lord has been in the midst of us. Oh! we have had a precious season, and trust we have renewed our strength for many days.

"It has been proposed to-day that two of the missionaries go from station to station, and labor among the children by turns."

LETTERS FROM HOME.

"The doctor returned late from Odooville, and found me ill with the headache, brought on by a fall. He did not make me acquainted with the treasure which he brought with him. This morning, as soon as the day appeared, he told me that I now should have the privilege of reading letters from America. He would not give them to me last night, for fear I would sit up the remainder of the night. Soon were we gathered around the precious little box, the doctor, myself, Henry, and Amy being the company, and little Willie peeping round for his share. Henry had his feet pinched into the red shoes, and, though they hurt him, he did not mind it, but seized the handkerchief sent to the doctor, put it round his neck, and turning to me, says, 'Poctavaviane, mamma' —that is, 'good-by'—and went off singing grandmamma. Every thing sent us was prized as a grand treasure, and all we shall find very useful. And the letters—what a feast!"

NEWS OF THE CONVERSION OF A SISTER.

"Oh, my dear S——, to have evidence that you are pressing into the kingdom—yea, that you are already there—that your name is enrolled among the followers of Christ—enables me in more exalted strains to magnify the name of the Lord. Go on, my sister; may you never lose sight of Jesus, but endeavor to be the consistent follower of your divine Master."

E 2

ONE OF OUR GREAT DAYS.

"We have had what we call one of our *great days.*
We expected all our missionary friends, and all came
but three, who were prevented by sickness. Mr. and
Mrs. Knight were also with us. All the children from
the other stations were here. Most of the native members of the Church were here. I had to make provision
for about one hundred and eighty. Their dinner consisted of rice, and curry, and fruit. All seated themselves upon mats, and took their food from the plantain
leaf. The two who were admitted to the Church were
Bloomfield, a boy who has been, we hope, truly concerned
for his soul for nearly two years. His conversation and
conduct is that of a Christian. The other, whose name
is Moloe, is a most remarkable child, twelve years of age.
He was awakened to some sense of divine things by hearing a tract read to him, and was desirous of coming to
Panditeripo school to learn more of the Christian religion. He had not been here above six weeks before he
was convicted of sin. He is the finest boy we ever had
in the school, and is perhaps the brightest and most active member of the Church at this place. He is very earnest in bringing others to accept the Saviour."

DR. SCUDDER LEAVES FOR MADRAS.

"The missionaries, at their late meeting at Manepy,
consulted upon the expediency of the doctor's taking a
journey for his health, which has for some time past been
very feeble. They all thought it best that he should go
to Madras, and from thence to Bengalore, about two hundred and sixty miles from Madras, where the climate is

cool and the place considered healthy. It was also left to my choice whether to accompany him on this journey or remain at home. I will not attempt to tell you what have been my feelings in view of my dearest friend being separated from me on account of his health. I will only say the struggle has been a powerful one between self and duty. I have thought in times past, should it be necessary for him to leave, that I would accompany him at all events. But when I looked around upon my charge at Panditeripo, and saw the sacrifice which must be made if I too left the station, my cry was, 'Lord, strengthen me to take up my cross.' (Her prayer was answered.)

"*September* 11*th*. We have parted. Oh, how painful the separation! God grant that we may meet again. I am unable to say much.

"*September* 14*th*. I returned this afternoon to my solitary home. On entering my room, I found myself quite overcome at the thought of remaining here alone for such a length of time. I found relief in committing my all into the hands of Him 'who doeth all things well.'"

ADMISSION OF FORTY-ONE MEMBERS TO THE CHURCH.

"To-day we attended a meeting at Manepy for the purpose of examining those who were candidates for admission to the Church. Forty-one will be received. It has been a day of deep interest to us all. A very large bungalow was erected at Santillipy, about two and a half miles from this place. We all assembled there from our several stations. A multitude of people were collected to witness the solemn ordinance instituted by our Lord and Saviour. The doctor preached, Mr. Poor addressed the candidates, Mr. Meigs read the Confession of Faith

and Covenant, Mr. Winslow administered the bread at
the table, the doctor the cup, and Mr. Woodward made
the concluding address.

"Each missionary baptized the children from his own
station, and Mr. Meigs baptized the adults. Praised be
the Lord for this increase! I pray that they all may be
found to walk worthy of their profession."

CHOLERA RAGING—A SCENE.

"Rode with the doctor this afternoon to visit some
poor people who were this morning taken with the cholera. Oh, the misery and distress we witnessed! The
mother met us, having but a few minutes before followed
her child to the grave—her husband apparently dying,
her father in the same situation, her only child sick, lying by the side of the old man—no human being near
them, no comforts, scarcely a cloth to wrap around them!
We spent four hours there in administering medicine,
applying hot sand, and rubbing them. The young man
appeared to be a little relieved before we left them, and
but little hope of the old man. Their neighbors lived
very near, but none dared to come to their assistance."

HEATHEN CHILDREN AT PRAYER.

"I do wish that friends at home could hear the sound
of prayer within our garden as I do at this time. Many
of our children are now at the throne of grace. 'The
Lord heareth the ravens when they cry,' and will he not
hear and answer the prayers of these little ones? There
is at present much seriousness on the minds of many of
the children, and I trust all are eventually to be brought
into the kingdom."

These extracts from the journal of Mrs. Scudder—which was a minute diary of daily life, and transmitted to her friends in America—show the energy and self- . denial which the women of the mission had to put forth. It was no languid or idle life; for, besides the domestic burdens pressing upon them, they were engaged also in the schools teaching and training both boys and girls, and providing for them food and clothing.

In Mrs. Scudder's case there was a more than usual draft on her strength, as her husband had hospital duties at home, and calls from every quarter to attend upon the sick; yet she seems to have met all these responsibilities with a cheerful energy, and scarcely ever complains of any thing but occasional fatigue and exhaustion.

The secret of all this lay in her patient spirit, her calm, collected energy, and most of all in her spirit of faith and prayer, by which she drew strength from above. "God was her refuge, her present help in every time of trouble."

In that part of Mrs. Scudder's journal where the addition of forty-one young converts to the Church is spoken of, it should be stated that they were the fruits of a powerful revival. A description of this work of grace is given with considerable minuteness by Mrs. Scudder in the letter which follows, addressed to her relations in America.

CHAPTER VII.

THE GREAT REVIVAL.

"Panditeripo, March 18th, 1824.

"DEAR MOTHERS, BROTHERS, AND SISTERS,—I will now endeavor to give you some account of what the Lord is doing and has done for our mission. His stately steppings have been in the midst of us, and the blessed influences of the Holy Spirit have been experienced at our several stations. On the third Sabbath in January an awakening commenced in the school at Tillipally, principally among the boys; then among the girls at Odooville. From thence the gracious influence was experienced at Manepy and Batticotta. The glorious work is still going on at all these several stations. As you will probably have accounts of each, I will not go into any particulars, but proceed to tell you of the wonderful display of divine power at Panditeripo. On the Sabbath of the awakening at Tillipally, a young man in our service (formerly a heathen) was baptized here and admitted to the Lord's Table. It was a most interesting Sabbath to us all, and a number of our boys appeared more than usually solemn, though we saw nothing very special. The following three weeks we were much encouraged with the appearance of things around us; but the evening of the 12th of February will ever be a memorable night to us, and, I believe, to all who witnessed what we did. On that day the doctor (in company with myself) went to Batticotta in the afternoon, to converse with the boys in that school. A meeting was held with our boys in the evening, as was directed, before we went. After the meeting, it being moonlight, the boys, many of them, were engaged in playing. They left their play, and began to prepare for rest by spreading the mats upon which they sleep. Amy called Whelpley, told him to go to the children, and talk to them about their souls, for they were all going to hell, and their blood would be required at his hands if he was not faithful. He accordingly went, spoke a few words to them, and then left them. Very soon the voice of prayer was heard in the garden; this increased, until from every part of the garden was heard the cry of 'What shall I do to be saved?' When we returned home, how awfully solemn was the place! It appeared none other than the house of God and the gate of heaven! We came in the house; the doors and windows were all open; the moon shone brightly. Our servant was weeping in the veranda. Philip Whelpley (a member of our Church) and Amy were walking the room in silence, and the heart-rending cry was heard from every part of our garden, 'To whom shall I go?' 'Have mercy upon me, Lord Jesus!' 'Oh, give me thy Holy Spirit!' 'Descend, I entreat, upon me!' 'Holy Spirit, forgive my sins!' 'I have been a great sinner!' and many more expressions of great earnestness, which seemed to proceed from broken hearts for sin. You may judge of our feelings. We sang a hymn of praise, knelt down, and returned thanks to Him whose was all the power, and to whom all the glory was due. After learning that they had been in this affecting way crying for mercy more than an hour, the doctor thought it prudent to ring the bell and call them to the house. They came in with tears streaming down their cheeks, and some of them appeared quite exhausted. Upon looking round upon the precious flock, we found twenty-nine in number, including all in our school with the exception of four, and they all appeared awakened to a sense of their state—that they were sinners and needed a Saviour, and felt that Jesus Christ was the only deliverer from the wrath to come. We conversed and prayed with them. Our meeting was truly a heart-melting one. We saw those among our children who were very proud and stout-hearted humbled down at the foot of the Cross, and we wept for joy. I must tell you that, on the afternoon of the same day, the doctor sent word to the boys—for those who were willing to forsake all for Christ—to come to him. Sixteen came. One proud boy said 'he would not give up all for Christ;' but in the evening it would almost have melted the heart of stone to have seen this same boy bowed down like a bulrush, and scarcely able to speak for sobs and tears. 'Oh that men would praise the Lord for his goodness, and his wonderful works to the children of men.' You will wish to know how things have appeared since that evening. It would have been interesting to you had I from time to time given you an account of our meetings with the children, which have been, most of the time since, two and three in a day; *but this duty I have neglected,* and you will not, in consequence, know so fully the state of things here. I rejoice to say that the Lord has carried on his work, and a number of the children give evidence of a change of heart. Among the brightest, you will rejoice to learn, is Gideon Waterbury, though, as I before wrote you, his serious impressions have been of long standing. How many of

these children will remain steadfast time alone will show.
We do hope that many of them will be jewels in the
Redeemer's crown. It becomes feeble creatures to be
humble; and humble we desire to be, and say, 'Not unto
us, but unto God be all the glory.' I have stated some
facts simply as they have taken place. I am aware that
I am not writing for the inspection of the public. What
I have written has been in great haste, and not without
some fears that I might say *too little* or *too much* about
the influences of the Holy Spirit here. The work commenced in *our own hearts*. Our meetings at our several
stations have been for a long time back very interesting,
and previously to the awakening in our schools there was
a day observed by all our members for fasting, humilia-
tion, and prayer. Amy has been much engaged in this
work, and I think she has been instrumental in doing
good. Her health is not very good, but better than it
has been. Pray for us. Call upon all our friends to
pray for us; and may we all be enabled to bring our
tithes into the store-house and prove the Lord therewith,
that He will open the windows of heaven, and pour us
out a blessing until there will be no more room to receive it. Oh, dear friends, there are clouds and thick
darkness round about us. The heathen rage, the people
imagine a vain thing. Those without our gates remain
stout-hearted and stubborn; but we long, we wait, we
pray for the blessed Spirit to apply the Word preached
unto their hearts."

ADDITIONAL REMARKS BY DR. SCUDDER.

"I have informed you before that the first-fruits of
our revival have been gathered in. Forty-one were ad-

mitted at one time, and a more interesting day I never
beheld.   The baptismal exercise was calculated to make
more than ordinary impressions upon our minds.   Among
the lambs of the flock was a hoary-headed old man of
sixty, the most interesting sight I witnessed on that ever
memorable day.   My heart melted to see this aged sinner, who had been worshiping idols above half a century,
come forward and be baptized in the name of the Triune
Jehovah.   Though I have mentioned several particulars
respecting that meeting, I will mention them again, as
my former letter may not reach you.   It was held in a
temporary bungalow, which was one hundred feet long
and sixty wide, and lined and ceiled (if I might use the
term) with white cloth.   My pulpit was carried there, and
placed upon a frame, which was concealed by white cloth
from the eyes of the people.   The exercises were commenced by Brother Woodward.   Brother Stead, Wesleyan
missionary, made the introductory prayer.   As Mr. Poor
did not arrive until late, I preached from the words,
'Verily I say unto you, ye must be born again.'   Brother
Spaulding delivered the address to the candidates for
baptism.   Brother Meigs read the Articles and Covenant,
etc.   Brother Winslow administered the bread at the
table.   I administered the wine, and Brother Woodward
gave the last address.   Brother Poor addressed the candidates for admission to the Church after they had been
publicly received.   When we came to the table we sung
an English hymn (a part of the seventh of Watts's first
book, which begins 'Let every mortal ear attend'), and
after the services of the day another English hymn was
sung.   These were our only English exercises.   With the
divine permission, we expect to hold a similar meeting at
the same place in about two weeks.   I should be glad to

tell you that as many more were about to be admitted, but not so. We, however, do not repine. Nearly thirty have expressed a desire to be admitted, and most of them would perhaps rejoice much if we should give them permission so to do. But we find it necessary to be cautious. About half the number we hope to admit. Some of whom we have hoped well have met with such violent opposition that they conclude that they can not follow Christ. You can form no idea, beloved parents, of the current of blasphemy and opposition which our native converts have to meet with. Your son knows something of the opposition and blasphemy from his own experience. Both your son and your daughter have been stoned. I have been hit, but. my dear Harriet has escaped. What would you think of a female speaking to a white man, who in general is somewhat respected, 'You ought to have your head broke.' 'Why do you come here barking like a dog?' This language has been addressed to me, and that by Catholics, our most violent opposers in *these latter days.* Judge a little, then, what those in some cases have to meet with who forsake all for Christ, whose opposers are not afraid to persecute them. Pray much for them. Pray much for us. I would by no means give you the idea that we meet with much of the abuse I have above mentioned. Far from it. In general we are treated with the greatest decency, and in many cases even with politeness.

"I wrote a very long letter to you a few months ago, of nearly eight pages, mentioning many things which will interest you. In that you will learn how great have been my enjoyments in spiritual things with our young converts, and what our prospects at that time were. We are now longing, I trust, for another visit from on high.

O that we might soon be favored therewith! My dear Harriet and myself were at a prayer-meeting at Odooville last evening. We reached home a little after midnight. One of the hymns of Dobell, which begins 'Saviour, visit thy plantation,' I hope we were enabled to sing with some degree of feeling. I hope, too, that our Saviour was with us. We often have very precious seasons of prayer in our mission. Unite with us. If you feel disposed to sing as well as pray, and if you should like to sing a hymn of your son's composing at any time, you will have the opportunity, as I will now write it for you."

Dr. Scudder's absence was of essential benefit to his health, and afforded him an opportunity to survey the continental field to which afterward he was assigned. He formed quite an extensive acquaintance with British officials at Madras and elsewhere, and scanned with close and interested observation the vast field of heathenism which he hoped, with some of his brethren, soon to occupy. Ceylon was the school where Providence had taught him the social and religious characteristics of the heathen, and where, by close study and constant practice, he had acquired a facility in the use of the Tamul language spoken by millions on the continent. On his return his heart was full of this new mission, and he communicated his zeal to the rest, so that, after due deliberation and communicating with the Board at home, it became clear that the time for establishing an American Mission at Madras was fully come.

In 1836 it was determined that Rev. Mr. Winslow and Dr. Scudder should make a beginning, with headquarters at Madras, and thence, as Providence should open the way, push their labors into the interior.

CHAPTER VIII.

Revival in Madras.—Tours, and Towns visited, etc.

MADRAS AND ITS SURROUNDINGS.

MADRAS is the chief city of the Carnatic, and lies on the eastern shore of Peninsular India. In it, Oriental magnificence is mingled with the activities of British military and commercial life. It has been the centre of stirring events. In the interminable and bloody wars, waged by the Saxon conquerors to extend their dominion, this city has been the *point d'appui* of their operations. This was the scene of the Nabob of Arcot's wily transactions with British officials, which required the genius of Edmund Burke to unravel and expose.

But now the horrors of war had been succeeded by an abject submission, the princes and people simply asking to be allowed the enjoyment of a languid existence, and the observance of their absurd and cruel idolatries.

The policy of England has been varied toward these poor heathen, sometimes conniving at their horrible rites, and at others legislating against them. It has, at length, under the constraining pressure of public religious sentiment, settled down on the principle of gradually undermining the power of paganism, and substituting, as fast as possible, the mild and merciful sway of the Christian religion. Hence Juggernaut and the suttee have gone down, and the missionaries are encouraged to prosecute ·their moral warfare against the antiquated forms of paganism.

A more important centre for missionary operations than Madras can hardly be named. Radiating from it are innumerable towns and villages, swarming with population, and readily accessible. But the city itself affords a vast field of usefulness. Dr. Scudder, writing under date of October 3d, 1836, says, "You will be surprised to hear that I have been removed from Ceylon to the continent of India. Such, it appears, has been the will of the Lord, and I have only to add that I rejoice that it is so. I am pleasantly situated in a pleasant part of the great city, on the borders of many thousands of people. It is nearly a central situation. I say central, for the whole population of Madras is not in one place. It is a city of cities, if I may so call it. It is supposed that there are 400,000 people in it. We expect to have a large printing establishment here, for the purpose of printing the Bible and religious tracts. We are expecting large funds from the American Bible and Tract Societies. The way is open to distribute immense numbers of religious publications among the Tamul people."

REVIVAL OF RELIGION AT MADRAS.

"I like Madras very much. I have enjoyed some precious seasons, as I have been in two revivals of religion since I came here. One occurred in Mr. Smith's congregation, where Winslow and I have labored, more or less, for some time past. The other occurred in the fort. This has been more extensive. There are seven or eight hundred soldiers there. Among them wickedness has prevailed to a shocking degree, and among most of them it still prevails. Drunkenness is one of the most

conspicuous crimes. Perhaps one hundred and fifty attended our meetings.

"There is a very pious, devoted military man in the
fort, whose house has been opened years to them who
would come to hear the Gospel which he proclaimed.
Generally but few attended. Now many of them who
are in the habit of attending have, as I hope, found the
Saviour.

"There is at the fort a chaplain of the Church of England. I do not know him. I am glad to say that he
has made no opposition to my private labors. Would
that I could tell you of a revival of religion among the
poor degraded natives. Alas! they are sunk in sin—fast
asleep in the arms of the great adversary."

After Dr. Scudder had become settled at Madras, he
pursued the same general plan of missionary operations
as at Ceylon. By the aid of a printing establishment,
under the superintendence of his colleague, Dr. Winslow,
tracts were prepared adapted to interest and enlighten
the heathen; and, with these and the Scriptures in Tamul, Dr. S., loading his bullock bandy, went forth among
the swarming population of the interior towns, preaching
the Gospel in the highways and hedges, and supplying
the greedy applicants with reading matter adapted to
make them wise unto salvation. Sometimes he was rude-
ly assailed, and often obliged to retreat before the surg-
ing masses. In a letter to his father he says, "When you
think, my dear father, that you have a son engaged in
the blessed work of endeavoring to ameliorate both the
moral and physical condition of such wretched and benighted beings, you should rejoice. Would that we could

see a general disposition to embrace the great salvation that we preach. But, alas! how few are there who receive it. Instead of meeting with a hearty reception, in many cases we must meet with ridicule and reproach, and sometimes even with bodily abuse. I was, not long since, stoned, and the soreness of the bruises continued for some time. We should soon be torn to pieces could the desire of many be gratified. But, notwithstanding all these trials, we often meet with encouragements."

Such was the spirit in which this heroic Christian, separating himself for months from his family, went out into the dark surrounding regions, carrying the lamp of salvation to the benighted. The extracts from his journal which we insert will be read, we are sure, with deep interest.

TOURS, AND TOWNS VISITED.

"Coonatoor is a village of considerable size. I went out into its streets this morning proclaiming the only name given under heaven whereby we can be saved. Distributed a few tracts. Sent out three native helpers on the same business. Several persons have come to the bungalow and received portions of the Scriptures. A native catechist ought to be stationed here.

"Some people have objected to the distribution of the Scriptures among the heathen as a useless thing. But facts go to prove the contrary. My own experience is in favor of their distribution, on the principle that, if one in a hundred is, by the Holy Spirit, made effectual to the conversion of a heathen soul, we can afford to lose the rest. But there is other than my testimony that the distributors of the Scriptures have not labored in vain. Let me adduce one instance. 'Some years ago, Mr. Ward, a Christian missionary, in going through a village near Calcutta, left at a native shop a Bengalee New Testament, that it might be read by any of the villagers. About a year afterward three or four of the most intelligent of the inhabitants came to inquire farther respecting the contents of the book left in their village. This ended in six or eight of them making a profession of Christianity. Among these, one deserves particular notice—an old man named Juggernaut, who had long been a devotee to the idol of that name in Orissa, had made many pilgrimages thither, and had acquired such a name for sanctity that a rich man in Orissa was said to have offered him a pension for life on condition of his remaining with him. On his becoming acquainted with the New Testament, he first hung his image of Krishnu, or Juggernaut, which he had hitherto worshiped, on a tree in his garden, and at length cut it up to boil his rice. He remained steadfast in his possession of Christianity till his death. Two others, being men of superior natural endowments, employed themselves in publishing the doctrines of Christianity to their countrymen in the most fearless manner, while their conduct was such as to secure their universal esteem.' Here more conversions were hopefully produced by a single New Testament than many missionaries have been permitted to see, after years of labor in preaching the Gospel."

THE CHOLERA—CAUSE AND CURE.

"Sterembatoor has lately lost a number of its inhabitants by the cholera. The reason assigned for it is that the goddess Ammarl, who has a temple in this town, has

F

been neglected for the last twenty years, and has been taking vengeance upon the people for this sin. For the last two days I am informed that she has ceased her work of destruction, in consequence of the vows they have made to give her her due. On the coming Sabbath their propitiatory offerings are to be made. Alas! how are these wretched beings taken captive at the will of the devil! May the ever-blessed Spirit open the eyes of those who have this day been supplied with portions of the Scriptures and tracts, to see the vanity of their system, to clear away their refuges of lies, and lead them to the Saviour."

SPLENDID TANK.

"*Rayya, June* 24*th.* Reached this place this morning. Rayya is quite a small village, but situated in a very charming spot. It has a large and beautiful tank, with flights of steps down to the water's edge, corresponding with the number of its sides, and is surrounded by large tamarind-trees. Native rest-houses face it in each direction except at the west. As there is but little correspondence between the village and this tank, it is difficult to conceive how one of so much expense should have been cut and built here. Its steps are of hewn granite, and must have cost very large sums of money. Went out into the village and proclaimed the Gospel. A few Gospels and tracts were distributed."

DISTRIBUTION OF BOOKS AND TRACTS.

"*Conjeveram, June* 26*th.* Reached this place on Saturday evening, and took up my quarters at the government bungalow. Yesterday morning I went out into the streets preaching the Gospel and distributing the Word of Life. In the afternoon the people thronged the bungalow for books. Was busy most of the time from three until six o'clock in distributing them, and was quite tired when my work ceased. As every person to whom a portion of the Scriptures is to be given must be examined as to his ability to read, much time elapses before all who come can be supplied. This morning I did not go out into the city, as I had an abundance of labor within doors. Continued the distribution of books and tracts this afternoon. The throng for books was so great that no small noise and confusion took place. The confusion is heightened from the circumstance that I have different kinds of tracts. The 'Songs of Praise,' the 'Blind Way,' and the Almanac are much in demand; and, as many have each their favorite tract, they will not rest satisfied until they are supplied."

TOUR OF INSPECTION.

"*June 27th.* Took a walk early this morning into the city to see something of its dimensions. Found but little to recommend it as a place of residence for a missionary, except its population. The city is wholly given up to idolatry. There are six different kinds of temples dedicated to Siva, Vishnu, Kalle, and so forth. In this we see the worldly policy and craft which actuated the framers of the present debased system. All is on the plan of the theatre. The same scene of show and parade would become tiresome, and cease to arrest attention. The system is admirably adapted to fleece the people and please the Brahmins. Last evening, as I was obliged to leave the government rest-house in consequence of the late enactment that travelers must not occupy them for more than two days, I took up my quarters in a native choultry. Constructed a small room in its veranda as well as I could, into which persons who wished to receive books and tracts were admitted and examined, as has been before mentioned, as to their ability to read. When the crowd is great, nothing can be effected without something of this kind. This afternoon I left Conjeveram, or Great Conjeveram as it is called, for what is called Little Conjeveram. They are connected by a long row of houses on each side. I am now at the latter place. Have distributed the Word of Life to many to-day, who, I believe, will carefully preserve it. This morning, as I was passing through the streets, my attention was arrested by a young man whom I heard reading. He was reading a tract. I invited him to come to the choultry and receive a Gospel. He very gladly availed himself of my offer. Had an application for a book from a female. She was a little girl. As she could read nothing but Tellogoo, to my great regret I was unable to supply her. Gave her a tract. She is destined, I suppose, of course, to become a dancing-girl. So far as I know, no others are taught to read.

"*June* 28*th*. Yesterday I referred to the craft of those who framed the system of faith embraced by this people. Last night I had an opportunity to witness the truth of what I then asserted. The cholera has lately made its appearance here, and those who have in charge the temple of Ammarl have of course given out word that she has sent it, and that the *sine qua non* of her removing the scourge is money, or other offerings. In order effectually to secure their object, they endeavor to make the people believe, and do actually make them believe that the goddess comes down, enters certain of her votaries, and speaks through them. Such a visit, it appears, she has been making to-night. The votary she entered has been parading through the streets with a large collection of flowers resembling the haystack upon his head. Incense was carried before him, and two persons with swords acted as his guard. He was also accompanied with drummers and dancers. When he reached the house opposite to the place where I now am, he stopped. One of his attendants spoke for him. He declared that the goddess had not been honored as she should have been, and that offerings must be made at the approaching festival to appease her. I need hardly add that the people are so much afraid of this terrible goddess that they will hardly dare to refuse the demand made upon them. A part of all that is given at such times goes to those who have charge of the temple, the people never for a moment thinking of the fraud which has been imposed upon them. This morning neither my native helpers nor myself went out among the people. We remained at the rest-house to attend to the multitudes which flocked to us for books and tracts. There is a great press for the Almanac, and my stock is nearly exhausted. This is a very popular tract, from its mere name. It contains much on the subject of Christianity, as well as science. Many Brahmins, who would be unwilling to touch any of our other publications, would be glad to obtain this—an important reason why such works should be largely circulated. Indeed, truth in a written form can not be brought before them in any other way. To-day a Brahmin came in front of the rest-house, and showed his enmity to the cause in which I am engaged by tearing up three tracts, which he obtained from others than myself. Among those who obtained tracts were a dumb man and two little girls. The tracts received by the latter were in Tellogoo. The dumb man received also a portion of the Scriptures. I ascertained that he could read by his writing the Tamul letters on the floor.

"*June 30th.* The cholera is raging in this place, and the votaries of Ammarl are more vigilant, if possible, than even those in Conjeveram. Money, and nothing but money, or its equivalent, will appease her. And if she does not get a good supply, she is not backward in reminding those who give it that she is dissatisfied. I had an opportunity of witnessing this a few nights ago. One of her donors gave her but a quarter of a rupee. She received it with murmuring. Last night there was a parading of the idol of Siva through the streets, accompanied as usual with music, firing, and so forth. The expenses of the ceremonies, I understand, were borne by *oil men, for the purpose of inducing Siva to espouse their cause, and constrain the people to give them a good price for their oil. Wallajabad is a good place for a missionary.

"*Chingleput, July 1st.* There are native choultries in most towns, and in some of them it would be pleasant enough to be, provided they had front walls, windows, and doors. Some are in such a state that I prefer rather to sleep without than to enter them for the night. In the work of distributing tracts and the Scriptures I find it especially of importance to have a place to which I can have recourse for a little rest occasionally—a place of freedom from the noise and bustle, which so much oc-

* *Guild oilmen, no doubt*

cur in open rest-houses after the news of the object of
my visit have gone abroad."

A GOOD PLACE FOR A SCHOOL.

"This is a good place for an English school. Two
missionaries should at least be in Great Conjeveram, and
one in Little Conjeveram. The streets of importance
are very wide, and cocoa-nut-trees in abundance grow in
them. Some of them are streaked with white and red
for about six feet above the roots. There are three most
splendid—if the word splendid may be used in such a
sense—temples. Two of them are dedicated to Siva,
and are in Great Conjeveram. The other is dedicated
to Vishnu, and is in Little Conjeveram. I have never
before seen so spacious a wall around any temple. It is
probably as high as the wall you may recollect to have
seen in Trichonopoly around the old rajah's palace. It is
difficult to conceive what could have induced the people
to erect it so high. For twenty or twenty-five feet it is
of cut granite (blue), that is, the two sides I saw, and on
this there is some brick-work. The wall from north to
south is probably a quarter of a mile long. In the three
temples now mentioned and their walls, there are probably enough materials to build as many native churches
(so far as the stone-work is concerned) as the place will
require; and they will come in place in good time. The
large granite stones will greatly lessen the expenses to be
incurred to build them when the idols shall all flee away.
I do not know how many of our Gospels of Luke we
have left in Conjeveram; perhaps eight hundred or a
thousand."

A BUSY DAY.

"Yesterday I had a busy day, at least in part. In the afternoon I walked out to see something of the extent of the place after giving out books and tracts. When I returned many were waiting to see me. I attempted again to give out the Gospel of Luke and tracts; but the confusion from the crowd was so great, and so forth, that I desisted. I gave no more out until it was nearly dark, and quite dark. Several came to get them by night, so that I had to have them examined as to their ability to read by lamp-light. After reaching Little Conjeveram I had an opportunity of witnessing something farther of the abominations of heathenism. I allude to a procession which passed the rest-house where I put up about eight o'clock at night. It was that of Ammarl. She, it appears, entered into a man, and he, of course, became, in fact, the goddess herself. Whether to call the man him or her I do not know; I will call it him. On his head was a great stack of flowers. Preceding him were drummers and dancers. The dancers carried little hollow circulars in their hands, with something within to make a noise; I will call them rattles. On each side of him was a person carrying a sword. Behind him was a man holding an umbrella over his head. Directly opposite the rest-house, in front of the house of some native whom the fellow expected to fleece, he stopped. One of his votaries then began to speak for him. He declared that the goddess was angry because she had been neglected, and that the people of the house must make their offerings at an approaching festival to appease her. Last night the goddess made her appearance again, and stop-

ped again at the same house, when she received four *an-
nas.* Loud was the cry that it was not enough. Whether
she obtained any more I do not know. Yesterday my
stock of Almanacs became exhausted. This is very popular. Through it, access for communicating religious
truth has probably been gained to not a few Brahmins
who might otherwise have never come near me. Am-
makus songs are also very popular. I could almost have
wished that I had procured ten thousand copies of this
instead of the Heavenly Way."

THE PALANKEEN MAN.

" The palankeen bearer, whom I prefer to stand ——
with me, is a strong man, and he has, I dare say, never
been in such hot water of this kind before. He has
come very near having a battle two or three times. But
I keep all pretty quiet at such times. I have come to
the point to put all the *pushing* part on his shoulders,
and of this, I assure you, there is not a little. Indeed, if
there was not some of it I should have ——'s enough.
Great numbers try to get up into our rooms, which
are only about four or five feet wide, and notwithstanding two stand ——, the little boys slip between us, or at
our *other* sides, and get in, and my man *Friday* will not
always allow them to remain. The fact is, you must
witness one of these scenes, or you can not form a proper
view of our case. I have to keep another of the palankeen bearers —— in the other part of the rest-house to
keep the people out, and as we give no tracts or books
to any body over the sides of the walls of our rooms, we
have less —— here than we should otherwise experience."

F 2

AGED MAN AND CONSEQUENTIAL MAN.

" I kept the doors of the bungalow closed until about
six, when I allowed the few visitors present to come in.
Among these was an interesting man, seventy-five years
of age. He said that he wished to know the truth—and
he heard it from my lips. I also supplied him with truth
in its inspired form. He expressed an uncommon degree
of pleasure in having met with me. Among those who
came to see me in the afternoon was quite a consequential man. He had read one of the tracts which had been
distributed, and this led him, as I suppose, to the bungalow. The subject of our conversation, of course, was religion. He associated me with Roman Catholics. I told
him that I was not of that faith, and endeavored to show
him that in several respects they differed but little from
the heathen. After he could say no more on this point,
he endeavored to make me believe that, with the exception of worshiping idols, his system of religion and mine
were the same. From this position I made the attempt
to drive him. I pointed out, to his great annoyance, three
of the particulars in which Krishnu—the god whose
mark he had on his forehead—differed from Christ, viz.,
that he had stolen butter and so forth, and was therefore
a thief; that he had taken upon himself the form of a
woman, and committed adultery with Siva; and that for
lying he was changed into a snake. He said that all
these were lies. Whether from shame or from what
cause, I shall not advance an opinion, but he denied what
is considered by the heathen in general as of unquestion-
able authority. He left me, I presume, with less consequential feelings than he had when first entering the
room.

" *Carungooly, July 4th.* In this village I came to a well's mouth, where some women were drawing water. I opened my mouth and proclaimed the name of a Saviour to them. It recalled to my recollection the time when the Lord Jesus addressed the woman of Samaria while sitting on Jacob's well."

PRAYS ON A HILL-TOP.

"*July 5th.* Came to Atcharepankum this morning. I remained at the rest-house to attend to such as might call to see me until about five o'clock, when I went to the top of the mountain mentioned yesterday. On the highest part of it there is a conical heap of stones about four feet high, on which a light is placed on a certain night once a year. I found a carved image in stone, about three feet in length, lying with other stones at the base of this cone. In days that have long gone by, it probably had an erect position, and received the homage of the mountain visitors. Time, however, has laid it low, and its history probably is unknown. I mounted the cone just alluded to, sat down, and took a view of the surrounding country. The sight was indeed beautiful, especially the rice-fields at a little distance, in which some of the grain presented a golden appearance, while other parts of it were perfectly green. While on this cone I endeavored to plead with heaven in behalf of the immense multitudes embraced within the compass of my vision, that they might enjoy my happy privilege—the privilege of knowing the only true God, and Jesus Christ, whom he hath sent. I endeavored also to intercede for the influence from on high to descend upon the colleges in England, and Germany, and America, that laborers may go forth from them into the immense harvest. Alas! alas! what are these and other dying millions to do unless by such an influence multitudes of their young men are constrained to leave all to tell them of a Saviour? I would that those Christians in India who view the desolations with which they are surrounded would frequently bring this subject with them to the throne of grace. Why should not the colleges of Oxford, and Cambridge, and so forth, become pre-eminently schools of the prophets?"

PILGRIMS.

"My native helpers gave away several of the Gospels to Brahmins who were returning from a journey they had taken to Bonarias, or Casey, as it is called by the natives. Each of these Brahmins was bearing upon his shoulders two pots of the water of the Ganges. They are on the way to Rammisseram. May the ever-blessed Spirit open their eyes, while reading of Jesus, to see that he is the object which they in vain sought for at the end of their long pilgrimage. In addition to the Gospels, each received a tract entitled the Heavenly Way. This tract gives an account of a Brahmin in Bengal, one of those ascetics who would never speak, but whose attention to Christianity was arrested by a book which a minister of Christ had sent him."

SUPERSTITIONS.

"*Wallakoor, July 6th.* Reached this place this morning. The country from Atcharepankum to Wallakoor is principally covered with jungle. Yesterday I was in danger of losing one of my bandy-men, and might have

been reduced to great straits had he left me, in consequence of a cat's happening to cross the path in which
he was walking. He looked upon it as a sad omen, and
wished to return home. This people are an exceedingly
superstitious people."

IDOLATRY HARD SERVICE.

"It is now past two o'clock, and a man has just been
to me to beg something to bury, or, rather, burn the
corpse of a poor Brahmin, who died, he tells me, this
morning in the cook-room of this rest-house. It appears
that he was on his way to Casey. He has gone, as there
is every reason to believe, to await the doom of idolaters.
Idolatry is a hard service. Vast numbers die on such
pilgrimages."

PERSEVERANCE.

"*Pondicherry, July* 10*th*. Rose yesterday morning
with a violent sick headache. It unfitted me to tell even
the few who came for books of the precious Saviour.
About twelve o'clock I began to experience relief, and in
the afternoon was enabled once more to proclaim the
name of this adorable being."

CONFUSION.

"*July* 11*th*. Yesterday we commenced our operations
in Pondicherry. Distributed a large number of books
and tracts, as has been the case also to-day. This afternoon the rush for them, and the excitement produced by
so dense a multitude coming together, were so great that
I had either to run the risk of distributing them injudi-
ciously, or of suspending my operations. I chose the lat-

ter. Indeed, the scene of confusion was so great that I hastened to leave the rest-house. No personal violence was offered, but I was apprehensive of an attack upon the bandy which carried my books and tracts. I was followed by what I may almost denominate a mob for some considerable distance. Among these was a drunken Roman Catholic, who conducted himself in the most shameful manner. He pulled out some of the straw from the back of the bandy; broke the rope which passed over the baskets of books, and so forth; and also broke one or two of my cooking utensils. I am now at a rest-house about a mile and a quarter to the northeast of Pondicherry, called Nullacherttee's Rest-house, and am glad to feel myself once more on English ground."

MODE OF DISTRIBUTION.

"As to its eligibility, Pondicherry, as a missionary station, when compared with other large cities in the Tamul district, I will not pretend to decide. Any person who attempts to reside there will have great trials to encounter from the drunkenness of Roman Catholics. Alas! that this corrupt faith should have made the people even worse in this respect than they would have been had they remained in their heathenism. After my return from my walk we commenced giving books and tracts to the people. That order might be preserved, I stood upon the veranda of the rest-house, and gave tickets to such as I thought might worthily receive them. I gave twelve or fifteen at a time. These were presented at the door of the rest-house, and the persons who presented them were permitted to go within. Such as could read were supplied with Gospels and tracts. By this means order was preserved to a very great extent, and I would add that in no other way could it have been effected. He who has never attempted to distribute tracts and books (under ordinary circumstances) among large collections of people, can have but little idea of the difficulties to be encountered. We are frequently obliged to stop our operations entirely. I think it probable that if an agent of the Bible Society should attempt to sell them a number of copies of the whole Bible, his attempt would not be made in vain. At all events, the trial should be made; of course, he would be obliged to offer them at reduced prices. Should such an agent be sent, I would advise him by no means to go into Pondicherry. He might be deprived of all his books by *force*, as I was deprived of some of mine. No less than three attempts of this kind were made, and each attempt was successful. Two copies of Luke were seized and taken from the hands of one of my assistants standing by me. The other two attempts were made upon my baskets. Instead of going into Pondicherry, let him take up his position at Nullacherttee's Rest-house. It is, as I before said, in the Company's dominions — a circumstance on which I lay great stress. The people from Pondicherry will flock to him there."

REFLECTIONS ON THE CLOSE OF THE TOUR.

"The words of inspiration are now in the hands of five thousand or more of the persons among whom I have for a month past been preaching the Gospel. Most who have received them have received them with great desire, though probably this desire proceeded, in a great majority of cases, from curiosity. But, even though this may be the case, may we not hope that, as Zaccheus's curiosity was instrumental in leading him to embrace the Saviour, theirs may be equally blessed to them? God is honored by the distribution of his own word. I feel more and more impressed with the importance of giving the Scriptures to every individual who can read throughout the districts which come within the sphere of the operations of the Madras Bible Society. Indeed, what are the immortal beings within these districts to do unless we can put into their hands the directory to the kingdom of heaven—the directory to the kingdom of life—the only directory, I may say, with regard to most of them? No voice are they destined to hear proclaiming 'Behold the Lamb of God, which taketh away the sin of the world.' They grope the dark road to death with all the lights of heaven extinguished upon their path, and the shades of eternal night now hang over their undying spirits. The Bible, and, I would add, the Tract Societies of Madras, have the destinies of many of the heathen, for heaven or for hell, suspended upon them— at least we ought to judge so, when we remember how the ever-blessed Spirit has honored his written word in the times that are past. And will not the societies go forward? Will they see the millions under their care, as it were, go down to the chambers of eternal torment without giving them that light which may illuminate their path and lead them to heaven?"

CONTINUANCE OF DR. SCUDDER'S JOURNAL.

"*Ponnamallee, September* 12*th*. Left Madras yesterday afternoon about five o'clock, and reached this place
after a ride of four and a half hours. I slept in the bullock bandy in which I came, in front of the native rest-
house where I now am. Went out this morning into the
streets and told the people of a Saviour. My fatigue
and exposure to the sun laid me up with a sick headache. I am but comparatively little able to bear exposure to the sun as I once was. Indeed, I never was very
able to do it at any time. It was such an exposure, together with the fatigue accompanying it, which shattered my constitution in 1821. I shall never look back to
that long tour I took on foot without regret. Had I had
a house at the time, or had I gone in a palankeen, much
labor might have been secured in the missionary field."

PILGRIMS.

"Saw a number of persons who are on a pilgrimage
to Tempathy, four or five days' journey from this place.
The object for which they are going is to make a dedi-
cation of the hair of their heads to the temple. This is
shaved, and offered to the god for the purpose of obtain-
ing the pardon of their sins. Vishnu is the god to
whom it is dedicated. Alas! how are these poor creatures taken captive at the will of the devil!"

FREQUENT LABORS.

"*Parumbaucum,* 16*th*. Yesterday morning one of the
pious pensioned soldiers called upon me and requested
me to preach in English. I complied with his request.

In the evening I addressed a large number of persons, consisting principally, as I suppose, of pensioned soldiers and their families. Immediately after preaching I got into my cart and set off for this place. Reached it about midnight. In Trippasson and its vicinity we distributed about seventy portions of the Scriptures. This morning I went out into the town adjoining the government bungalow. Finished my work in it about half past nine o'clock, and returned; glad, on the one hand, that I had been doing good, and, after it was done, glad on the other to obtain a shelter from the scorching rays of the sun. My native helpers went to several villages in the vicinity of Parumbaucum."

ROMAN CATHOLICISM.

"This morning I was visited by a young person rubbed with ashes, and whom I, of course, considered a heathen. This afternoon he made his appearance without his ashes, and declared himself to be a Roman Catholic. He came for the Old Testament. As might be supposed, I immediately questioned his being of the Catholic faith, when one of my native helpers told me that he had the mark of the cross on his arm. I found this to be the case. It appears that he is a Roman Catholic belonging to Trichonopoly, and rubbed himself with ashes that he may be allowed to tarry in the town, or rather to be entitled to the privileges of common heathen travelers. Were it known that he is not of their faith, they would not give him so much as a drink of water."

SEVERITY OF LABORS.

"*Kaaverybaucum, 19th.* Reached this place this morning, after a ride of several hours.· Am in a comfortable bungalow provided by government for travelers, and prize the privilege the more after my confinement yesterday in the noonday heat in a veranda four or five feet wide. To-day I have had many visitors, and preached the Gospel probably to a larger number of people than on any other day since I left home."

VELLORE.

" This morning I went out to view the size of Vellore. As it is situated at the base of a mountain, I thought I would ascend it. After half an hour's hard labor, I had nearly reached the top of it, when I came to a fortification which surrounds the peak of the mountain. I went up to the gate of the fortification and found it locked. The noise I made brought a Sepoy to the edge of the rampart above me. I asked admission. He told me that he could not let me in without a passport. I opened my mouth, and entreated him to unlock the door of his heart and admit the Saviour. I had little idea, when I began to ascend the mountain, that I should find any one to whom I could make known his adorable name. May it be found, in the last day, that my messages were not delivered in vain. The view of the plain from this mountain is most charming. I had a most commanding sight of the whole city. It is very large; not, however, to be compared to Black Town as to size. I also had an excellent view of the villages in the vicinity of Vellore. The tops of trees, which appeared at a distance; the pad-

dy fields, in perfect green or yellow; the white bed of
the river, which is nearly dry; the shades cast over a
part of the plain by the passing cloud, while the full sunshine was on other parts of them; the fort, with its surrounding water and so forth, presented a scene which
beggars all description. Add to all these the distant
mountains, with which every part of this delightful prospect is surrounded; the azure color of the atmosphere
before those which were most distant, as well as the different shades of these mountains, the darkest of which
are caused by the passing cloud, and you may well suppose it is a pleasant spot for all the admirers of nature
to visit. Vellore is not entirely surrounded by mountains, but you would be led to make such a supposition
had you been where I was. I came down from the
mountain by a route different from that by which I as-
cended. When descending I came to an excellent spring
of water, near to which washermen were busily engaged
in washing clothes."

LABORS AT VELLORE.

"*25th.* On Saturday afternoon we began our operations in Vellore. My native helpers went out into the
city with a few Gospels and tracts, and this is the only
time they went out, as the news soon spread that we had
books to distribute. Yesterday I had an uncommonly
busy day. I took my position at the gateway of the native choultry, where I now am, at a quarter before seven
o'clock in the morning, and did not leave it a moment
until after six o'clock in the evening. The work of distributing the Scriptures is a very arduous one, from the
fact *that every one, before he receives them, must be ex-*

amined as to his ability to read. I gave out more than a thousand tickets to persons for such an examination. To those who could read a different kind of a ticket was given by my helpers. This, when presented to me, was redeemed by a Gospel. Of course two thousand tickets and more passed through my hands, and a thousand Gospels, with the same number of tracts. You will not, then, wonder at what I say, that to distribute the Scriptures is an arduous work. This morning I again commenced the distribution of books and tracts, and continued the distribution for about five hours. I then suspended my labors (as I saw but few new faces) until the afternoon, when I disposed of most of the stock of Gospels remaining. I thought proper to reserve a few for distribution on my way home. I have had, on the whole, a quiet time. I have spoken about the use of tickets. I have found that the only way to prevent confusion when the multitude is great is to have the different kinds I have mentioned above. Under such circumstances, should we attempt to examine whether the people can read, nothing could be effected. The pressure of the throng would oblige us to desist. In the giving of tickets, too, I find that I must be in an elevated position. But on this point I will not dwell. I will only observe that those who engage in the business of distributing the Scriptures when the numbers of the people are great will have difficulties to encounter which will put their inventions to work to know how to remedy them.

"As I consider my work in Vellore at an end, I shall, with divine permission, leave it this afternoon, with my face homeward. We have distributed probably not far from fifteen hundred Gospels and a large number of

tracts. Vellore is an excellent place for missionary labor. It needs a dozen laborers, as there can not be less
than eighty or ninety thousand inhabitants in it and its
vicinity."

"This morning I again commenced giving out books
and tracts, and continued to give them for about five
hours. As I saw but few new faces when I wished to
give them, I suspended my operations until this afternoon, when I disposed of nearly all the remainder of my
Gospels. I reserved a few, which I wish to give out on
my way home. A few, also, of the portions of a part of
the Old Testament remain. I have had, on the whole, a
quiet time. The gateway, I am glad to say, had four
posts of granite in an erect position, which so filled up
the passage into the yard that I was easily enabled to secure the inner yard from the crowd by ropes and sticks,
and so forth. I sat some time on the top of one of the
granite pillars, or stood on the tongue of the cart, the
cross-piece of which forms a part of the yoke, if I may
so call it, of the oxen, and which was forced out of its
place, and stood in a perpendicular direction to fill up
one of the little openings between the granite posts. Of
course I was elevated above the people, which gave me
a good deal of facility in giving out tickets. Indeed,
nothing could be done without such an elevation without
great pressure from the crowd. I have found that the
only way to prevent confusion when there are such multitudes of people is to have two kinds of tickets, one as
a passport for examination as to the capability of reading, the other to receive books. The pressure from the

throng would entirely prevent us from ascertaining who could and who could not read. Yesterday morning, while the people were before me, and I at my post, the question passed through my mind, With what kind of aspect must the angels view the scene?

"27*th*. Distributed several of my remaining Gospels. One of them I gave to a woman, the first I have found in my present tour who can read. Endeavored to plead that she might be a Mary Magdalene in her renewed condition. She probably has been, if not now, one of the devotee prostitutes of the temple.

"30*th*. Reached Madras this morning. The whole number of Gospels, with other portions of the Scriptures distributed, were about three thousand two hundred and fifty."

CONTINUATION OF DR. SCUDDER'S JOURNAL

WHILE DISTRIBUTING PORTIONS OF THE SCRIPTURES.

CHILDREN AND MODE OF BEGGING.

"*March 3d*. Left Madras yesterday morning, and came on to Tempporeoor (the meaning of which is the holy fighting-place), where I now am. Tempporeoor is much celebrated from the alleged circumstance that Conduasisammie, one of the sons of Siva, came to it in a fit of anger after one of his battles with a giant, whom he conquered, and upon whom he rode in the form of a peacock.* Passed a great multitude of people, both male

---

* It appears that he afterward went to a place which is called Temtarneki, from the circumstance that there his anger was appeased. Both Tempporeoor and Temtarneki are places of much celebrity.

and female, this morning, on their way to Madras, who had, I suppose, been attending the ceremonies at the temple on the preceding night. It would be rather a novel sight to foreigners could they observe the different ways in which females carry their children on such journeys. Some are swung upon their backs, entirely wrapped up in a cloth. Some sit upon the shoulder, their legs hanging down by the breast and back, while they take hold of the mother's head. Not unfrequently they recline their heads upon theirs and go to sleep. Some are on the back, clinging to the body by their feet and legs, which pass over the hips, and by their arms, which encircle the neck. Some sit on the hips, and not unfrequently are nursing at the same time. Some are carried in the arms. This afternoon I began to give out the portions of the Scriptures which I brought with me. Gave away about two hundred, with a number of tracts.'

BEGGARS.

"This place abounds with beggars, many of whom are most unworthy of receiving charity. Most choose to go alone. I, however, saw a procession of them this morning. The company consisted of five adults. The one in the middle had an umbrella over his head, to command, as I suppose, the greater veneration and respect. Their music was both vocal and instrumental. Before them were three boys, who acted the part of Merry Andrews. Their gestures were of a most ludicrous nature. All were clothed in yellow garments, and proceeded at a very slow pace, in order to afford time for the people to come out of their houses and bestow their charity. Great is the supposed merit of giving to these vagrants."

CAR BASKETS.

"While the car was standing in front of the choultry, I observed a Brahmin who was mounted upon it very busily engaged in letting down and taking up a basket. This, I perceived, was for the purpose of receiving the offerings of cocoa-nuts made on the occasion. Seven poor infatuated creatures rolled after the car, a most distressing sight to all lovers of humanity."

WORSHIPING A BOOK.

"This morning, while distributing books, a young man came to the choultry who said that a man belonging to Chempankum, who had received a book, had taken the covers from it, had covered it with boards, and kept and *worshiped* it. Whether he has absolutely made an idol of it, or whether the idea of his worshiping it has arisen from his attention to its perusal, I did not learn. I suppose he took the covers off because they were leather— very defiling in the estimation of many of the heathen."

PREACHES UNDER A TREE.

"*Coverlong, 7th.* I left Tempporeoor last night and came to this place this morning. As I could find no choultry, I took up my abode under a large tamarind-tree. Here I received my visits from the people, and supplied those who could read with a portion of the Word of Life.

"10*th.* Left the mount about six o'clock, and reached Madras about nine. During the eight days of my absence I distributed about one thousand eight hundred portions of the Scriptures and three thousand tracts.

G

Was very sweetly impressed while on my tour with the 10th and 11th verses of the 55th chapter of Isaiah: 'My word shall not return unto me void, but it shall accomplish that which I please, and it shall prosper in the thing whereto I sent it.'"

CHAPTER IX.

CORRESPONDENCE.

WHILE absent on these tours, a correspondence was kept up between Dr. Scudder and his wife, which served to mitigate at least the trial of separation. By it may be seen how a Christian may live in the atmosphere of heaven while yet he retains the sweetest charities of earth; how piety in its purest aspects and loftiest flights, forgets not the claims of social and domestic love. Dr. Scudder was not only a self-denying missionary, but the tenderest and most devoted husband and father. We supply the proof of this in extracts from the correspondence alluded to, without burdening our pages with the whole.

"June 29th, 1837.

"MY DEAREST,—That little kettle and lamp which you put up for me is one of the finest little affairs. It affords me a nice cup of tea. By-and-by I shall be very comfortable on my tours, that is, if I have a tent and bullock bandy long enough to stretch myself out when I lie down, and which I can close up, to be alone when I wish.

"My bread and butter are getting low; and as my man Friday has made the tea part of the way, I find my canister rather lower than it would have been had I taken the management myself; my sugar-bowl also is well lowered. Indeed, I would be called intemperate in tea-drinking by many. Something hot is a great comfort to

me, and bread and butter is my staple in the eating department.   I find the salt fish you put up a great relish.
I quite forgot to bring my old scissors-knife—the one
which Sister Winslow gave me, and which traveled with
me to the Neilgherries.   I have felt the need of it to
snuff my lamp.

"*June 4th.* Hope you and the children are all well.
I am far from it.   However, I have much to be thankful for—thankful that I can do something for Christ.
But one thing: I must travel in the best way I can.   My
health is too important to be sacrificed for a few rupees.
Shall expect to take my tour to Tanjore with bearers
throughout.   Must have a set by the month, as I did last
year.   Then I can go comfortably.   I could go in a
common cart, but it is too much for my head.

"*June 5th.* I wrote you yesterday, and filled much of
my letter with groans, lamentations, and woe.   I am,
through mercy, better to-day, and think I shall be able
to eat my dinner, having had no appetite yesterday for
my rice and curry, but made my meal on fruit—mangoes.
I have not been able to get a lime in so great a place as
this.   The boy had but one, and this I used in water as
lemonade.   I have felt quite a craving after acids, and I
have needed something to hide the bad taste of the water.

" I commenced giving out books myself this morning.
For two days I had my own concerns to attend to; besides, it has been raining, and but few people have come
for books.

" The rest-house is pleasantly situated on the borders of
a large tank.   It was, in the days of yore, probably quite
a splendid tank.   It is a great place of resort for persons
to bathe, wash their clothes, and draw, or rather dip up

water. This is the water I have to drink. It does *pret-ty* well, as the water I drink is a little way removed from that portion of it where the people wash their dirty clothes.

"Hope, my love, that you can stay your mind on Je-hovah Jesus while I am away from you. I have been thinking since I left you that you and I do not talk to-gether so much of our precious Saviour as would be ben-eficial to us. We talk too much about the world, and too little of Him. I think we do not prove as much 'helpmeets' to each other as we might. We are apt to keep too much of our Saviour to ourselves. Do you not think so? We have Him alone in our closets, but not together enough with us. Good-by. The Lord bless you and the dear children. May our separation prepare us for a union in the better world, where sorrow and tears shall all be done away.

"The people are preparing for the ceremonies of the great idol festival of to-day and to-night. Pray that the Word scattered may not be in vain. J. S."

"June 7th.

"My DEAREST,—Yesterday was quite a busy day. We had large numbers of people to see us, and distributed probably not far from seven hundred books. My Alma-nacs were all spent last night. The demand for this is amazing; the news of it seems to fly. I regret that I have not a thousand of them. To-day many books have been given out, but less than yesterday. The only great day remaining is Sunday, when the car is to be drawn. I am not in the most favorable part of the city for dis-tributing books, as the feast is at Little Conjeveram, as I

told you before. If I had a good rest-house there I
should soon be in it; but there is nothing but open native rest-houses, and it seems not right hardly to take
them from the people at such a time, and it is not pleasant to be in them; so most of what I do must be done
here. I suppose we have distributed at least a thousand
of our books.

"We have had a very quiet time, on the whole. Have
met with several turbulent Brahmins. One got a book
from some other person and tore it up. Several young
Brahmins came for books yesterday afternoon. As I refused to give them books, they went off in a rage, if I
may judge one for all. He stormed, and whether he got
any thing to tear up from any others I do not know.
The Word, however, is received by many with pleasure,
and doubtless it will be carried in every direction. This
morning two young men brought back books which had
been received before. I took them, and gave each a
whole New Testament.

"It is about a week since I left you. How rapidly
time flies—and let it fly! It can not fly too fast if we are
only doing our duty. I rejoice in my work as I am now
doing it. I hope good may come out of it. Many hear
of Jesus as well as receive his Word. Good-by for to-
day. To-morrow, with divine leave, I will add a word
before I send off this letter. Now, my dearest, may Jehovah Jesus be your stay and support. Bear up under
all your trials with more than ordinary fortitude, and *rejoice that you are called to suffer any thing for Christ.*
Did he suffer for us, and shall we not suffer for him?
Good-by.

"*8th.* To-night will be a week since I left you. A

few days more, and I hope to meet you. You speak of
these tours wearing you and me out. We must not think
of wearing out this thirty years while so much land remains to be possessed. These tours, if I do as I should,
may do me good on the whole. I must not, however,
travel to my injury. As to your wearing out, you must
not *think of it.* You should, if more cares come upon
you by my absence, *rejoice* in being considered worthy
to suffer for Christ.

"My dearest, do you recollect that this is the 8th of
June? Hope you and Winslow will together celebrate
this *twentieth* anniversary of our leaving America. Great
mercies demand great gratitude and praise.

"Now, my dearest, farewell till we meet. Let your
prayers ascend that the Word given may have free course
and obtain the rain from heaven. I feel much pleased
with much of what I have been doing. Not merely do
many receive, but *hear* a preached Word. Hundreds
have *heard* at this time who never heard it, I suppose,
before. Much love to the children and Brother Winslow.
Edward—does he love Christ? Ask him.

"Ever yours most affectionately, J. SCUDDER."

"Sethemparum, June 27th, 1838.

"MY DEAREST,—I reached this place this morning
about nine o'clock. After I left you I intended to travel
without cessation until I reached Alampuray, sixty-five
miles from Madras. I was quite tired, and had a headache during the remainder of the day and all night, and
just as I reached Sethemparum I was almost well of it.
What a mercy it did not go on until I was made distract-
ed by it. This I might have expected from the inces-

sant shaking of the palankeen, for I was shaken, I assure you, at no small rate. The bearers sometimes almost flew, as we say. After reaching this place I had
some good coffee, with milk, and I am *next* to being spry
as a lark this afternoon; so you see I have to sing of
mercies which I could not expect to have received. All
my carts but one reached me Monday afternoon. There
are but few people in Sethemparum as yet, while to-morrow is the day for the drawing of the car. The river to
the south is very much swollen by the rains, and a vast
number of people are detained on the opposite shore.
They will not be able to get over at all. A lady came
to the bungalow this morning who says she was detained
two days there for want of a boat. So Swammie will
not have so many to bow down to him, nor the doctor so
many applications for books. There have not been very
many applications for books—nothing of the press when
I was here before. To-morrow may, however, be, and
probably will be, different. I shall, with the divine blessing, move on toward Mayaveram. I shall move on from
this place in a cart, as I must move very slowly in distributing books.

"I hope you and the dear children are well. You
must, my dearest, endeavor to cheer up under our separation. I tell you, as I told you some time ago, eternity
will be long enough for you and me to be together. We
ought to rejoice to suffer all we possibly can for God's
glory. I believe we shall rejoice in it much; yea, just
as much as we do it for *his* glory. I rejoice to think
that I have *more* of your prayers for the divine blessing
upon my labors than when I am at home. Absence
makes you pray more; so you see one good fruit of my

being away from you. I enjoyed myself much after leaving you in the afternoon. Yesterday I had but little, as I was just poorly enough to be good for about nothing. I gave away all the books I had which I got from Brother Winslow—I mean the Acts of the Apostles and the *little* books which came from Jaffna. Now, my dearest, do try and pray, especially at *eight o'clock* each night, as we spoke about; and when you have company, as you will of Brother Winslow and Miss S—— on Wednesday night, all of you must think of me. I should like to have a season with you at twelve o'clock at night—as near as we can wake up—on *Saturday* night. You must take up with this short letter at this time. I shall, D. V., write you next week some time, but when I can not tell, as I probably may not come across a post-office before next Thursday or Friday, so do not be in trouble if you do not hear from me for *many* days. Now, my dearest, stay your mind upon Jehovah Jesus, where *mine* is. Grow in grace while I am away, and then you will hereafter rejoice much in my having been called to be absent. Much love to all the children, and most of all to yourself. I will keep open my letter until to-morrow morning, and may add a word then; so good-by for to-day, with much love. The people are now coming in numbers.

"*28th. Early.* To-day we shall probably be very busy. After the car is drawn, crowds will, I suppose, press upon us for books. I am in rather a good place to distribute them, so far as *place* is concerned. I have a high veranda, and have it inclosed by the palankeen. My helpers are busy in putting tracts within the leaves, or rather covers, of the portions of the Scriptures. I rather think I shall go to Tranquebar, but can not definitely say

G 2

—must go as the Lord leads. And now, my dearest, farewell. May you have much of the divine blessing. Tell the children to be *good* and obedient to mamma.

"Ever yours most affectionately,   J. SCUDDER."

"Shearly, July 2d, 1838.

"MY DEAREST,—I reached this place this morning about half past seven. Had a headache, as is very common, but feel better after having had a good breakfast on *oppers* and *milk.* So you see I am living on the fat of the land. The fact is, I get very tired of my hard bread. When I get to be *seventy,* should I have no teeth, I must have something besides *hard* bread. I told the boy to buy me some oppers. He went out and brought in three great oppers, about *nine inches* in diameter, as large about as *the plate* on which he brought them. I gave him a *scolding* for bringing such a load. But I found them quite tolerable as to eating. As they were cold, I got my little tin kettle belonging to my lamp, and put in it piece by piece, with a little milk, to warm it, until I had devoured more than one of my oppers. The boy must have, for aught I know, been astonished to see me make such havoc in the oppers he had bought after I had scolded him as I did. I had a good cup of coffee also, and some salt beef. Indeed, I did remarkably well—spent about an hour in getting through. Had it not been for my breakfast, I should not have been able to write you. But to go back. On Friday, the day after I wrote to you, was the great day for bathing, and the people numerous, of course. The crowd for books in the evening, or rather afternoon, became so great, and the confusion became such that I suspended giving books until Saturday. On Saturday I had a very quiet day, and on that day and on Sunday gave out thirty or forty, or perhaps fifty of my New Testaments. Most of these were given to *choice* men from the *country;* and I re-joice much in the thought that the *whole* New Testament has thus gone abroad into different villages. I do not know exactly how many books we gave out—probably two thousand three hundred. We left Sethemparum yesterday morning, but made but little advance on our journey in consequence of two rivers we had to pass. The bandy upon which I have *embarked* is higher than the others, and this could pass without my trunks being taken out; all the books were taken from the others, and went over in a small boat. Near this river is another still wider. It is passable now with bandies unloaded. I passed over in my bandy most of the way, unloaded. I took off my stockings, and stood in the water a part of the time where the water was deepest. It was so deep that the poor oxen did not like their plight any more than John Gilpin did his steed. So they were in won-derful straits. At last one got loose from the bandy, and away it went, Gilpin-like. The poor bandy-man was in a sad plight, as you may suppose; so he undertook to be *one of the oxen.* He got hold of the yoke, but all would not do; *over* went the bandy into the river by the force of the current. The doctor, you may be sure, made haste to get into the river without a moment's loss of time, as he would by no means go under with the bandy. Thus I was in a sad state, for I had my watch to take care of, and in my fob were bank-notes. I soon got my watch into my jacket pocket, and in order to save my bank-notes, which were pinned within my fob, I tried to get out the pin (this I did, you must know, upon one of the wheels which was out of water, upon which I got up). But alas! the head of the pin was *inside* the fob, and I could not get at it. I therefore got off my pantaloons as soon as possible. I was in the water for so *short a moment* that my bank-notes did not get wet at all. So I went to the shore, and reached the rest-house in good order. My bandy-men, with the boats, did not reach me till evening. I had tied up about twenty of the Gospels in a handkerchief: these were not wet as much as might have been expected; they were not wet inside at all, except a leaf or two near the covers. But how, you may ask, did we succeed with our old bandy? There were men in the river to help with bandies loaded with cotton; so some of them came to our help; not, however, was any thing done *until* an agreement had been made as to the *price* for help. One fanam was the bargain between the bandy-men and the others. So we soon had our old bandy on its *legs* again. At the rest-house I took off my pantaloons a second time and dried them in the sun. My shirt also dried, and I was in quite a dry condition in a short time. I put my books to dry, but got rid of them before I could finish drying them, the comers were so anxious for them.

"I am engaged in a blessed work. The Lord, by the distribution of his own Word, will make way for his coming to take possession of this land as his own. Jesus shall reign, and it will be found at last that his reign was hastened by his servant, whom he has privileged to sow so largely of his Word.

"I have had some of my shirts washed, and washed my dark pantaloons myself. I am quite a washerman."

"Shearly, July 6th.

"MY DEAREST,—I am now at Mayaveram. On Monday afternoon I left Shearly, and reached Vittesuremkovil in time to do something for my Master, though I was unfit both in body and mind. I seemed to long for the coming of the night, and when it came was soon in my bandy, and after looking upward went to sleep. If various trials have reason to make us praise God, and look upon them as our choicest mercies (my doctrine, you know), I think I have much to praise him for so far as regards the work in which I am engaged. It is certainly 'through much tribulation' of one kind and another that I engage in the work in which I am now busy. I have a most distressed headache most of the time, at least so great as to make me unfit in some measure for my work. I have a ticklish stomach. I have opposition to meet with from Satan and from the natives. Now and then a tract or book is torn up. I have the opposition of some of the committee of the Bible Society, and I lastly have something of the unwillingness of my dearest wife to contend with. 'Who is weak, and I am not weak?' Instead of writing to me as you did about my separation from you, if you had told me to go forward, that you rejoiced in the separation, and hoped that it could not be otherwise than the will of God, I should then have been delighted; but I am quite willing that all should be as it is. You say, 'If this is your duty, and the labor which the Lord would have you perform, I do trust it may be made more plain to *me*. I would not oppose (as is known to my heavenly Father) if I could see your duty plain,' etc. But I will not continue the subject. Now, my dearest, do not think I am complaining too much. No, I feel strong. I had a good day yesterday—one upon which I shall look back hereafter, I hope, with great pleasure. I will leave my complaints.

"10*th.* Yesterday morning I removed to that part of the city called Mayaveram, where I continued to preach the Gospel and give out books. I give out most all of the books with my own hands. Yesterday the boys tried their *fun* in throwing little bits of brick or *chunam* at me. I went out to the boy, my cook, and told him to go up privately into the veranda opposite to the one where I was, and lay hold of the person in case he should throw again. He soon caught a young Brahmin boy, whom he hurried off to the police. I left Mayaveram yesterday afternoon, and came here (that is, at Teduktrayyoor) this morning. I shall be so busy, perhaps, to-morrow that I shall not be able to write much, and I must do the most of it to-day. I shall probably be at Tranquebar at least three days, one at Paneor, one at Cancal, one at Nagoor, perhaps two at Negapatam. From thence I will endeavor to go as the Lord shows the pillar of cloud. I shall, with divine permission, write you from Negapatam on Wednesday or Thursday week. I shall probably visit Temvallor, a town about twelve miles from Negapatam, before I set my face homeward. I hope you will continue to pray much, that my labors may not be in vain. Good-by for to-day, with much love.

"*Tranquebar*, 11*th.* As you will see, my dearest, I am now at Tranquebar, and I seize a moment to write to you. I have the prospect of a busy day after we begin fairly to give out books. I am near Mrs. Cameron, as I am told. I shall probably, D.V., call there to-night and see her. I am in the part of the city where the population is large, near one of the Christian churches. I do not certainly know when I shall leave Tranquebar—I suppose not before Saturday, at least. I must remove into the fort after my work in this part is done. Probably may finish it by to-morrow night. Hope to hear from you at Negapatam, if I do not find a letter from you here. I have had excellent health for the last week; the more busy the better, if I do not strain the point. I was a little poorly on Sunday morning, but soon got better by rest and *coffee.* I find my coffee a great comfort. I like it much *without* milk. I shall have to buy some sugar, as I sweep off so much. I shall buy some coffee too, probably. Now, my dearest, I must bid you good-by until next week. Again I say, trouble not yourself about me, as to my being in the path of duty. Let this subject be at rest, and pray without ceasing that the rain of the Spirit may come down upon the seed sown."

"Negapatam, July 21st, 1838.

"My Dearest,—As you perceive by the above, I am now at Negapatam, safely moored in the house of the Rev. Mr. Hardy. I did not leave Tranquebar (as I wished) on Saturday. I had so many applications for books on Saturday morning that I could not make up my mind to set off, so I remained until Monday morning. On Sunday morning, with the leave of the governor (for Mr. Knewtson, the German, or rather Danish missionary, at the earnest entreaty of one or more of the native Christians, wrote to him and gained his permission), I preached to the native congregation in the Jerusalem Church, built more than a hundred years ago by Tiegenbuly. I had a very considerable number of country-born people. These I addressed in English after I got through the Tamul. I came on *hastily* through Cancal and the next city, which are under *French* influence, and was rejoiced when I got on *English* ground again. See what I wrote in the inclosed to Winslow. I will not take up *your* letter with it, but you all must think it is written as much for you as for him. To go back, you seem to think that I keep you in the dark as to the places where I go, and on this account you have not been able to tell your inquirers where I had gone or was going. I am not aware that you have been more in the dark, my dearest, than myself. I do not know that, when I left home, I had any more idea of visiting Negapatam than I have of going to the *moon* to-night. The thought first probably entered my mind at Sethemparum. Now I wish you just to answer those who make inquiries as to where I am going, that I am going just where the pillar of cloud by day and the pillar of fire by night lead me; that I have no place but that which my divine Lord and Master points out. I thought when I reached Negapatam that I should not go farther; but I see that I must visit a town five or six miles below. I expect, God willing, next week to go to Temvallor. So far my way appears plain, but beyond that I can not tell what I shall do. Perhaps I shall go right straight to Sethemparum on my way home, or I may go to Coembacoonum, and from thence to Sethemparum, Cuddalore, and so on home. I shall probably not leave Negapatam until Wednesday next *for good and all.* I have about two bandy-loads of books remaining, and it depends upon the number given here and at Temvallor whether I go to Coembacoonum. I shall write you, with divine permission, again before leaving Negapatam, and may, perhaps, be better able to tell you whether I go to Coembacoonum or not. But enough of all this. Now as to myself and helpers. I have had hard work for a week. Raaman has, until yesterday, been laid *aside* —could do nothing. I have had to preach, and preach, and preach, and this, too, with a bad cold, so that my lungs are most worn out, and I feel that I ought to give them some rest. Raaman helped me some yesterday. We preach all the time, we may say, as well as give out portions of the Scriptures and tracts. Cornelius and Timothy, too, have had colds, but nothing like Raaman's sickness. My cough is so bad that I have sent out the boy to buy me some liquorice-stick. It would be well for us if we could all be quiet to-day, but this will be impossible. We shall have crowds of people before night. I do not know, my dearest, when I shall see you. It will, I think, take up my full six weeks before I can in any way reach home, though I thought possibly I might be back sooner. But all is well. I shall be back just when the Lord sees best. I am doing a most blessed work. I have (aside from Sabbaths) preached the Gospel more within the last month than for the whole previous year in the streets of Madras. The precious name Jesus is sounded far and near.

"*Negapatam, July 23d.* The distribution of God's own Word is calculated, with the divine blessing, to break down heathenism to a great extent. It may be an excellent *John the Baptist* to go before and prepare the way for the coming of the Son of Man.

"J. Scudder."

"Rayya Rest-house, near *C*onjeveram, Dec. 17th.

"My Dearest,—This is a memorable day. *Twenty* years ago to-day we reached Tillipally. I have been looking out the passage, 'Hitherto hath the Lord helped us.' 1 Sam., vii., 12. Truly *we* may say, hitherto hath the Lord helped *us*—helped us in sickness and in health, in trials numerous and sometimes not a little severe. He has been with us; and what above all demands our gratitude is that he has not allowed us 'to fall away' and perish. Twenty years have we had the supports of divine grace. The hope of heaven which we had twenty years ago remains until this day. Until this day the desire remains to look to Jesus. And shall we not this day inscribe the name Ebenezer upon our dwelling-place, and look up and say, 'Hitherto hast thou, O Lord, helped us?' And as this grace has hitherto been vouchsafed, shall we doubt whether it will be continued unto the end? Instead of yielding to such doubts, rather let us lay hold of the skirts of our precious Redeemer's garment and say, In thy strength, we resolve never to leave nor forsake thee. When you receive this letter, just turn to the passage I have been alluding to, and the passages in its connection, and then turn to Joshua xxiii., 14.

"It is now past twelve o'clock, and I have been, according to our agreement, at the throne of grace, praying for you and for the children. May Jehovah Jesus be your stay and support, and comfort you. I know you feel most keenly on account of our separation; your time of rejoicing on this account, perhaps, will be reserved for the day of the winding up of the affairs of the universe. Then, if not before, you will rejoice—oh yes, for you will see then that, in consequence of our separation, great glory was brought to the name of Jesus. And when all your and my trials are over, and when nothing but the glory which has been brought to this, our adorable Master, will strike us fully in the face, then shall we lift up our voices and praise him for these separations as among the choicest blessings he ever conferred upon us. Let the remembrance of this, my dearest, assuage your grief, and dry up those tears which you so plentifully shed when the thoughts of our separation come over your mind. How many tears did you shed just before I left you? Well, Jesus allows you to shed them, for he wept himself. Would that you, would that I, in all our trials, could look more into the eternal world, and view things when under them as we shall view them by-and-by. Would that we had more of the feelings of our adorable Master, of whom it is said, "Who, for the joy set before him, endured the cross and despised the shame." But alas! human nature is human nature, and it seems that an abundance of joy must be reserved for the house not made with hands, eternal in the heavens. Perhaps the joys then to be experienced would not be duly appreciated unless by the discipline under which we have to be trained for heaven. Indeed, we may say they could not. How should we know how to value health of body unless we had been deprived of it? May we, my dearest, but safely reach the shore, and oh, what a time for rejoicing will it be with us! It will indeed be a time of rejoicing—of fullness of joy, for there will be nothing to mar it; there will be no alloy mixed with the gold.

"Now, my dearest, good-by for to-day. Kiss the dear children for papa. Call Louisa, and tell her that papa sends her a kiss for both cheeks. If you previously ask

her how papa kisses, she will probably point you to both
sides of her face.   Tell all the children to strive who can
comfort mamma most.

"*Malianoor, December* 20*th,*1839. A little before sunset I left for Tayyill, where we arrived probably about
seven.   Though it was night, the people soon found out
that I had come, and I had as busy a season for night
distribution of portions of the Scriptures, tracts, and Almanacs as I ever before had.   It was a beautiful night,
with nearly a full moon shining upon us, and by the light
of the moon I discovered who could read.   There were
two persons who could not see the letters, so I examined
their *thumbs*.   I found the *notch* in the nails of each, so
I had no hesitation in giving them what they wanted.
To one man I gave also what he wanted, though he could
not make out the letters, and though he had not a notch
at all in his thumb nail, or so small that I could not tell
whether there was one or not.   I gave what he asked
for, taking him at his word.   He told me he could read.
I closed my labors with the people in this village a little
after nine o'clock, and felt much the need of rest.   This
morning I came on to this place, where I have been at
work in preaching and distributing portions of the Scriptures and tracts.   It is a large village; but few of the
people can read.   As I did not get a cup of tea until
late (probably not far from half past ten), and as I was
very busy before getting it, I am now writing with a little of my old companion—a sick headache.   Most of the
people who can read, or who wish for books, have been
supplied, and I shall, D. V., leave in about two hours for
Tyyanoor, where I shall spend the night.   It is now one
o'clock, and I hope to labor there a while before the night

sets in. Good-by, my love, to-day. Have been a little home-sick.

"*Tinvannamaly, December 23d,*1839. *Half past six o'clock in the evening.* I have had a very busy time of it for most of the time since I reached this place. Have had many visitors, and distributed above three hundred books and tracts together. Of these, twenty-five at least were Tellogoo Gospels, and one hundred and twenty-five Tamul Gospels. As I have but one native helper, I have found the work rather hard—that is, the work to examine people whether they can read, to give out the books, and to preach the Gospel. About three o'clock he began to help me so far as the examination of persons as to their capacity to read is concerned. We continued our work till nearly six o'clock, when it began to grow dark. I have seen no disposition to tear up any of the books. This part of the country needs a missionary very much, as there is no person near to whom an inquirer can go. This would be an excellent place for his abiding-place, and he might visit various places of note within a few miles of it. But I must hasten to bid you good-night. I wish it may be a good and a happy one to you. It is just one week since I saw your face for the last time before leaving you. Time flies, and eternity presses on. I am not disposed to catch hold of the wheels of the former and stop them. If we are to be housed in safety at last, it seems that time can not speed its flight too fast to get us into the haven. Good-night, my dearest, with much, very much love. *Christmas day.* How should our hearts flow out in love to our Jesus, dying for us, choosing us while others are left to perish, being with us, whipping us into heaven — all love from first to last! I am

now encamped for the night at a very small village, called, as you have read, Sankyyum, under a tamarind-tree,
as there is no choultry.

"*Trivettoor, December* 28*th,* 1839. To-morrow morning, with divine permission, I reach Chetpul. I find that
my palankeen, like myself, is getting rather old. One of
the screws of the middle iron, which holds the palankeen
up, has fallen out. Downer, I think, must have picked it
up, as, just before I left, he brought me a screw which
looked *old enough* to belong to it. That you may think
I have not brought up a bad report of my establishment,
I would observe that *it leaks;* it does not keep out the
rain *at the sides; the middle piece*—the piece of wood
which goes under the rattan to keep the sides of the palankeen from pressing inward by the weight of the person within—*has given away; another screw* at the *other*
end of the palankeen *is shaking,* and may soon fall out.
But enough. If I get home safely, I must make better
provision for next time. If I break down, I must get
some small bamboos, or something of the kind, and *tie*
up my concern. I am so *lengthy* that I need a longer
palankeen than the one I now have. I want one, too, a
little wider. You see I am always talking about what I
want, and yet never get any thing; but you will see that
it will not all end *in talk.*

"*Chetpul, December* 29*th,* 1839. Hope you and the dear
children are well. For your comfort and joy, think of
the number of precious souls who will probably hear of
Jesus from my mouth while absent from you. Put yourself, my love, in their places. Suppose you had never
heard this name, *would you not wish some husband to
leave his wife to come and tell you of him, and to put*

in your hands his Word? May Jehovah Jesus support and bless you abundantly. We shall meet in due time with the permission of our heavenly Father, who has the *directing* of all our concerns. Are the children obedient to mamma? Please to call them all to you and ask each of them the question, and ask them also what answer you must give when you write. Love to the Housingtons, Meigses, and Winslows, and the largest share for yourself. Remember me to Amy.

"Ever most affectionately yours, J. SCUDDER."

"Meyyoor, December 28th.

"MY DEAREST,—I sent off a letter to you yesterday from Temkoviloor through the Tapildar of that place. As I told you, I reached Temhovil on the afternoon of the 26th, and soon began my work. This I continued yesterday. I began before sunrise, and continued till after sunset to preach and distribute books and tracts. I gave away, in the two days, above two hundred Gospels, and more tracts. Of course, as I began my work so early, and continued it so late, I was abundantly tired at night. I had two intermissions—one for breakfast, of twenty minutes, and one at about noon, of an hour and a quarter. After dinner I caught a little nap. I was in a good government bungalow, where there was a room into which I retired. I mentioned that I could not get a book into the village where I staid on Wednesday night, at Sankyyum. Two men who came from that village to Temkoviloor (one of whom I saw there and would not take a book) came and received books; so the written Gospel will have a place there, contrary to my expectations. I did not mention that I found a very interesting woman in that village. I could not but think of Lydia of old, and prayed that she might be a Lydia.

"*Monday, December 30th.* I am now at Temvamanal-loor. I left Meyyoor on the afternoon of Saturday, and called at the villages of Puthuparlium and Panipankum on my way to Marnakoopum and Erluntary, two villages adjoining each other, and merely separated by a street. I do not know exactly how many books I gave at Mey-yoor; perhaps sixty of the Gospels, and as many, or near-ly as many copies of the Blind Way, with other tracts. Left ten books and two copies of the Blind Way in the village of Puthuparlium, and one or two in Panipankum. After I left Puthuparlium, a young man came running after me for a book, which I gave him. On Saturday evening, rather late, I had to run about the place where I expected to spend the Sabbath to find a place in which to tarry during the Sabbath. I went in quest of a large tree, and at last found one, but did not put up under it, as I was told that the veranda of the building in front of Karle's Temple was at my service provided I did not go *within*. I took up my abiding-place there, or rather in front of the veranda, where I placed my palankeen. On Sunday I sat in the veranda in the morning, and preached and gave out books. As my applications for books had ceased pretty much by noon, I resolved to go to a large village, as I was told it was, in the afternoon. Accordingly Kesay, and the boy, and I set out on foot. We were told it was one —— distant; but it was a long narlekay. I was an hour in walking the road to it, and, when I reached it, found it to be a small place. Preached Christ to the people, and gave away seven Gospels and as many copies of the Blind Way. Re-

turned with *aching legs.* Gave away yesterday, altogether, between forty and fifty books and tracts. This
morning I went to Erdyyaar, a village on the main road
to the north of Marnakoopum. It is a large village; but
my *wares* were little esteemed by most. Gave away
only three books and as many copies of the Blind Way
to the villagers. Two or three other persons received a
book and a tract also this morning. The place where I
now am is said to be large. In going through the country, I feel that I am doing no justice to what may be
called a general distribution. There are hundreds of important villages which ought to have copies of the Word
of Life in them. But what can be done? Very little
for them until you and I sojourn in tents. What do you
say to it? A double tent—a great *big house* with *out-
tents*—*outhouses.* How would you like to take a ten-
months' trial, to see how the thing would work? It is an
easy thing to visit places on a main road, but what are
these (cities excepted) to the vast number of villages with
which the whole plain (by-the-by, I believe I spelled this
word *plane* the other day) is skirted?

"MEMORANDUMS.—1. *Short of Bread.* Eat an immense quantity. Not two weeks gone. Think my dearest
did not calculate on my having such an enormous stomach; but she must remember that I have to eat from this
store three times a day. Cook rice but once. Next time
must have two weeks' supply of bread laid in.

"2. Find my old black inkstand an unspeakable comfort, instead of that little *red, long* pocket-inkstand. No
danger of the present inkstand tipping over and daubing
all things around it with ink.

"3. My *old, uncouth-looking, long-legged, bagged,*

H

black pantaloons, excellent for the ticks to creep up un-discovered and feast on my *flesh*. These old grand-father, nine-different-ways-cut, two-legged bags come down so low as to cover my stockings, and give me no chance to see the ticks when they make a sally upon my legs. Never want any more such articles on my legs. The ticks have bitten me as I have never been bitten be-fore. Great blotches—put me in mind of the blotch oc-casioned on the arm by the cow-pox. Must take the pre-caution, when I encamp under a tree again, to draw my stockings (as I have done) over my pantaloons, thus making the best I can of my predicament, not having more than two pairs of clean white pantaloons, and the old *stand-bys* having given out, having a great long slit in one of the knees. Good-by, my dearest love, for to-day.

"I forgot to tell you that yesterday morning a woman came up in great rage to Karle's Temple, and prayed most fervently that she would destroy some persons who had been beating her. I had an opportunity of witness-ing the devotion of one of her worshipers both yesterday and this morning before daybreak. He came up with a small drum, and said over, in quite a solemn tone of voice, his prayers in the Tellogoo language. He would beat the drum, and then stop and pray, etc. I think he might have made some nominal Christians, to say the least, ashamed. After hearing what I did, I could not but be struck with those lines of Dr. Watts, 'Why was I made to hear thy voice, and enter while there's room,' but did not feel that I could apply the last two lines until after I had made known a Saviour to him.

"31*st*. *Anotoar*. Came to this place this morning.

Distributed at Temvamanalloor about seventy-five Tamul Gospels, and about as many copies of the Blind Way. Gave away also several Tellogoo Gospels. Found, when the night closed upon me, that it was high time that my *lungs* should have rest. Nothing occurred yesterday of particular interest out of the common way, except that a little girl came and received a Tellogoo Gospel and tract. Her father came with her. He told me that he had devoted her to the Temple. This information made me eloquent. I enjoined it upon him not to fulfill his vow, but to marry her—to have her married. He probably felt the force of what I said to some extent, for he said he would not adopt the course he had adopted with this daughter with another and a younger which he had. All I said to make him break his foolish vow will probably be disregarded, and this modest, well-behaved, and pleasant, if not beautiful child, will probably be doomed, after four or five years, to become a prostitute of the Temple. I endeavored to operate upon his feelings of honor, and told him that it would be disgraceful for him to do so, and, moreover, that the curse of God would rest upon him if he did. One of the by-standers seemed to think that it would not at all answer to withdraw his vow when it had been made to God. I told him it had been made to one who was no God. But, as I before said, probably all I said will be disregarded; though, probably from the earnestness of my manner with the father, it will not be soon forgotten. May Jehovah bless the Word in her hands to the salvation of her soul! She has a directory which few females have in their hands. I gave her father also a Tamul Gospel and a copy of the Blind Way, and I believe also of the Spiritual Milk. I am drawing near now to Tividy, and shall leave this place this after-noon, having nearly done my work here. So I shall take leave of my dearest with saying what a horrid state of things is it when it is considered as *honorable* to dedicate children to a temple to become prostitutes. What must we think of such a vile system of religion which will countenance and encourage it but that it is eminently fit-ted to prepare subjects for hell!

"*Tividy, January 1st,* 1840. I bid my sweetest a hap-py new-year—an important season in two respects. The first is because we are brought one year nearer to eterni-ty; the second is because another tenth of a century has passed. Instead of 1839, we have to substitute a four before the nine, and make it 1840. I had some expecta-tion of spending this day in a very different manner two months ago; but we know not what a day brings forth. I expected, as we talked it over, to have a prayer-meeting at our house to-day to pray for the best interests of our fel-low-men. Yesterday afternoon I left Anotoor, and came on to Puthapertly, where I encamped under a tree at the side of a tank for the night. As I had distributed books here before, I refused to give any except to a few who were from villages near. This morning I stopped at Lingared-deparlium, and distributed about sixty books and tracts. Most of the tracts were of the Blind Way. Yesterday I gave away probably about thirty books and as many tracts at Anotoor. Have met with nothing on all my journey thus far until this morning which indicated that a book would be misused. This morning I met with a very vile person. He came to the place where I was, and was free in his abuse of *our Beloved.* He called him a thief and a *player,* meaning that he had done as Sciva is said to have done. I took no notice of him so far as speaking to him was concerned. He spent all his spite and then went away, but came back again with a copy of the Blind Way, which he had got from some other person, for I had given him none. As I would not speak to him, he spent his spite so far as words were concerned, and then tore out the first leaf of the Blind Way. I flew to him, and took away the book from him in a moment. Thus ended our interview. I inquired his name, but nobody *knew.* He was a *foreigner.* I begged for his name again and again, but in vain.

"I am now, as I said, at Tividy, and the natives are quite in a flock around me. I have been supplying a number with books, and stopped to finish my letter to you, which must go off to-day.

"*Memorandum.* My old cloak needs my dear wife's needle and thread very much. This old stand-by must yet be my companion, and must be rigged up."

To his Brother-in-law in America.

"Madras, January 15th, 1840.

"I lately returned from a tour of three weeks—a tour to distribute portions of the Scriptures and tracts. I was absent three months from your sister on this business last year. These separations your sister feels so sensibly, as well as myself, that it is not improbable we shall *quite* turn Rechabites. We now drink no wine. We have no vineyards; neither do we have field nor seed. Should we go out and live in *tents,* we shall be Rechabites to some extent at least. We could be very comfortable in tents for nine months of the year. The remaining three we could spend in a city, where there are good houses.

I find no one who is willing to engage in this great work of the general distribution of the Scriptures and tracts. The consequence is that much falls upon me. Winslow *prepares;* I *distribute.* I do not feel that I am doing justice to the work on my present plan. Harriet seems quite pleased with the idea of accompanying me in the manner just mentioned.

"Well, my dear brother, farewell. Think for Christ, speak for Christ, act for Christ, and may Jehovah Jesus be with and bless you and yours. Harriet sends much love to you and sister.

"Very affectionately,   J. Scudder.

"To Rev. J. B. Waterbury."

CHAPTER X.

FAILURE OF HEALTH—1841.

Dr. Scudder's abundant labors at length broke down a constitution almost Herculean. He seemed not to have considered the draft made upon his physical energies by the constant action of a debilitating climate. "In season and out of season," amid drenching rains and torrid suns, he still kept on his incessant preaching and book-distribution. Jolting along in his bandy-cart, or footing it amid sand ankle-deep, surrounded by insulting Brahmins or the wild and furious populace, he keeps on with his heavenly works, trusting in God, and weeping over the miseries of the heathen. At length his appetite fails; his headaches become terribly chronic. The strong buttresses seem to be giving way. He is obliged to admit that the arm so often stretched out with the Bread of Life is partially paralyzed, and that he must have a season of relaxation or die; yet how he hates to think of receding or relaxing when surrounded by millions needing his help!

"My doctor has ordered me off to sea, and advised me to visit America; but still I am somewhat strong to labor. Had I nothing but the swelling of the tendons, I should not regard it much. It is the inflammation which occasionally comes on which threatens to break me down.

I stopped preaching several weeks, but have commenced again. I have been very desirous of going out on a tour, taking H. and the children with me. We have as many tents or 'cloth houses' at our command as we wish. One of our pious friends, a civilian, who has been obliged to dwell more or less in tents, has offered us his. Unless we can so go out, there are vast numbers of persons who will never hear of the name of Jesus. Few are at liberty, or are disposed to engage in the work of taking extensive tours. The tour which I took a year ago enabled me to give away eight thousand of the bound volumes of the tracts, many Almanacs, etc., with five or six thousand Gospels. I wish very much to go through that region of country lying north of the Coloroon. The people there have probably never seen a missionary." But this project Dr. S. was never able fully to carry out.

JUNGLE FEVER.

This malady has features in common with our well-known intermittent fever, or fever and ague; but when it takes hold, it holds on; seldom is it ever entirely eradicated. This terrible jungle fever struck the first heavy blow on the naturally fine constitution of Dr. Scudder.

Having an important object in view—the establishment of a Christian educational institution—he made a long journey on one occasion, crossing the entire peninsula from eastern coast to western. He passed over the Neilgherries and through the Mysore district, encountering perils innumerable, and exposing himself to the malaria which spreads itself like a death-pall over the country. Unfortunately, the journal which he kept has been lost; but the writer will never forget the intense interest which that journal awakened in his mind. The scenery, with the grand and beautiful intermingled; the air laden with the perfume of flowers such as we cultivate in hothouses, but *there* growing wild; the impenetrable jungle, the abode of tigers and elephants; and, above all, the heathen in his blindness "bowing down to wood and stone," made the journey one of intense excitement.

Dr. Scudder displayed tact and courage throughout this excursion. Though alone, and with treacherous bearers, he managed to keep every thing under his control. He saw the men he wished to see; and, by letters of introduction from the officials at Madras, he gained access to wealthy and influential military and civil officers on the eastern shores of India. Naturally and educationally a perfect gentleman, Dr. Scudder found no difficulty in freely communicating with gentlemen of the highest standing. He received from them polite attentions and donations in money. But his great aim seemed to be to draw the attention of these military and civic officers of the government to a consideration of their personal responsibility to God, and of their need, equally with the surrounding heathen, of a personal interest in the blood of Christ.

No man was better qualified to do this than Dr. Scudder. His very look was that of a sincere Christian, and his manners indicative of high culture. He was known and recognized as a self-denying missionary of the Cross. What he said had weight; and, by studying the character of the individual, he seldom gave offense when pressing, in a Christian spirit, the claims of his divine Master.

On his return through the forests and jungles of the midland road he was seized with the jungle fever. His

H 2

life was despaired of. The sad news was transmitted to his wife, in the hope that she might be able, by traveling day and night, to reach him and receive his dying benediction. As a last resort, the surgeon placed him in a chemical bath, which operated favorably, and proved a means, under God, of saving his valuable life. But the shock to his constitution, as we have said, was felt to his dying day. The seeds of that disease were never eradicated. When at the writer's house during his visit to America in 1846, he suffered severely by its recurrence.

PERILOUS JOURNEY OF MRS. SCUDDER.

Mrs. Scudder prepared at once for the overland journey. A kind friend provided her with a tent, bearers were engaged, and provisions laid in. Then this lonely but heroic woman, accompanied by her little son, and just on the eve of giving birth to another child, started on her mournful way. The agony she endured can not be conceived. Nothing stayed her up but her faith in God. She still had a bare hope that she might find her husband alive, and possibly recovering. This faint hope lighted up her dark pathway across the Neilgherries. She had to travel in the *night* as well as by day, which involved personal peril such as few would dare to encounter.

In the worst part of the jungle road, as night drew on, the bearers became intimidated at the sound of wild beasts roaring after their prey, and suddenly fled, leaving Mrs. Scudder and her little one exposed to the most horrid death, and with none to protect them but Daniel's God. What could she do? There was but one thing. She held her little one by the hand, and spent that night on her knees in prayer. She heard the heavy tread of wild elephants, which could have trampled her and her little one to death. Then came the growl of tigers and other ravenous beasts, the sound approaching and then receding. They seemed to be circling round the little spot where she knelt, ready to spring upon their prey. But God held them back. Yes, He who shut the mouths of lions, and allowed Daniel to pillow his head on their manes, sent his angel in answer to prayer to guard these, his dear ones, from the death they dreaded. So they passed the night. Morning came, and the cowardly bearers returned and resumed their burden.

Mrs. Scudder found her husband convalescent. The immediate danger of death had passed, but long months were required to restore him to his wonted health.

DECIDES TO VISIT AMERICA.

After long-continued labors and wearisome journeys, Dr. Scudder was at length obliged to confess that his physical energies were no longer adequate to fulfill his duties as a missionary. That old jungle fever crept through his frame; exposure to the burning sun brought on headache and faintness; his arm hung paralyzed by his side, and no medical treatment seemed to afford relief. So, at length, by the urgent entreaties of his brethren, backed by the opinion of skillful surgeons, he decided to set sail with his family for home, or rather what was *once* his home.

It was supposed that a change of climate and of habits might renovate his shattered constitution, and give him still a number of years to labor for the salvation of the heathen. This, in a measure, reconciled him to the proposed plan. It cost him many a pang, however, to leave India even for a few years. Here he had come in 1820 to live, to labor, and to die. It seemed to him like a retreat before an enemy. For a while he could not bear the thought.

Writing to his mother, he says: " I have, as you perhaps know, been long experiencing the enervating influence of this warm climate. For the last year I have been afflicted with swellings of my arm, which have occasionally been attended with severe inflammation. Dr. Lane, an eminent surgeon of this city, considers my whole constitution to be materially shattered. He advises me to go to sea, and even to America; but of this I can not now even bear the thought. I require bracing up immediately, but think I may linger along, and do much work yet for some time to come. I do not want to fail in my material outwork of going forth to distribute far and wide the Word of Life. If I rally soon, He will go out with me."

But the hope thus expressed was not realized. After much prayer for direction, he decided to embark with his family—those still with him—for his native shores. He had some strong ties drawing him in this direction. Many of his relatives still survived. He had several sons whom he had sent to America for their education, whose hearts leaped for joy at the idea of seeing and embracing their venerated father and their beloved mother. But these inducements, howevever strong, were overborne by the grand consideration of duty. He might, by this change, add some years to his working life in India.

THE ARRIVAL.

After the usual incidents of a long sea-voyage, during which his health continued to improve, he was welcomed by a host of friends, some of whom, twenty-three years before, had witnessed his departure, and bidden him, as they supposed, a last farewell. To them it seemed something like a resurrection. They could scarcely, however, identify that young athletic form, and that look of sacred hilarity, which, as he waved them farewell, spoke of a heaven-inspired consecration. Disease and toil had made serious inroads on the physical man. He was bowed down under his infirmities, and called himself an old man when but little past fifty. But the same hallowed fervor spoke through his features, and the nearer vision of heaven likened him more closely to its perfected inhabitants. Trials had softened and sanctified his spirit, but had not abstracted one particle of his heroic self-denial. The writer can never forget the first interview after his return, when, having embraced each other with tears, he said, " Come, dear brother, let us retire together and give God thanks that, for more than twenty years, you and I have been kept from doing any thing that would bring reproach on the cause of our blessed Master."

CHAPTER XI.

Preaching Tours for Children.—Reminiscences, etc.

HIS WORK IN AMERICA.

IT might be supposed that, coming home with broken health, Dr. Scudder would have retired to some quiet country place, and there endeavored to recuperate. But no! He must "work while the day lasted." *Still* life was no life for him. His soul was full and overflowing with love to the souls of the heathen, and it must have vent in some way. He found that Christians generally, in this country, could not be made to feel the pressure of obligation to give the Gospel to the whole world, and that his only hope was to educate the next generation up to these important responsibilities. He resolved, therefore, that he would employ his remaining energies in preaching to the children of America, and so, if possible, and by God's blessing, raise up a generation to serve the Lord in this higher and nobler department of Christian consecration. With this view he at once laid his plans, nor did he swerve for an instant until he had, in almost every important city and town, called around him the children, and instructed them as to the heart-affecting miseries of heathendom and their own contrasted privileges, laying upon them the obligation to pity the heathen, to pray for them, and, so far as they could, to send them the Message of Salvation. For three or more years this was his constant work, traveling from place to place,

and every where received with open arms. From Geor-
gia to Maine, from East to West, he prosecuted this mission, until he had addressed over *a hundred thousand
children and youth.* By his conciliatory manners he
fascinated them; by his loving spirit he drew them; by
his touching appeals he melted them. He brought the
living pictures before them—told them what he had seen;
the representation making *them* shudder, as the reality
had made *him.* He dwelt on the love of Christ, alike
poured out on the heathen as upon us. Jesus loves *you;*
Jesus loves *them.* "He tasted death for every man."
This was the great argument which he used, alike cogent
upon youthful minds as upon those of adult years.

PREACHING TOURS FOR CHILDREN.

The testimonials in this field are numerous. We
shall select but a few. The following is from the Rev.
B. R. Allen, of South Berwick, Maine:

"REV. AND VERY DEAR SIR,—Your visit to us last winter is remembered with great interest, both by the young
and the old. I write for the purpose of communicating
some items of intelligence connected with that visit
which I know will cheer your benevolent heart. And,
first, the Juvenile Society, organized for purposes of benevolence just before you came, received from you a
specific object and an impulse of a very important character. They were laboring industriously to do good, but
had selected no one channel through which to operate.
They have adopted the course you so nobly advocate,
and to which your life is devoted, and are now laboring
with increased efficiency for its promotion.

" Another result of your visit has induced a gentleman and his wife—Mr. and Mrs. H.—members of my Church, to undertake the education of a heathen girl under your supervision.   They lost a daughter two years since, about sixteen years old, named Cynthia Ann, whose name they wish you to give to the girl, whom, for them, you will receive into the school.   She died in the triumphs of faith. They will wish to hear from the child through you, and when she shall be able to write, a letter from her *direct* will do great good, not only in that family, but in others, leading them to adopt a similar course.   The first annual donation for this object has been sent to the treasurer of the Board.   But I have another item of news still more interesting.   You recollect my little group of children and youth in the course of religious instruction in the *Old Catechism,* that you saw and addressed?   Well, God has, I trust, blessed that means of grace in the conversion of many of them to Christ.   About the first of February I found several of them specially interested. The interest has continued to the present, and twenty-four or twenty-five have found salvation."

                                   " Putnam, December 1.
    " Dr. Scudder will please accept my mite by the hand of my brother.   I have been keeping it for the purpose of buying a Geography; but, when I heard you preach yesterday, I thought I had better send it to you for the poor heathen.   SARAH F. B."

    " DEAR SIR,—I have often thought on the subject of heathenism; but this afternoon, since I heard you preach, I desire to become a missionary.   If ever I grow up, I will be a missionary, if the Lord pleases. I feel deeply for the heathen. Oh that thousands may be brought to the Lord! I have always been fond of reading mission- ary books. Oh that we may be missionaries!

"From your sincere friend,　MARY PAINE."

"DEAR SIR,—Your lecture this afternoon has made a deep impression upon my mind, more so than I have ever felt before. My companion and myself, that have writ- ten together this evening, have resolved to be mission- aries if we live, and the Lord is willing. We have never experienced a change of heart yet, but we (hope) soon to join with the people of God.　ELIZABETH SMITH."

"New Albany, February 16, 1846.

"DEAR SIR,—I would like very much to become a mis- sionary, as I am named after one. I hope I shall be one. I have been saving a dollar for to buy myself some books, but concluded to give it to buy some books for the heathen children. My age is ten years.

"HENRY MARTYN WOODRUFF."

"Lexington, Feb. 9th, 1846.

"DEAR SIR,—Inclosed you will please find five dollars, which I wish to give for the benefit of the poor degraded children of India. Yours very respectfully,

"HENRY T. DUNCAN, aged nine years."

"St. Louis, Feb. 23d, 1846.

"DEAR SIR,—I am a Sunday-school scholar, and went to hear your address to the Sunday-school children yes- terday, and was sorry to hear of so many children who suffer so much for want of the Bible and missionaries to tell them of a Saviour. With this I give you eight dollars, just as many as I am years old, which I have been saving a long time, by request of my grandma and ma, for some good object, and this I think the best I can ever give it for, and hope that it will help to make the heathen better, and save the poor little children. After I have saved some more, I will give that too.

"Robert C. Barnum."

"My dear Sir,—You told me last Sabbath about the little heathen girls, and I wish to send them my little savings. Although it is but little, I hope it may be useful to purchase them a few tracts. When I grow up, I hope to be a missionary and do some good in the heathen land. Please accept this trifle from   Lillie Lytle."

"Owego, Oct. 8, 1845.

"Dear Dr. Scudder,—After your visit to our place last summer, we *small girls* concluded to establish a society (as you recommended) for the benefit of the heathen. We met eight or ten times, and about four weeks ago had our fair. It was a *very rainy* night, but we managed to *clear* about *twenty-six* dollars. We had many of our things left, which we have sold since the fair, and have *thirty-one* dollars to send you; and as small favors are *sometimes* thankfully received, we hope you will accept of this from us. We *hope* we shall be able to send you *more* soon.

"Harriet L. Huntington, *Treas.*
"Elizabeth C. Platt, *Sec'y.*"

"Biddeford, Feb. 6, 1846.

"DEAR SIR,—When you were in Biddeford and addressed us on the condition of the children of India, we felt that we ought to do something to raise them from their ignorance, superstition, and misery, and confer upon them the blessings of the Gospel. Accordingly, we organized ourselves into a Juvenile Missionary Society in January, 1845. Our society is under the care of Mrs. Lord, the wife of our minister. It meets the first Saturday in each month; has collected thirteen dollars the first year, which we have forwarded to the Mission House in Boston, to be devoted to the mission of Madras. We hope to do as much or more the present year. We remember you with much interest, and would go a long way to hear another lecture from you. We should be much gratified to receive a letter from you, and if you write, please to direct to Mrs. Mary E. Lord, in behalf of the Female Juvenile Missionary Society in Second Parish, Biddeford.   M. C. BRADBURY,
S. L. MORRELL,
P. W. HAYES,
E. PINKHAM,
} *Com.*"

"Fair Haven, July 15th, 1845.

"DR. SCUDDER: SIR,—I inclose to you forty dollars for the use of the mission station under your immediate care. The donors are a few young misses connected with the Congregational Sabbath-school, and under my care as a Bible-class. I would add (with gratitude) that it is the result of your labor here in the fall of 1843. And now, dear brother in Christ, may God bless you, and return you in safety to your adopted country; and may you, by his blessing, be instrumental in winning many, very many precious souls to Christ.   Yours with respect,

"MARY GILLUM."

"Rome, N. Y., Sept. 1st, 1845.

"DEAR BROTHER,—On behalf of the scholars of the Sunday-school connected with the Second Presbyterian Church in this place, I forward you three dollars for the mission schools under your charge at Madras.   It gives me great pleasure to assure you that an interest has been awakened in behalf of your mission that will lead to a continued contribution.

"With my most ardent wishes for your prosperity and that of the mission with which you are connected, I am very respectfully yours,   BENJ. P. JOHNSON."

"*Cincinnati, March 12th.*   Yesterday went to Covington, Kentucky, opposite this city, and preached to two hundred and seventy-five children in the afternoon, though quite unwell.   Left fifteen copies of 'The Harvest perishing for want of Laborers' for the students in connection with a Baptist seminary there.   To-day gave to Mr. Rodgers seventy-five copies of my 'Letters to Sabbath-school Children,' for Sabbath-schools.   Wrote in one or two of them only, for want of time, for the Sabbath-school Library.   Have been quite unwell since I came to this city with a severe cold and cough.   Until yesterday had not preached for more than a week.

"*Steubenville, March 28th.*   On the morning of the 15th preached to the children of color in the African church in Cincinnati.   About one hundred were present. In the afternoon preached to about six hundred children in Mr. McDonald's church. Left Cincinnati the next day, and reached Marietta on Wednesday morning. No arrangements had been made for a Convention, as Mr. Bartlett was away, and did not receive the letter which had been sent to him, notifying him of my coming. Arrangements, however, were made for meetings in the place on Friday. On Thursday crossed over the river to Harmar, and preached to about one hundred children. On Friday morning went to the college, and spent two hours with the students. The most of the time was spent in asking questions and receiving answers. A short address closed my exercises with them. I then distributed a copy of 'The Harvest perishing for want of Laborers' to each of the pious students. Connected with the college are about forty students who are professors of religion. Most of them, I trust, have this tract now in their hands. I wrote their names in English and in Tamul in them. In the afternoon preached to one hundred and seventy-five children and youth, or more. In the evening lectured on the map. On Saturday went to Warren, and preached on Sunday to forty children there, and to more than this number at Belpre in the afternoon. Left Marietta on Monday night for Wheeling. Preached to three hundred children and youth at that place on Wednesday afternoon, and lectured on the map in the evening. On Thursday and Friday, until evening, was detained at Wheeling. Reached this place last night at about half past ten o'clock. Have sent answers to letters from Mrs. Allen, Miss Gillum, Mrs. Lord's Juvenile Society, to Miss Huntington, and to Mr. Johnson.

"*April 2d.* I should have mentioned that I left one hundred copies of the 'Letters to Sabbath-school Children' with Mr. Bartlett for Sabbath-school libraries; also one hundred copies of 'A Letter on the Formation of Juvenile Missionary Societies in Sabbath-schools.' From Wheeling went to Steubenville, Ohio. Spent the last Sabbath there very pleasantly. Preached to Christian mothers in the morning, to three hundred and fifty children and young persons in the afternoon, and lectured on the map in the evening. Next day visited Dr. Beattie's school, and had an interview with the young ladies. Many of them received books, and had their names in Tamul and English written in them. Left with Mr. Commingo fifteen copies of the Sabbath-school book for distribution at the meeting of his Presbytery, for Sabbath-school libraries; also fifteen of the 'Letters on the Formation of Juvenile Missionary Societies in Sabbath-schools.' Yesterday and to-day have been making arrangements at this place (Pittsburg) for meetings hereafter with the children. When visiting the Lutheran clergyman, he told me of an instance where a man was driven from the anvil to preach the Gospel through the means of one of my tracts.

"Have been preparing a letter for little girls about Juvenile Sewing Societies, as follows. It is entitled *Dr. Scudder's Letter to the Little Girls:*

"'You have often heard, my dear little girls, that the heathen of India inflict great tortures upon themselves. I will mention one kind of torture of which you, perhaps, have not heard. Some of these deluded people make a vow. With one hand they cover their under lips with mud. On this, with the other hand, they put some small grains, usually of mustard-seed. They then stretch themselves flat on their backs, exposed to the

dews of night, and the blazing and scorching sun by
day. Their vow is, that from this position they will not
stir; that they will not move, nor turn, nor eat, nor
drink, till the seeds planted on the lips begin to sprout.
This usually takes place on the third or fourth day.
After this they arise, and think that they are very holy.
Now many of the little girls in America, after having
heard of these miseries of the heathen of India and other places, have formed sewing societies to earn money to
send the Gospel to them. Since my return to this country I have received letters from some of these little girls.
I will give you a quotation from one or two of them.
One, who is the secretary of one of these societies, writes
as follows: "Immediately after you left us we organized
a sewing society for the purpose of aiding the foreign
missionaries in enlightening the poor degraded heathen.
We met at the session-room of the Presbyterian Church,
with Mrs. Ripley at our head. We succeeded very well,
and held our fair on the 13th of December. We realized ninety-three dollars, which we send you. I am a
little girl, and I hope I shall live to see the heathen converted, and all the world rejoicing in the light of the
Gospel." Another little secretary writes: "When you
were here last fall, and told us how much good little
girls had done in having sewing societies, we thought we
would see if *we* could not do some good in the world as
well as they; and, since October, we have met weekly,
and by holding a fair we have succeeded in raising sixty-
two ·dollars. We hope it may be the means of saving
some poor heathen children." These quotations must
suffice.

"'Since my return to America I have traveled several

thousand miles, and preached to more than ninety thousand children, half of whom I suppose are girls. Besides the little girls from whose letters I have made quotations, others, as I before said, have written-to me about the societies they have formed, and I have written back to them. And I hope that many more have formed societies from whom I have never heard. If you are of this number, will you not write to me about them before my return to India, which, with God's permission, will be in the coming fall? Or, if you prefer, you can write to me after my return to that country. I shall be glad to send an answer to all such letters.

"'I wish to say a word to all of you, my dear young friends, who have formed sewing societies. This is, that you will not allow them to fall through. After I preached in one of the churches in New York, the little girls formed a sewing circle, and met together for several months to sew. They then had a fair, and raised seventy dollars. After this their society *died*. Now this is not well. These little girls began well, but they did not end well. They should have continued as they began. I have heard of a little girls' society in Andover, Massachusetts, which has continued, I believe, ever since the year 1831. This is noble.

"'But perhaps some of the little girls to whom I have preached have not formed sewing societies, though I very much begged them to do so. If you have not complied with my request, will you not do it?

"''One word more. If any of you who have written to me about your little sewing circles will write again, I shall be very happy to hear from you. I long to hear how you are prospering.'

"*Pittsburg, April* 14*th.* Preached on the 5th in Dr. Riddle's church to seven or eight hundred children, and on the same afternoon to about the same number in Dr. Swift's church in Alleghany City. Attended the monthly concert of prayer in Mr. Bryant's church, and addressed the meeting. On Wednesday morning a letter came to Dr. Armstrong, in which Mr. Bartlett says, in speaking of my visit to him, 'Although he was but a very short time in my family, less than one week, all my children, except the very youngest—though of very different dispositions in other things—all are alike bent on going to India, if the Lord will permit. And one of them, a daughter of eleven years of age, seems to have given her heart to the Saviour since he left us, in consequence of his conversation with her on the great theme which so fills his soul. And this is by no means a solitary case.' On Wednesday evening preached to sixty children in Minersville. On Friday and Saturday, 10th and 11th, held a Missionary Convention in Dr. Riddle's church. Addressed the people on the map on Saturday evening. On Sunday preached in Mr. Fulton's church to six hundred and fifty children at two o'clock. At four, preached in Dr. Herron's church to nine hundred or one thousand children. Yesterday, at night, held a meeting in Dr. Riddle's church. Nearly the whole exercises consisted in asking and answering questions. Gave 'Appeals to Mothers,' 'Letters to Sabbath-school Children,' to Mr. Bryant for the members of his Presbytery, to the Lutheran clergyman for his Classis, and thirty of each to Mr. Speir for the members of his Presbytery. The 'Letter on the Formation of Missionary Associations in Sabbath-schools,' in all instances, perhaps, accompanied those books. Left at Dr. Riddle's last evening fifty copies of the 'Harvest perishing for want of Laborers' for the students of Cannonsburg College; also fifty for the college at Washington, under Dr. McConnoughy's care. Shall never forget the interest which some of the dear children of this place have manifested. Their little hands have been held out for the heathen.

"*Milan, Ohio, April* 23*d.* Left Pittsburg on Tuesday week, and reached Hudson, Ohio, the next day. On Thursday preached to the children in Mr. Hart's church in the afternoon. Seventy-five or more young persons were present. In the evening lectured in the college hall to the students of the Western Reserve College, on the map. On Friday morning met the theological students and other students, and was questioned by them on India. Wrote the names of more than forty students in the 'Harvest perishing for want of Laborers.' Delivered most of them on the evening of the lecture. I hope there is some missionary spirit in Hudson among some of the pious young men. On Saturday went to Oberlin, where I spent a delightful Sabbath. Preached in the morning to a congregation perhaps of fifteen hundred persons. Among these there were about four hundred students of the college."

Dr. Scudder's account of his visit to Mount Holyoke:

FEMALE SEMINARY.

"I have lately been on a visit to the Mount Holyoke Female Seminary, and a most delightful visit have I had—a visit which will be remembered by me long after I shall have been buried from the sight of its inmates in a heathen land. At the head of this seminary stands

Miss Mary Lyon, eminently fitted, both by nature and by grace, for the station which she occupies. She was the projector of the Seminary. She laid the first stone of its foundation, and that foundation, as she told me, was PRAYER. Upon this foundation a beautiful edifice of brick and mortar has been erected. But the external building, beautiful as it is, is of little notice or of consequence when compared with the noble structures wherewith it is internally adorned, even with a hundred and twenty temples of the Holy Ghost. Yes, to the praise of Divine Grace be it spoken, there are a hundred and twenty beloved youth who were once subjects of the kingdom of darkness, but who have been wrested from it, and whose names have been inserted in the catalogue of heaven.*

"I reached the Seminary on the morning of the 27th of June, and met with a hearty reception from Miss Lyon. She insisted that I should be a partaker of her hospitalities so long as I should remain in South Hadley. I availed myself of her kind invitation. It was not long after my arrival before the bell rang for dinner, when the inmates of the Seminary trod with quickened pace toward the great dining-room. This spacious room is fitted up with many tables, around each of which a little family of these inmates clusters (for they are all divided into little families), and at which, at the sound of a bell, they immediately take their seats. The blessing is then asked, and they proceed in the utmost order to partake of their repast. I had my seat at the table

---

* There are 180 young ladies belonging to the Seminary, 60 of whom are not pious—an uncommonly large number, I am told, to be found in the ranks of the impenitent.

where Miss Lyon presided, and before the young ladies rose from theirs she struck her bell as a signal that she wished to make some remarks. These remarks were, that if any of them would like to be introduced to their missionary (the missionary for whom they had so often wept and prayed), they could avail themselves of the opportunity of so doing at two o'clock in the afternoon and at eight o'clock in the evening. The young ladies then returned to their rooms. At two o'clock quite a number conferred upon me the honor of a visit; among these were the precious children of the beloved Goodell, and Thurston, and others of my missionary brethren. At eight o'clock in the evening a much larger number came. The hearty shake of the hand which we tendered to each other showed that we were not strangers, but children of a common Father—children all traveling to the same home, the house not made with hands, eternal in the heavens. After a short interview, in which I told them something of India, we separated for the night. On Sunday morning I preached to Christian mothers on the importance of training up their children for the great work of the world's salvation. This exercise took place in the beautiful church which has been lately erected in South Hadley, and which Miss Lyon and her pupils attend. In the afternoon, at two o'clock, I had a meeting with the children of the village. In the evening, at six o'clock, I addressed the young ladies of the Seminary. They were, at my particular request, seated in front of me; I said a word to no one else. That address, though I was the speaker, deeply affected my own mind, and the fountains of my eyes, as John Bunyan calls them, could not be kept from overflowing. And how could I keep

from weeping, with such a mass of cultivated mind before me—mind which was soon to be brought to bear in
a hundred and eighty different directions upon the destinies of souls, either for heaven or for hell—mind which
was to add to the hallelujahs of heaven, or which was to
swell the wailings of the lost forever! When I came to
that part of my address where I showed them the tears
of that poor man who went ninety miles to one of our
missionary stations to beg that a teacher might go and
reside in his village, to tell his dying countrymen of a
Saviour, but who was told that he must go back alone,
for they had no one to send with him, because the pious
young men of America had turned their backs upon all
their calls for help, I could not but exclaim, Alas! that
these young men should treat their Saviour so; and I
could not but add, that if the Saviour had committed the
preaching of the Gospel to females—to such as were before me—they would treat him differently—they would
flee in larger numbers to the heathen. Before my interview with them on Sunday was terminated, I remarked
that perhaps God might direct the feet of some of them
to heathen lands, and that, if they should come to my
destined station, I would bid them a hearty welcome to
share in my toils and labors; but if they did not come, I
hoped they would 'keep hold of the rope while I went
down into the well'—that they would uphold my hands
as Aaron and Hur upheld the hands of Moses. I then
bade them farewell, hoping that, if we should meet no
more on earth, we might meet on those shores where

" 'Adieus and farewells are a sound unknown,'

and where

" 'The parting sound shall pass our lips no more.' "

[*To be continued.*]

Mount Holyoke Female Seminary.

"The great object for which this seminary was founded, as Miss Lyon informed me, was to be the means of saving souls. And God has made it to be just such a seminary as its founder desired. Scarcely a year has passed without some tokens of the divine approbation. Most of the years have been characterized by very marked tokens. And what has been the secret of this success? The question is easily answered. Prayers and pains, with faith in Christ Jesus—labors with individuals to bring them to Christ, accompanied with exertions to bring the efforts of these individuals to bear upon the salvation of a lost world. After a description of the divine favors experienced in the fifth year of the existence of the Seminary, one of the teachers, in speaking of the revival of religion which took place in the sixth year, remarks: 'The following year, the sixth, was one rich in blessing. A more careful division of responsibility and labor was made among the teachers, and from the commencement of the year there was an increased personal effort in relation to every member of the family. God crowned these efforts with abundant success. From the first there was an attentive listening to instruction, and truth seemed to be taking hold of the understanding and conscience. But it was not till March that the Spirit of the Lord came upon us with great power, and at once a large number stood upon the Lord's side, having received the breath of life. The work was sudden, rapid, and powerful. We could only stand still and see the salvation of God in our midst. Some cases of conversion were of a very marked character and great interest.

Of the sixty-six who entered the school without hope, only six remained destitute of it.'

"I remarked that one of the causes of their revivals of religion is to be found in their efforts to save a lost world. I found the Seminary to be eminently a missionary seminary. The respected teacher, from whom I have already quoted, at my request penned a few remarks on the subject of their missionary operations. They are as follows: 'In order to promote the missionary interest in our school, we have several arrangements. One of these is our Missionary Society. The object of this society is to increase our knowledge in relation to missionary operations, giving the most prominence to the American Board, but occasionally directing our attention to the operations of other societies. This society is organized annually, and embraces all who wish to be regular attendants at its meetings, usually nearly all our school. The meetings are held once in two weeks, and are conducted by the teachers, who prepare themselves to give a connected history of some mission, aided by the use of missionary maps. Letters received from our missionary friends are read at these meetings, also any articles which may come to hand of unusual interest.

"'We have also an arrangement by which half an hour is devoted weekly to giving instruction on the same subject to sections of about twenty by the section teacher. Each teacher continues through the year with her section, thus having an opportunity to carry her pupils forward through a regular course of instruction. Ten numbers of the *Missionary Herald*, sixty of the *Dayspring*, and thirty of the *American Messenger* are taken for the use of the young ladies, and lent to them individually.'

The reading-room is supplied with the *Home Mission-ary*, the *Sailors' Magazine*, as well as the various relig-ious papers from all our large cities. Two missionary contributions are taken up during the year, when the duty of giving of our substance to send the Gospel to the heathen is inculcated, and the principles upon which this duty rests explained, thus endeavoring to let the in-structions given be impressed by the act of giving of their substance to the Lord's treasury. The amount raised each year has gradually increased. For the last three years it has somewhat exceeded $1000 each year, including the contributions of both teachers and pupils. About one third of this sum has been contributed to home missions, and the remaining two thirds to the American Board. About two thirds of the sum raised each year has been contributed by the young ladies, and one third by the teachers.'

"So far as religious operations are concerned, the sem-inary to which I have now directed your attention af-fords, as it appears to me, a beautiful model for other seminaries and for our colleges. Here, no matter what-ever may be the subordinate plans pursued, the great ob-ject is to save souls; and while the latter object is in such numerous instances accomplished, the former are thoroughly carried out. Of this seminary it is emphat-ically true that holiness is written on every study, and that, too, on every study well studied; and, until similar plans are pursued in the various literary institutions of our country, thousands of souls which, humanly speak-ing, might be saved, must be lost. Alas! how little in-terest, comparatively speaking, is taken in the spiritual welfare of the students in many of our colleges and seminaries. How many of them are suffered to pass through the whole course of instruction with scarcely any of that effort to save their souls which is manifested in the seminary of which I have just been speaking. The outer man seems the first object to be attended to; the inner man the last; and thus both body and soul are involved in one common ruin.

"Shall this state of things be continued? Has not the time come when, in all our colleges and seminaries, the religious influence of the Mount Holyoke Seminary shall be exerted? when it shall be the prescribed duty of their presidents and tutors to labor *individually* with the students in spiritual things? and when, too, they shall use every exertion to bring the energies of these students to bear upon the salvation of others? By these latter exertions how many streams of benevolence might be set in motion, and which would continue to run down through life; how much money which is now squandered by our young men and women might be transferred from a corrupt into a holy channel, and transferred, too, for their everlasting good. I say for their everlasting good, for I lay it down as an axiom that one of the best means to be made use of for the salvation of the souls of the impenitent is to set them to work for the salvation of the heathen. I did not ask the revered principal of the Mount Holyoke Seminary what bearings her labors in this department had upon the conversion of those under her care. Perhaps she would have related many instances similar to the one of which I lately heard, where a man was hopefully converted in consequence of his having become an annual subscriber to the Bible Society. I would that the presidents and professors of our colleges would

I 2

take this subject into their prayerful consideration. God has committed to their trust the care of a large body of the flower of our land, who are soon to go forth into the world to bless it or to curse it. Whether they will bless it or curse it depends much upon them. If they adopt that course of faithful individual labor (which obtains in the Mount Holyoke Seminary); if they make it a point as diligently to use means to save their souls as they use to cultivate their minds; and if they are successful in bringing their energies to bear upon the salvation of the souls of others, then may we hope that God will bless their labors—then may we hope that many who would otherwise prove curses will prove blessings to the world. There is a day of final reckoning coming, when these professors of our colleges and seminaries are to stand before the bar of God. Sad indeed will it be for them if it shall be found that they have neglected the religious instruction of the students under their care. It would have been well, perhaps, if they had never occupied their important trusts."

Dr. Aydelott writes from Cincinnati: "It will encourage your heart, and, I doubt not, rather humble you, to learn how deep and favorable an impression your labors among us have left upon the minds of Christians of all denominations. Your visit has done pastors good, and professors good, and above all has it left impressions on the minds of multitudes of precious youth, which, I feel assured, will lead very many of them to missionary fields, and still more to heaven. Be strengthened, dear brother, with the thought that many prayers go up here from all ages that God would largely bless you, and make you still more instrumental of usefulness."

CHAPTER XII.

REMINISCENCES.

THE two communications which follow may be very properly here introduced, as they bear on the labors of our missionary among children and youth of this country. Their perusal will awaken similar reminiscences in the bosoms of many others.

"347 West Twenty-first Street, New York, Feb. 25, 1869.

"REV. AND DEAR DR. WATERBURY, — In response to your request for reminiscences of Rev. Dr. John Scudder, I copy from my own private diary the following, penned in 1858:

"*Monday, Nov.* 29. My hearing Rev. Henry M. Scud-}) der preach last evening, and my going to hear Rev. Wm. Scudder deliver an address this evening, reminds me of the following reminiscences:

"I recollect that in 1844, when I was scarcely seven years of age, I came in contact with Dr. John Scudder for the first and only time.

"We were then living in Varick Street, near Spring, and I was a scholar in the Spring Street Presbyterian Sabbath-school, Rev. Dr. Wm. Patton being our pastor at that time.

"On a dull, dark-looking Sunday afternoon in May, 1844, our Sabbath-schools were seated in the spacious galleries of the church, while a large audience of parents and friends filled the pews below. The object of this gathering was to hear the venerable Dr. Scudder address us children.

"As for myself, I was in a front pew of the left-hand gallery, near the choir, and, as the doctor was speaking, I stood up, leaned over, and looked directly at him. Thus, unintentionally, I made myself quite a conspicuous object, and was made still more so when Dr. Scudder, who was urging the children to consecrate themselves to the missionary work, raised his voice and said, 'Perhaps a number of these children and youth now before me are yet to become missionaries—perhaps that boy yonder,' pointing to me, thus singling me out among hundreds of scholars, and causing many to look at me. I was somewhat abashed at being thus particularly noticed; yet, as I can well remember, though more than fourteen years have gone by since then, I said to myself in a moment, 'No! no! never! you are mistaken this time.'

"He invited all who wished to purchase the little book in paper cover called 'Scudder's Letters' to come to the lecture-room the next morning. 'I'll be there,' said he, 'and will sell them to the children for six cents apiece.' I was very anxious to have the book, and so, having obtained the money from one of my parents, I started off before breakfast, and went around the corner to the church. I found the doctor alone in the lecture-room, seated beside a little table near the door. He began to converse with me in a kindly manner, again urging me to become a missionary. My only reply was that I never would. Perhaps I was a little obstinate in my manner. So I made my purchase and went out. That was the last time I ever remember having seen Dr. Scudder. I am told he was at our next monthly concert, and made an address. Of this I have no recollection whatever.

"He was a tall, slender man, with a long yet not narrow head. His hair, which was gray and white mixed together, was cut short, and brushed up in front, giving him rather an unusual appearance. He must have been upward of fifty years of age at that time. He spoke distinctly, and with a loud, clear, shrill voice. His manner was open and familiar; his disposition seemed to be very fatherly and affectionate.

"Whenever he spoke the children were extremely attentive. He enlisted their interest and attention by plain off-hand remarks such as these: 'Now I want you to look right at me, and when you go home I want you to be able to tell your parents all that Dr. Scudder has told you about India.'

"Trusting these boyish memories may be of some service to you, your young brother in the Gospel ministry,

"JAMES A. LITTLE."

"30 Bible House, Tuesday, Feb. 23, 1869.

"MY DEAR SIR,—Your notice in the 'Observer,' calling for reminiscences of the late Dr. John Scudder, awakened many pleasing recollections of that good man and his family. On his visit to his native land twenty-five years ago, he stopped a while in Burton (now Leroy) Street, in the vicinity of the West Presbyterian Church, then in Carmine Street, now located in West Forty-second Street, the Church with which the writer was identified from its foundation. I well remember Dr. Scudder's appearance among us in Carmine Street, and the interest which his presence awakened. The remarks which he made in prayer-meeting and in the more public services were most impressive. Perhaps a peculiar interest was felt at that time in seeing and hearing this veteran soldier of the Cross, from the fact that in that church his son Henry had made his home for a while, from the fatherly care evinced for him by the pastor, the Rev. David R. Downer. In 1840, during a precious revival of religion in the Mercer Street Church, under the preaching of the Rev. Edward N. Kirk, Henry, with Thomas H. Skinner, Jr., Henry B. Elliot, and others of the senior class in the New York University, were brought to yield to the claims of the Gospel, and immediately commenced a course of preparation for the sacred ministry. Dr. Scudder came to America in time to see Henry, his eldest son, who had given him much solicitude, ordained and set apart for the work of the Master, and devote himself to the same cause which had engaged the father's heart and life.

"How often, in conversation with Dr. Scudder and his family in Burton Street, and West Nineteenth Street, where he afterward removed, would he most feelingly advert to the power of prayer, and bear testimony to the devotion of his beloved wife, who regularly observed special seasons of prayer on her children's birthdays.

"When Samuel, the third son, was suddenly stricken down while pursuing his studies at New Brunswick, the good doctor wrote home to us, ' If Samuel has a place in heaven now, it is owing to his praying mother.'

"The pervading atmosphere of Dr. Scudder's home was that of prayer, and for that reason I would say it was a home of cheerful, hopeful, warm-hearted piety.

"Never were husband and wife more thoroughly united. They were one in heart, purpose, and action, entirely consecrated to their life-work. They had trials with their children as others have. Their prayers in some instances seemed for a long time to go unanswered. But they believed that delays were no denials, and their faith persevered through all obstacles and discouragements.

"Dr. Scudder's whole soul went out after children, and during his stay in this country he visited and addressed hundreds of Sabbath-schools and children's missionary meetings.

"He gave away thousands of books containing his autograph and some word of good advice, and embraced every opportunity of directing young people to the Saviour, asking them to give their hearts to Jesus, and give themselves to the missionary cause.

"I doubt not that there are numbers of persons now grown up who can remember writing down in some book, twenty-five years ago, 'Dr. Scudder, the missionary from India, asked me this day if I would not give my heart to Jesus, and, if I grew up, if I would not be a missionary and come out to India.' It would be interesting to know how far the beloved missionary's wishes were realized. Perhaps some correspondents may give you light on this point.

"It has been refreshing to run over these recollections of one of the earlier and most devoted missionaries, whose name is so precious to the Church of Christ. I might greatly extend these notes, but my sheet is full.

"Yours very respectfully,   LEWIS E. JACKSON.

"Rev. Dr. Waterbury."

EFFECT OF DR. SCUDDER'S LABORS AMONG CHILDREN IN
AWAKENING A MISSIONARY SPIRIT.

Naturally the children were interested in his representations. Their young and tender hearts were moved, and
tears in many cases fell like rain. Some of them resolved
to deny themselves the childish luxuries which they had
been wont to enjoy, and give their spending-money to aid
in sending the Gospel to the pagans. The mission-box
was duly installed, and many a stray coin found its way
into it. Doubtless this first enthusiasm cooled off, and
the frivolities of youth drove the subject out of their
thoughts. But the good seed in some cases fell into good
ground. Impressions were made which never wore away.
One of the secretaries of the Board of Missions said to
me, referring to Dr. Scudder's labors among the juve-
niles, "Sufficient time has now elapsed to test the effect
of these appeals in awakening and strengthening the missionary spirit among the young, and our experience is
that not in vain did this venerable missionary call upon
his young audience to consecrate themselves to this noble
work. In putting the question to the applicant for missionary appointment as to what first led him to entertain
thoughts of going on a mission, the reply, in some instances, has been, ' *Dr. Scudder's addresses and appeals
to me when a child.*' " Thus was the seed sown, and
thus in after years did the fruit appear.

A MISSIONARY FAMILY.

Dr. Scudder and his wife regarded themselves and all
theirs as consecrated to Christ and to the upbuilding of
his kingdom. God had given them fourteen children.

Four of them he had taken to himself in their infancy, and ten remained—eight sons and two daughters. All these at length became active Christians, and some of them missionaries to India. The fourth son, Samuel, died while prosecuting his theological studies at New Brunswick, November 15th, 1849, just three days before the death of his mother at Madras. He was a young man of deep piety, superior talents, and of a very amiable disposition. His death was sincerely lamented by all who knew him, and especially by his classmates, who erected a beautiful marble monument to his memory in Greenwood. He, too, intended to have followed his brothers to India. The two daughters, Harriet and Louisa, have inofficially also been missionaries, both having resided in India the most part of their lives. Having married English gentlemen, they live together on the Neilgherries.

The eldest son, Henry Martyn, was sent to this country at the age of eleven, with William, the second son, to be educated here, in the hope that they might return and preach Christ to the Hindoos. Great was the trial when Mrs. Scudder kissed a mother's farewell, with gushing tears and a breaking heart, as she placed them under the care of the ship's master, who promised to paternize them on the voyage.

By previous arrangement, Henry was to reside with his uncle in Hudson, N. Y., and William with his grandmother at Westfield, N. J. Happily for the aged and infirm grandmother, William proved a modest, docile, and obedient child, ever ready to acquiesce in her wishes and commands. But in striking contrast were the mental and moral traits of his elder brother. He was impetuous, headstrong, self-reliant, and disposed to throw off all moral restraint. In one word, he was reckless. Highly gifted intellectually, his talents were prostrated under the impulse of passion. A hard task was thus imposed on his guardian, and many a heavy hour of anxiety weighed upon his spirit. But God had him in charge. Daily and constantly prayer arose in India and in America for this child of the Covenant. At length the hour came when "the strong man armed" was to be cast out. He struggled under conviction for several days, when light broke in upon his soul, and he laid his all at the foot of the Cross. Grace had seldom made a more signal triumph, or brought into the ranks of the redeemed a more decided and valiant soldier.

It should be remarked in this connection, as illustrating the power of prayer, that just about this time the mother and father had devoted a week to fasting and prayer for the conversion of this son. William, while in college at Princeton, also became a decided Christian; so that now the two brothers were ready, when duly qualified by theological training, to join their father in India.

It seems appropriate to notice more particularly in this connection a chain of providences illustrative, on the one hand, of the covenant faithfulness of God, and showing, on the other, how instrumentalities are interwoven in his plans and purposes.

Dr. Scudder's Christian influence is blessed to the conversion of the only son of the widow in whose house he goes to reside. That youth, during his senior year in college, under the influence of a powerful work of grace among his fellow-students, has his heart so warmed that he resolves to spend his vacation in laboring for the conversion of young men in New York. The Spirit of God goes with him. Frequent meetings are held, and many are awakened to a sense of their sins. One evening there came a youth, about eighteen, and fixed his eye on the *E.N.I* speaker with a sort of fascination in his look. The latter grew intensely interested, and directed his remarks especially to this young stranger. At the close he came forward, and, with a countenance almost of despair, seized his hand and said, "Do you think there can be mercy for *me?*" "Yes," was the prompt reply—"there is mercy for the chief of sinners." Night after night he came. At length, after much personal conversation as well as public appeal, he took his seat as usual. Looking closely, his countenance seemed to wear a calm expression, significant of a change within. The meeting ended, he came forward, took the speaker by the hand, and, with his whole soul in the sentence, said, "Yes, you were right; there is mercy for me, and I have found it."

Years passed. This converted youth became an evangelist. His power in the pulpit was acknowledged by the crowds which sought to hear him. Meanwhile Dr. Scudder's eldest son—the wild youth before spoken of—was finishing his collegiate course in the New York University. A great revival was in progress in the Rev. Dr. Skinner's Church (Mercer Street), during which the son of Dr. Skinner was converted. He was the intimate friend of young Scudder, and his classmate. At this time Dr. Kirk, the evangelist before mentioned, was aiding Dr. Skinner, and preaching powerful and pungent sermons to the careless and impenitent. After much entreaty, Skinner induced Henry to accompany him to church. The sermon interested him—penetrated his conscience; and when the invitation to enter the inquiry meeting was given, Henry Scudder, overwhelmed with a sense of his sin, was found among the inquirers. Here is a remarkable chain of providences, embracing three families, including four ministers, and extending over many years. Who can calculate the good which this chain incloses, or the good which prospectively it *may* inclose? What a powerful motive to labor for the conversion of young men!

Successively the other sons followed in the train, so that nearly at the same time seven of them were laboring in different parts of India for the conversion of the heathen. In their visit to America, Dr. and Mrs. Scudder found great satisfaction in the reunion of their scattered family, gathering them all around the family altar, and consecrating them anew to their covenant God.

CHAPTER XIII.

Madura Mission.—Caste.—Successful Treatment of Cholera.

RETURNS TO INDIA.

Dr. Scudder's health having to some extent been restored, yet still far from being reliable for future labor,
he prepares to bid adieu to his friends in America,
and wend his way back to the land of his adoption.
Often when here, enjoying many comforts and even luxuries, he would sigh for a return to his field. "There is
no place," he would exclaim, "like India. It is nearer
heaven than America."

Glad was he, then, when it was announced that he
must be ready to embark in the first vessel that should
leave Boston for the East in the coming fall—1846.

And now the adieus and farewells had the emphasis
of *finality*. We sorrowed most of all that we should
see their faces in the flesh no more. They felt it as well
as we; and still the glow of sacred joy lighted up their
countenances, the sure presage that on other shores and
amid brighter scenes we should again meet, "where
adieus and farewells are a sound unknown."

On their arrival at Madras they resumed their mission
work with renewed interest and unflagging zeal. Knowing how short the time would be, this veteran laborer
pressed into the work all the remaining energies of soul
and body. He preached, and prayed, and wrote, leaving

himself but little time for relaxation, while the younger
members of the mission gathered about him for advice
and encouragement.

He undertook, also, to send contributions to the religious papers of America, and keep up a vast correspondence with the numerous Christian friends he had left
behind.

THE MADURA MISSION.

Soon after Dr. Scudder's return to India, it was
thought expedient that he should, for a short time at
least, take up his residence at Madura, and give the
brethren there the benefit of his long experience as a
missionary, and his eminent skill as a physician. This
removal met his wishes, and he proceeded to this new
field with high expectations of increased usefulness.
Here he labored with his usual assiduity and success.
His heart was cheered by finding a woman who, fifteen
years previously, had been converted by reading a tract
which he had given her. The following is copied from
his diary:

"*January* 17th. Since my arrival at Madura I have
met with a woman who is, I trust, devoted to her Saviour;
who told me that she was, as she hopes, born into the
kingdom of grace by a tract which was given to her by
myself at least fifteen years ago. The tract is entitled
'The Loss of the Soul.'"

CASTE A GREAT IMPEDIMENT TO MISSIONARY LABORS.

Hindoo caste is perhaps the most formidable barrier
to Christianization in India. It is a deep-laid plot of
Satan, by which human pride and prejudice array them-

selves against the humility and common brotherhood required by the Gospel. A high-caste man would no sooner touch a low-caste than he would touch a viper. The
low-caste trembles lest his shadow should cross the path
of a high-caste man. Every thing possible is done to
maintain these social and religious barriers. Even when
converted, the high-caste can with difficulty be persuaded
to sit or associate in any way with the low-caste. Our
missionaries in the schools and churches have taken
strong ground against this caste system, as they have
found it more potent in its power to thwart their efforts
than any single element in the Hindoo system. Some
good men have proposed to tolerate it, or at least to con-
nive at it, until gradual enlightenment may enable them
the more easily to put it down.

The policy of the successive magistrates in India, from
the governor general down, had been sometimes tolerant
of it, and at others sternly opposed. Dr. Scudder's
whole heart and soul was enlisted *against* it. He saw
no hope of success for India but in its abolition. He
would give it no tolerance in school or church, inasmuch
as, according to his views, it warred against the very
foundations of the Christian faith. He was conscientious in his belief; and if, at times, he spoke so strongly
as to seem uncharitable toward others who may have differed from him, it was but the strongly expressed convictions of an honest heart. But as this caste controversy
will not interest our readers, we will enter no farther
into it, hoping that one day this Hindoo pharisaism will
yield to the combined action of civilization and a pure
Christianity.

SUCCESSFUL TREATMENT OF CHOLERA AND OTHER COM-
PLAINTS.

One of the reasons for Dr. Scudder's transfer for a
while to the Madura Mission was owing to a prevalent
idea that it was an unhealthy station, and that the mission families were peculiarly exposed to cholera and other dangerous epidemics; but, after making himself acquainted with the region, he considers it one of the most
salubrious in India. " I consider it," he writes, " to be a
healthy station, even more so than I thought it before my
arrival here. Within a short space of time, it is true, several persons have been swept off by cholera; but the
cholera rages every where in India.

" Madura has an advantage over both Madras and Ceylon. In its district are the Pulney Hills, which are very
high and cold, and are very healthy. It is even cold
enough to produce ice. To these hills we can have access from Madura City in twenty-four hours. They have
proved to be very beneficial to children who have been
sent there on account of ill health. Some of our invalid
brethren have been greatly recruited by a visit of a few
weeks to these hills."

Dr. Scudder was eminently successful in his treatment
of cholera. He relied on strong doses of opium and cal-
omel, accompanied by the usual frictions with hot sand,
etc. His surgical skill also was constantly called into
exercise. The blind came to receive sight, and he was
almost invariably successful in couching. Enormous tumors also were removed, and the patients sent on their
way rejoicing.

HEATHENISM *VS.* MEDICAL SKILL.

There was a case of a man of high caste affected with a ponderous tumor. It must be removed or he must die. This was the alternative. But the difficulty lay in the fact that he must submit to the skill and touch of the polluting surgeon. This stood religiously in the way of its removal. The Brahmins were consulted. Much debate was had over the important question. At length the following device was decided upon. The gods must be consulted; but as wood and stone, "though they have ears, hear not, and mouths, speak not," there must be some other way contrived to find out their will in this juncture. It was decided to ascertain it as follows: Two bouquets of flowers, one red and the other white, were to be laid before the god; then a little child was to be sent in, and told to pick up one of the bouquets and bring it out. If she selected the *red*, it was a token that the god said *nay* to the amputation; if *white, yea.* The white flowers were brought out, and so, the will of the god having been ascertained, Dr. Scudder proceeded with the amputation, and it was successful. No doubt he improved the opportunity to recommend them to put their trust in something better than wood and stone. He never let an opportunity like this slip to preach Christ and salvation to the applicants for his aid.

K

CHAPTER XIV.

Witchcraft and the Demetrians.—Pulney Hills.—Routine, etc.

"HE SHALL STAND BEFORE KINGS."

In a tour through the Madura district, with a view to preaching the Gospel, distributing books and tracts, and affording medical aid to the poor suffering natives, Dr. Scudder and his family reached a famous bungalow erected by the King of the Tondiman country for the accommodation of such of the English who may wish to visit the chief city of his dominions. It is situated near the borders of Poothacortly. Food, as well as a furnished house, is provided for the guests. The following description of a regal entertainment will interest the reader:

"Some time after my arrival, his majesty's manager, as he is called, intimated that I might have the privilege, if I wished, of visiting the king at his palace. Accompanied by my youngest daughter, about eleven years of age, I went at twelve o'clock to the palace. As I entered the inner court, where his majesty was seated in the middle of his throne, he arose and came toward us. After shaking hands with us, he took my daughter by the arm and conducted her up the steps, and seated her next to him at his right hand. The king's brother waited upon me, and conducted me to a seat nearly opposite to that which my daughter occupied. The steps to the throne were guarded on each side by four officers with staves in their hands, gilded, as I suppose, with gold and silver. After chatting with his majesty for about fifteen minutes, I proposed to leave. He requested me to stop a little while. Wreaths of flowers were then brought, and put over the necks of my daughter and myself; bracelets of flowers were also put upon our wrists, and so forth, and so forth. After he had sprinkled our pocket-handkerchiefs with sweet-scented water from a silver vase, we sat down a few moments, and then retired. In the afternoon his majesty called to see us at the bungalow, and, after spending an hour, he took a long ride in his carriage with Mrs. Scudder and my daughters. I rode in a buggy with the king's brother. On Saturday I examined the English schools in Poothacortly. The two native free-schools were together in the same place. Afterward, by a particular invitation of his majesty, Mrs. Scudder, my daughters, and myself visited his palace. The same ceremonies with flowers, and so forth, were gone through as were observed with my daughter and myself the day before. His majesty took us through several of the apartments of his immense palace. In one of them he has quite a large English library. He speaks the English language with a great deal of fluency. In the afternoon he again visited us, when I had an excellent opportunity of opening to him the plan of salvation through Christ. I entreated him to read the New Testament, a copy of which, in English, is in his library, and which he says that he keeps merely for the inspection of the English who may visit him. He told me that he was not at liberty to read it, meaning by this that he was under the control of his priests. I told him that he was second to no one but God. In temporal things he acknowledged that this was the case; in spiritual things he said that there was a difference. His lord bishop, as he calls him, who resides in Coembacoonum, visits him once a year; he is, probably, entirely under his control. During his majesty's visit I performed a surgical operation on one of the eyes of one of his principal men. On Sunday I preached to the native Christians in Poothacortly, and afterward distributed tracts and portions of the Scriptures, and preached to such as visited me during the day. The diseased found me out, and came to me for relief. On Monday afternoon his majesty addressed a letter to me, requesting me to do what I could for the relief of the commander-in-chief of his army. His eyesight is quite dim. This gentleman called upon me at the bungalow. He is quite advanced in years, and will not, I fear, live long. I thought it not proper to do any thing to his eyes. I merely recommended him to take a little nitric acid drink for his general health. While his excellency was with me, a young man, who lives in a village ten miles off, hearing that I was in Poothacortly, came to me for relief. A splinter had entered the transparent part of his eye, and would, probably, soon have destroyed his vision; I took it out, to his great relief. Left Poothacortly on Tuesday morning for Parungkaloor, where I now am. It is about thirteen miles from Poothacortly. His majesty kindly lent me a tent, which I sent on to this place on Monday afternoon. This was pitched, and in readiness for our reception. Immediately on our arrival the villagers flocked to see us. To them I preached the Gospel, and gave books to such as I thought worthy to receive them. These labors I continued until the time had come for me to take my breakfast. After breakfast we received many visitors, among whom there were not a few women, who, perhaps for the first time in their lives, heard of the Saviour. Mrs. Scudder thinks that, in the course of the day, more than one hundred of these women visited her, besides a large number of girls. Had she not been with me, perhaps not half a dozen of them would have heard the Gospel preached. I can give no estimate of the number of men who visited us. At four o'clock in the afternoon we went to Mertlypertlee, about a mile from Parungkaloor, where there is a small village congregation of professed Christians. There were ten adults and several children, amounting in all to fifteen or sixteen persons. I preached to them from the words 'Verily, I say unto you, ye must be born again.' We have a school in this village. Gave a few Gospels to the children who could read. When we returned to the tent we had a large congregation of men and women in front of it, to whom the Gospel was preached. This morning early we went to Lurchamepurum, a village about three miles distant. We have a school also in this village. Examined the children in the Catechism, and so forth. Returned afterward to the tent. Since I came to this place quite a number of diseased persons have been to me for relief. To-day I cut out an immense tumor from the upper part of the arm of a man, and operated upon the thigh of another on a tumor of smaller size.

"24th. *Karampakurdy.* On Wednesday afternoon we went to Maantaankoordy. From curiosity, a crowd gathered around us. Among these there were probably seventy-five females. After preaching Christ to them, I went into the school-house and addressed the people. Left Parungkaloor yesterday morning for Kuluppunpertly. We have a school there also. Examined the school, and preached the Gospel to many visitors. Yesterday came to this place. Had my tent pitched this morning near the market. Preached the Gospel to many persons. I counted nearly one hundred in the tent at one time. Distributed tracts and portions of the Scriptures to such as could read. Continued this work till after twelve o'clock, when I returned to the bungalow at which we had put up. We have a school in this village, which I examined this morning before going to the tent.

"27th. *Aalungkurde.* On Friday afternoon, while at Karampakurdy, I went again to the tent and spent a short time there. Afterward went to the school-house and addressed the native congregation of Christians. On Saturday morning left for Raasamungalum, where the mission has a school. Had a good congregation to preach to immediately after our arrival. The women probably had never seen a white face before. This village has about sixty houses in it. Early on Saturday afternoon came to this place. As the people immediately began to crowd around me, I began my labors among them. Distributed all the remainder of the tracts and portions of the Scriptures which I brought from Poothacortly with me. This is a large town, containing probably more than one thousand inhabitants. Yesterday had a very busy day, and large numbers of visitors. Preached the Gospel at twenty different times to the people. The diseased flocked to me for help. Performed six surgical operations. Declined operating upon the eyes of two different persons for this morning.

"*Poothacortly,* 28th. Yesterday afternoon left Aalungkurde about half past two o'clock, and reached this place at eight. From eight o'clock in the morning until the time I left, with the exception of a short intermission for dinner, I was surrounded by a crowd of people. Probably as many as eighty persons applied to me for medical aid. Performed *fifteen* surgical operations. One was on the eye, with the cataract needle, three were tumors, and so forth. Was very much worn out. To-morrow morning I expect to leave for Vayalokum, and return in the evening.

"30*th*. Yesterday morning I went to Vayalokum. It is a large village. I examined the mission school, and addressed the native Christians and some Roman Catholics who were also present. Preached the Gospel to others also. Performed two surgical operations upon the eye with my couching needle. In the evening returned to the king's bungalow, where I now am. To-day many persons have applied to me for medical aid. Performed ten surgical operations. Two of these were operations on the eye. The king's brother-in-law visited me this morning for medical aid. I am to take some blood from his arm this afternoon.

"The king has appeared to be very friendly to us. On our arrival here on Monday night we found a letter from his majesty, addressed to Mrs. Scudder, in which he entreats us to remain several days longer. I think it probable that he would be willing to receive missionaries in his dominions, but I do not think it proper to speak to him directly on this point. Should I do so, he would take no steps in this business without consulting the collector of Madura, who is the political agent of the British government to his majesty. Poothacortly is a good place for a missionary station. The king understands several different languages. He speaks and writes English well for one who has had no better advantages of learning it. The following is a copy of his letter to Mrs. Scudder:

"MY DEAR FRIEND,—I have seen Mr. Scudder's letter to my manager, informing him that you intend to come to bungalow this evening for dinner, and I hope you will find every thing ready for you. I drove this evening from palace to this bungalow, and I hope to see you to-morrow noon, if convenient for you and Mr. Scudder and children, at my palace at twelve o'clock. If you want, I will send my carriage to you and lead you to my palace. I pray you and Mr. Scudder to remain here for four or five days more. You may go to Madura after you pass a four or five days here with us. I shall be very much obliged if you will comply with my request. With my compliments to Mr. Scudder, etc., I remain, my dear friend, most affectionately and sincerely yours,

"RAJAH RAMEHUNDIA TONDIMAN BAHADOOR.
"Bungalow, Monday."

"31st. Yesterday afternoon I performed several more surgical operations. Have performed two or three this morning. We expected to leave Poothacortly this morning, but have been disappointed in consequence of a failure to procure bullocks. Last evening his majesty took leave of us. He put wreaths of flowers on our necks, wrists, and so forth, and went through the same marks of respect which characterized our visits to the palace. Before he left I once more told him that there is but one God and one Saviour, through whom we must be saved. "You will excuse me on this point," he observed. Sunk in heathenism, he does not want to hear of the only deliverer from the wrath to come. This morning he rode up here, and said he was on his way to his temple. This he visits at least once on Friday. He has paid us much attention. For several nights he has had his band of music here to contribute to our gratification. This band is a fac-simile of an English band. His carriages are constructed after the manner of the English. He even wears gloves, so much does he appear to be desirous of conforming to English customs. On no account whatever, I presume, would he ever ride out in his carriage with a native female, but has no hesitation in riding out with English ladies. I have not ventured to give him any of our publications except an Almanac. I understand that the former collector of Madura offered him a Prayer-book, which he would not receive. If he will read the contents of the Almanac he will find some of the best of religious truth in it. I before said that he has an English Bible. He is very young—not yet eighteen years old. I fear that he is entirely under priestly influence; but his heart is in the hands of Jehovah. Would that we could indulge the hope that his intercourse with Europeans may lead him to examine the truths which they profess to believe."

WITCHCRAFT AND THE DEMETRIANS.

"*August 2d.* In consequence of the flocking of the people to me for medical and surgical help, the physicians of the city, it appears, are in great straits. Their gains are, to a considerable extent, gone. To put a stop to our operations, I understand they have been resorting to witchcraft to destroy my life and the life of my medical helper. The latter has lately been quite ill, and probably they thought they were about to succeed with him. However, he is now again well. I understand, also, that they have been bewitching a tree in Mr. Chandler's yard. The tree is dead, and it is said that it died in consequence of such a bewitching. They have not succeeded in doing me any injury. Some think, I believe, that a white skin is impervious to witchcraft. To succeed to good advantage with their black art, I understand that they have called two powers well skilled in the art from a far village. They have received ten rupees each; and, if they succeed, they are to have each twenty rupees more. The manner of their proceeding is as follows: they killed a calf, took its blood, cooked it with rice, brought it into the street near our compound, spread it out, and then made an image to represent my medical helper, and another to represent me, and placed them near it. After this, one of the conjurors took a nail and drove it into each of the images. They expected that as soon as they did this we should be destroyed.

"The tree of which I before spoke has probably been destroyed by some enemy, as a wooden nail of a poisonous tree was found to have been driven into it. How long these deceivers, these conjurors will continue to try their efforts to destroy us, we can not say. They have tried for one month, and, though they have not succeeded, probably not a whit of the confidence of the people in them is destroyed."

THE PULNEY HILLS.

"*September* 15*th*. I am now on the Pulney Hills, where our Madura brethren have two houses for invalids. The place is very delightful, and the climate is peculiarly advantageous to such as have suffered from the effects of a hot climate. They are about fifty miles from Madura City, and about sixty from the Neilgherry Hills. Ice is to be found on them in the winter season. I came here three weeks ago in consequence of the illness of my little granddaughter. With the hope of saving her life her mother lately brought her here, and a most surprising change has been effected within three weeks. We have every reason to believe that she will recover. With divine permission, I shall go down into the plain on Monday next."

COMMUNION.

"Yesterday, being the day on which the American Board meet to celebrate the Lord's Supper, I, with my daughter-in-law and daughter as a part of the Madura Church, had the privilege of celebrating it also. The wine which we used was prepared by letting water stand on raisins until it extracts from them the vinous qualities. This we did rather than use the vile compounds sold here under the name of wines. The Jews are well satisfied with the delicious wine prepared from raisins for their Passover, and those who try it when celebrating the Lord's Supper will, I am persuaded, be not less satisfied with it in this ordinance.

"After the celebration of the ordinance we went to a place called Mount Nebo, from which there is a most

charming view of the low country. The grandeur of
the sloping mountains until they are lost in the plains—
the immense ravines between these mountains affording
a receptacle for the waters from a hundred different
fountains—exceed all description. There we were, more
than a mile above these plains, in the region of cold,
while below us the people were scorching, as it were, with
the heat. Looking over these vast and beautiful plains,
and knowing they were promised to the Redeemer, we
sang together—

> " ' Jesus shall reign where'er the sun
> Does his successive journeys run ;
> His kingdom stretch from shore to shore,
> Till moons shall wax and wane no more.

> " ' People and realms of every tongue
> Dwell on his love with sweetest song,
> And infant voices shall proclaim
> Their early blessings on his name.

> " ' Let every creature rise and bring
> Peculiar honors to our King:
> Angels descend with songs again,
> And earth repeat the loud amen.'

When are the soldiers of Immanuel to go up and con-
quer this land in his name ?"

ROUTINE OF WORK.

" An old missionary finds it somewhat difficult, from
his familiarity with heathenism, to make out a journal.
I will mention the labors of the coming month day by
day, to let you see something of my routine of work.
" 2d. Yesterday attended to the sick ; preached in the
morning from the parable of the rich man and Lazarus,
and, as Mr. Chandler is absent from Madura, in the afternoon from Hos. xiii., 9. Had he been present I should

have gone into the highway to preach. Was present a few moments at the Sabbath-school in the morning. Attended to the sick this morning. Went out this afternoon into one of the highways, and preached and distributed two copies of the 'Blind Way,' and several Almanacs. This evening attended the monthly concert of prayer with the natives.

"3d. This morning prescribed for the sick after two tracts had been read to them, and after I had preached to them as usual. While attending to them I was called away to visit Mrs. Tracy at Pasaimalee, who is ill. Returned this afternoon.

"4th. Preached and attended to the sick this morning. The dressings were removed for the first time from the leg which was taken off by me on the 3d of this month. This afternoon went out into the highways and preached the Gospel. The difference between my congregations in the streets and those who assemble to receive medical aid are often very marked. It is most trying to behold the utter indifference or opposition which is manifested very often in our street-preaching. Generally the people hear the Gospel with great civility when they come to have their maladies relieved. It is only now and then that we have much opposition manifested. Many assent to truths under these circumstances who under other circumstances would oppose it.

"5th. Preached and attended to my sick people this morning. Afterward examined a number of witnesses respecting a quarrel between two Church members. Am so unwell this afternoon that I shall not venture out to preach, nor shall I attempt to attend our weekly prayer-meeting. Have been taking a dose of medicine.

" 6th. Preached as usual to my sick people in the morning. This afternoon went to the river side and preached to the people who came round me. Gave but two copies of the 'Blind Way.' Perhaps I might have given the remainder which I had with me, but, as I had some of the baser sort round me, would not give them out.

" 7th. Attended to my sick people in the morning. Went out this afternoon and preached by the wayside.

" 9th. Yesterday morning went to the Sabbath-school; afterward preached from the history of Paul's conversion. In the afternoon preached by the wayside. Gave but one copy of the Bible away, for the reasons mentioned in my journal of the 6th. This morning preached and attended to the sick; performed two surgical operations. This afternoon went out and preached to the people by the wayside.

" 10th. Attended to my sick people at the usual hour. At eleven o'clock met the Bible-class from the schools. This class comes weekly to Brother Chandler's. This afternoon preached by the wayside. Addressed quite a number of persons. Met with as little opposition as could be . expected. Gave away three copies of the 'Blind Way.' Some attention was apparently paid by two or three persons or more to what was said.

" 11th. Preached and attended to my sick people. Went out this afternoon in the streets and preached to numbers of people. Gave away seven copies of the 'Blind Way.'

" 12th. This morning preached to my large company of sick people. There were about twenty women among them, several of them with their diseased children. After preaching and attending to the sick, went out into the highway, on the borders of the great market which is held in this city once a week. At this time the people come in from the country to dispose of their produce. One of the native helpers accompanied me. Had, toward the last, a very *tempestuous* time. We were obliged, for a season, to hold our peace on account of the noise. The people raised a great outcry when I left. My native helper was stoned. Little does a Christian community at home know what we have to endure in our preaching in the highways and streets. I refused to give books to any except from the country. Gave but two.

."13*th*. Attended to my sick people this morning. This afternoon have been attending the weekly Friday meeting which Brother Chandler holds with the girls of the boarding-school and others. Have been sent for by Brother Cherry to visit his child on the Pulney Hills. She has been very sick. Leave (D.V.) to-night, hoping to reach Padra Koorlum by to-morrow morning eight o'clock, and immediately ascend the Hills.

"18*th*. Left home on Friday afternoon last week to visit Brother Cherry's child, ill with jungle fever, now on the Pulney Hills. Reached the hills about nine o'clock on Saturday night. Left them yesterday morning, and reached home about ten o'clock to-day. Have been quite poorly part of the time with sick headache. On Sunday my son and self had quite a congregation of adults on the Hills—at least forty persons. Had a long interview with them.

"19*th*. This morning attended to the sick. Afterward went to Pasamale to visit Mrs. Tracy, who continues poorly. This afternoon went out into the highways and preached the Gospel. This evening attended our weekly prayer-meeting.

"*20th*. It is my practice to prescribe for the sick but once a day. All are to come at eight o'clock in the morning, when two tracts are read to the people. They afterward receive a ticket, which entitles them to receive medicine after I have prescribed for them. Those who come too late, *except new-comers*, have to go away unsupplied until eight o'clock the next morning. It is *entirely* out of the question for me to attend to the sick in any other way. My whole time would be broken up if I were to allow the sick to come at any time they pleased. Some come while I am prescribing for the company present, who have been here before. To them I also refuse to give medicine for the day. They have not been in time to hear the Gospel preached, the main object I have in view in prescribing for the sick. *New-comers* are attended to. To-day I preached, as usual, to my first company. Afterward to another company. Among them were several Mohammedan women. This afternoon, when about to go out to preach, a man came for me to visit a native woman with an immense tumor in her neck. She was in great distress. I merely opened the upper part of it, and let out a quantity of coagulated blood, etc. I had seen the tumor before. Possibly I may venture to remove the whole of it, though I fear the operation. It would be a very sad thing should she die under it. Proclaimed the Gospel to those who were present.

"*21st*. Preached to my sick people this morning. This afternoon went out into the highway and preached the Gospel.

"*23d*. Prescribed for the sick. Said a word, and only a word, to the Sabbath-school children. Preached from

Numb. x., 2. In the afternoon went out and preached by the wayside, and in the evening attended a meeting at Brother Chandler's, with such of the girls as professed to be serious. This morning preached to the sick. This afternoon preached to one company in the street, to one in a native house, and afterward went to visit Mrs. Tracy at Pasaimalee.

"24*th*. Preached to my sick people this morning. This afternoon went out as usual, and preached to the people by the wayside. Distributed several of our little publications. At eleven o'clock attended to the Bible-class of Brother Chandler's schools.

"25*th*. Attended to the sick this morning. At half past three o'clock went to meet Dr. Colebrook in consultation at the house of Judge Baynes. His little daughter is ill. Immediately on my return went to visit a native woman, who is probably not far from the eternal world. She heard the Saviour's name. Addressed a few people who were present on spiritual things. After this went to visit Mrs. Tracy. She is getting better.

"26*th*. Preached to my sick people in the morning. Afterward went to the market, or rather just beyond it, and preached by the wayside to the people. This afternoon went out by the wayside to preach. Made but one attempt to speak, on account of the mob with which I was accompanied. After remaining still for half an hour or less, I turned my face homeward, glad to escape without personal violence. I much feared it. Yesterday the oldest elephant belonging to the temple of Mccnaache in this city died. It was drawn through the streets to-day to its burial-place, accompanied with music. Probably there were several hundred engaged in drawing it, so immensely heavy was its carcase.

"27*th*. Attended to my sick people this morning. Was detained at home this afternoon by the rain.

"28*th*. Preached, as usual, to my sick people this morning. This afternoon went out and preached the Gospel by the wayside.

§ "30*th*. Yesterday morning preached to my sick people. Then went to the Sabbath-school and catechised the children. Afterward preached from Numb. x., 29. In the afternoon went out and preached by the wayside. This morning preached to my sick people. Gave religious instruction to the children of two schools, which have this day been examined on the lessons of the month. This afternoon went down to the river side and preached the Gospel.

"31*st*. Preached to my sick people. Addressed the children of Brother Chandler's third school on the concerns of their souls. This afternoon went out to a village about three miles from Madura, and preached the Gospel to two different companies. Stopped at another village on my way home, and preached the Gospel also."

CHAPTER XV.

Black Town.—A Liar, etc.—White Ants.—Queen Ant.—Publications.
—Present to a Prince.

BLACK TOWN.

UNDER date of May 10th, 1849, Dr. Scudder makes in his journal the following entry:

"My son and self, with our families, moved into this part of the city last week. It is an excellent missionary station. We have had large congregations in front of our door in the evenings. We stand on an elevation of chunam-work, while the people stand a little below us. Crowds of people have already heard the Gospel. I have commenced my medical establishment also. Performed my first surgical operation this morning on a Brahmin. Shall probably have great crowds for medical and surgical assistance. Had two patients early this morning."

HE WAS A LIAR FROM THE BEGINNING.

"A gentleman called here and mentioned a lying report which has been put in circulation. It is that, with my two sons, I was near the car of one of the idol temples in this vicinity preaching, and that I had become so animated as to spit on the idol; that I was then seized by the Brahmins, and rescued from them by the peons, or public officers of government.

"This is a specimen of the falsehoods which are propagated. Neither myself nor my sons saw their idols or were near them. Thus it is that the great adversary supports his kingdom by falsehood and deception."

WHITE ANTS ONE OF THE SCOURGES OF INDIA.

"One of the most destructive little creatures in India is the white ant, which is about half the size of the common black ant. It is impossible to preserve wood floors if they can get at them. They will go through walls even up to the timbers, and destroy them. It is said that the queen ant is always to be found in the neighborhood of a house infested by white ants, though not under it, and that her destruction causes that of her subjects.

"Many years since Dr. Carey invariably dug up the ground in the neighborhood of any building so infested, and killed the queen, and the plan proved in every instance successful. A general order has lately been issued. It is as follows:

"'It is hereby notified that, whenever public buildings are infested with the destructive white ants, their nests, containing the queen ant, will always be found in the immediate neighborhood; and as the destruction of the queen destroys the colony—and this having been found an effectual remedy wherever properly tried—there is, therefore, no reason why any building should hereafter suffer from this destructive insect. All officers, civil or military, occupying or in charge of public buildings, being held responsible for the same, it is their duty either to take immediate measures for discovering and digging up white ants' nests within one hundred yards of the building, and destroying the queen ant, or to report to the proper authority the existence of the white ants' nests within that space from the building.'"

THE QUEEN ANT.

"She is a very curious creature. She is found in a very secluded spot of the nest. If we dig into the ant-hill we shall find many rooms, sometimes hundreds of them, where the ants make their home. If we dig near the centre we shall find a room shaped like two saucers put together; within this lies the queen. She is like a white worm, somewhat transparent, and grows to the enormous size of a man's little finger. To this body is attached the natural-sized head of the small ant. All around her room are very small entrances, about the size of a pin's head, and at each of their doors is stationed a sentinel to guard her from any insect intruders. These sentinels are very watchful, and, if disturbed, they show their attachment to their sovereign by striking out of the hole their little nippers; and, if in their power, they will cut their enemy into two parts as with a pair of scissors.

"The queen lies quiet, not being able to move her great body; and, if she were able, she could not get out of her palace. It is said that the ants bring her food and supply all her wants, while she, month after month, continues to fill up her little world with her mischievous brood."

NUMEROUS WRITINGS AND PUBLICATIONS.

The pen and the press were put under contribution by this good man to forward the great interests of piety and evangelization. His correspondence was very extensive, and related to the one important subject that filled his thoughts. A very large volume would not suffice to contain the letters which he wrote on missionary topics.

But we do not think it would be expedient to give more than here and there one, or an occasional extract from some of the most interesting.

He was also a constant contributor to some of the Christian journals published in India. The articles furnished by him have a pith and power, which made them not only readable, but effective in pulling down the strong-holds of heathenism. He found time also to address successive appeals to the young men of America, with a view to influence them to consider and decide as to their duty to become missionaries to the heathen. His appeals also to his own Church (the Reformed Dutch) are calculated to rouse both clergymen and laymen to a consideration of the claims of the millions perishing in darkness. These, we hope, will be given to the public in a separate volume, following this brief sketch of his life and labors.

His little books and tracts, issued by the American Tract Society, have been scattered broadcast over the country, and thousands have been stimulated to Christian duty by reading them, and some have decided to follow him into the field of foreign missionary labor. "The Redeemer's last Command," the "Address to Christian Mothers," and "Tales about the Heathen" are doing their work in the Church and in the Sunday-school, while the hand that penned them has long since been paralyzed in death. That beautiful and touching little volume, "Provision for passing over Jordan," has inspired many a timid saint to enter the dark valley and to cross the swelling tide, singing "I will fear no evil," or "Thanks be to God that giveth me the victory."

A PRESENT TO A PRINCE.

One of the volumes relating to the practices and principles of the millions under the rule of her majesty, Queen Victoria, was sent by Dr. Scudder as a present to the Prince of Wales. He hoped to arrest the attention of the young prince, and make an impression on his mind favorable to the needful reforms in Southern India.

Quite a correspondence ensued on the subject. Our minister at the Court of St. James, the Hon. Abbot Lawrence, after stating that he had forwarded the parcel to the queen, adds: "I have no doubt that I shall soon receive an acknowledgment of its reception, when I shall have much pleasure in transmitting it to you. I have a lively and happy recollection of Mrs. Winslow, and knew Mrs. Scudder by public report. Both were persons of extraordinary personal attractions and high Christian attainments. I have long known through the press of your public labors in India, and of the success that has attended them. I need not, perhaps, say that no one entertains a higher respect for your character and services in the cause of our common religion than, reverend and dear sir, your faithful servant, ABBOT LAWRENCE."

The following epistle was subsequently received by Mr. Lawrence from her majesty's secretary, and transmitted to Dr. Scudder, dated Osborne, May, 1852:

"I have had the honor to submit to her majesty the queen the letters of Dr. Scudder, together with his work which accompanied them, and which has been given by her majesty to the Prince of Wales.

"I am commanded to request that you will have the

kindness to convey to Dr. Scudder the assurance of her high appreciation of the kind motives which have induced him, from so great a distance, to direct this attention to the Prince of Wales, and to request him to believe that the queen is very sensible of the terms in which he has addressed her majesty.

"I am commanded to request that you will have the goodness to take the trouble to communicate this to Dr. Scudder, instead of writing to him directly, as the address upon his letters, 'Madras,' might, perhaps, be hardly sufficiently defined to assure a letter reaching him. Believe me, my dear sir, sincerely yours, C. B. Phipps." .

CHAPTER XVI.

A sudden and severe Stroke.—Woes cluster.—Effect of these Bereavements.—One Labor more.—Sketches, etc.

EVENING SHADOWS.

By his sojourn in America, Dr. Scudder's health, although much improved, was not re-established. On resuming his labors he found that he was soon fatigued, and that his power of endurance was much impaired. His eyesight also began to fail, and it is affecting to read from his journal the reflections which this new calamity suggested.

" My eyesight has begun to fail; but, though I should become blind, if spared, I trust that I shall be able to preach. My voice is good, and though, under equal circumstances, I should much prefer losing my voice to my eyesight, still, under my circumstances, I would sooner lose my eyesight than my voice. I could do nothing without the latter."

A SUDDEN AND SEVERE STROKE.

Next to God, his strongest prop was his beloved wife. When his children died, he exclaimed, with a sort of prophetic agony, " What if it had been their mother!" The idea of losing her was insupportable. If such a cold shadow crossed his mind, it made him shudder far more than if his own death-knell had sounded in his ear. Every thing seemed to indicate that he should first pass over

Jordan. How terrible, then, to see her suddenly seized and prostrated, and in a few short hours brought face to face with death! Medical skill is vain. Man can do nothing but bow before the fiat of God. "I was dumb, because *Thou* didst it." However agitated other bosoms were, his was perfect peace. Life's labors were ended. It was simply entering into rest. But the following tribute will better describe the event and its immediate consequences than any thing which the writer can say.

DEATH OF MY DEAR WIFE.

"*November* 29th, 1849. On Monday night, last week, the dear companion of my youth and of my later years fell asleep in Jesus. This event called forth the following communications to Dr. Anderson and others:

"'Madras, Nov. 22d, 1849.

"'REV. DR. ANDERSON: MY DEAR BROTHER,—My precious wife has entered into her rest. On Thursday last she was taken seriously ill, and on Friday was attacked with severe cramps, which were followed by extreme exhaustion of her whole system. All the means that were used to cause her to rally failed, and on Monday evening last she left the world for that "house not made with hands, eternal in the heavens." It was not until after midday on Monday that I became much alarmed about her. I called in Dr. Shaw, one of our most able surgeons, who very kindly rendered all the assistance in his power; but death was at hand. After we found that her disease was about to terminate fatally, we assembled around her dying couch and heard her last words. The righteousness of Jehovah Jesus, which had been her joy and support in life, was her only trust in death. She retained her senses nearly or quite to the last, and, although very weak, she conversed with us till within a few minutes of her departure. The same ardent love for Christ and for dying souls which she exemplified in her life, shone forth brightly during her last hours. When asked what message she had to send to her son Silas, she replied, "Tell him that I have written to him all that I would wish to say in my last letter. I spent half of his last birthday in prayer for him." This birthday had occurred about two weeks before.

"'When I asked her whether she wished all her sons to become missionaries, she said, "Yes; it has been my constant prayer that they might all come to this land to preach the Gospel. I do not desire that they should come unless they are prepared; but I wish them to be fitted for this work.

"'On being asked what message she had for her son William (who is a missionary in Ceylon), she answered, "Tell him I shall soon meet his beloved Kate. Tell him to be faithful, and to live to win souls. Tell him not to seek for comfort from any thing in this world, but to look to Jesus."

"'In addition to the messages of love which she sent to her own relations and to her connections on her husband's side, she added a message to such of them as are still out of Christ, exhorting them to seek him.

"'She said, "My only burden in dying is the thought that three* of my children are yet in an impenitent state;" and she besought her daughter Louisa, in the most affectionate and impressive manner, to yield her

---

* These three have since professed their faith in Christ.

heart to the Saviour; adding, " This is my dying request. I have done all that I can for you." She also told her to read the twenty-seventh Psalm. Seven out of her ten children have made a profession of their faith in Christ.

" ' Again she said, " I hope my being taken away will stir you all up to greater activity in the Lord's service."

" ' In respect to herself, she remarked, " I am a poor, miserable sinner, full of imperfections. Heaven will be glorious, because there will be neither sin nor imperfection there."

" ' Twice with great emphasis she said, " What a wretched place is a death-bed to prepare for eternity! What a miserable being should I now be if I had not Jesus to rest upon!" and then added, " Precious Saviour!"

" ' Again she said, " I have had seasons when I felt that I knew I loved the Saviour—that he was very precious to me."

" ' Again and again she exclaimed, " Precious Saviour!" and on one occasion, " Thou knowest all things —thou knowest that I have desired to love thee."

" ' By a repetition of the four following lines, she showed where the place of her refuge was:

> " ' Jesus, lover of my soul,
>   Let me to thy bosom fly;
> . While the billows near me roll,
>   While the tempest still is nigh.'

" ' She repeated also the following verses of Scripture: "Yea, though I walk through the valley of the shadow of death, I will fear no evil: for thou art with me; thy rod and thy staff they comfort me." "Surely goodness and mercy (have) followed me all the days of my life." —Psa. xxiii., 4, 6.

"'Just before she died she opened her eyes and exclaimed, with peculiar energy, "Glorious heaven! Glorious salvation!"

"'Soon after this she voluntarily closed her eyes and sweetly fell asleep in Jesus.

"'When gazing upon her, as she lay a corpse before me, I exclaimed, "How many prayers have come out of those lips!" She literally prayed her children into the kingdom.

"'And now what shall I say about my loss? I must sum it all up in one sentence—it is *irreparable!* In the prayer which was made at her funeral by Brother Spaulding, after Bro. Winslow's address, he used the expression that she had been to me " emphatically a help-meet." Thirty years have we been permitted to travel together and to labor for the salvation of souls. Now I am left to travel and labor alone, so far as this beloved help-meet is concerned. But all is well. Christ lives. I told her, when dying, that we should not be long separated.

"' May it be my lot, my precious companion, to meet thee on those happy shores, where

"' "" Adieus and farewells are a sound unknown,"
and where

"' "" These parting sounds shall pass our lips no more!"

"' Your affectionate brother, J. SCUDDER.'

"'Madras, Nov. 23d, 1849.

"'My precious Children, Silas and John,—Oh, how will your hearts be torn in pieces to learn that your dear, dear mother is no more! She has gone; yes, gone and left me alone; and left you too—left off her tears and her prayers for you. Only last week she sent letters to you in her own hand-writing. That hand is now stiffened in death. We buried this precious one day before yesterday. We kept her corpse with us longer, perhaps, than any corpse has been kept for a long time in this city—nearly forty - eight hours. I rejoice in this, that we were enabled to keep her so long. Oh my children, my dear children, what a loss have we sustained! But our loss is her gain. Can it be that you are never again to see your dear mother on earth? Oh, then, will you not meet her in heaven? Will you not give up this vain world—its pleasures, and live for Christ? Oh, become His, and by-and-by come out, as your mother expressed the desire, to this land to tell the heathen of a Saviour. Write me, my dear children, and tell me that you have given yourselves to Christ. Then my joy will be full.'

"'Madras, Nov. 24th, 1849.

"'My dear Brother, and Sisters Sarah and Sophia, —We all have a new song to sing, and this is, that my precious companion and your dear sister has triumphed over death, and has entered through the gates into the city of the New Jerusalem above. This event took place on Monday evening a little before eight o'clock. Clothed with the all-glorious righteousness of that Redeemer in whom she trusted, she is now *at rest.* And what shall we say? Shall we not say "The Lord is righteous still?" Shall we wish the beloved one back in this vale of tears? "Glorious heaven! glorious salvation!" were among her last words. Shall we wish to call her from that "glorious heaven?"—from that "glorious salvation" of which she is now in the possession? Would we have her any

more wet her earthly couch with her tears? any more
struggle with a heart of unbelief? any more encounter
the storms of this tempestuous world? any more contend
with the world, the flesh, and the devil? No, no, my
precious companion, no. I wish you joy in your new
habitation. Then, if such be *my* feelings—the feelings
of one to whom she was more dear by far than she was
to you, should you not acquiesce with me in saying " All
is well?" How desirous should we be to have the sanctified effect of this sorrowful but joyful bereavement! Yesterday in a note from Colonel Brown is the following expression : " We sympathize with you sincerely, but we
feel that your sorrow must be full of joy. Your beloved
wife is now with Him whom, having not seen, she loved
and served, and her works shall follow her." I would
that all our dear nephews and nieces might take warning from the death of their aunt. Say to our nephews
and nieces in Boston that their father's request to make
them the special subjects of prayer for a week was attended to by their aunt and myself. Oh that they would
listen to the voice which now calls upon them from the
grave! Dear Harriet Scudder, how would her aunt,
whose name she bears, sing the song of joy in heaven
over her repentance, and with what joy would she sing it
over the conversion of all those dear to her *yet*, belonging to the Waterbury, the Cheeseman, and the Downer
families!'

"'MY DEAR JOSEPH AND SAMUEL,—What more shall I
say? Is our beloved gone? Yes, gone; but gone to
rest. Oh that we might be stirred up to live more emphatically for Christ! What is this vain world to us

any more? You will never see your dear mother on earth again, but you can come and *see her where she lies in our burying-ground.* Last evening we went to pay this dear departed one a visit in her new habitation. . There we placed her on Wednesday evening. We kept her corpse for forty-eight hours, a thing not often done in this climate; but I would not bury her soon. Harriet, Louisa, and myself will go and pay another visit to her this evening, if God permit. Louisa wishes to take some flowers and put them on her grave. The spot where she lies will ever be dear to us. It will be dear to you; and, if you come out to this land, as she expressed a wish for you to come to preach the Gospel, you will delight to visit her also. My dear sons, let the death of your mother stir you up to live for Christ. What is there for us, in this vain world, but Christ? and let us labor for Christ. Oh! is it not worth laboring for to introduce one such saint, as is now your dear mother, into the kingdom of heaven? Write me, my precious children, and tell me all about yourselves and your prospects. Are your thoughts strengthening as to your coming to India?'

"*November* 23*d*, 1849. Oh that I may never forget the softened feelings which I have had since my precious wife died! Father, my heavenly Father, graciously be pleased to make me more humble. Oh! shall I ever have any more pride? ever stand up with pride *to resent an injury?* Shall I ever again speak pettishly or harshly to one who has injured me, or show any cool feelings toward him? Yesterday I wrote in the blank leaf of my Bible—

"'See that none render evil for evil unto any man.

" ' Be kindly affectioned one to another, with brotherly love.

" ' Overcome evil with good.'

" My heavenly Father, give me, I beseech thee, mildness and gentleness in all my carriage, with my friends, my children, my servants, and with the heathen. Let me never be vain in my conduct, or speak against any one, unless duty requires it; and help me often to examine myself whether or not I thus act. Thus shall I adorn the doctrine of my precious Saviour. I wish I had given my precious wife something on her birthday. She presented me with a smelling-bottle on mine, perhaps with reference only to its relieving my headaches. Precious companion! Perhaps if she were with me I should show her more kindness.

"*November 24th.* If my precious wife were to come here this evening, how careful would I be not to do any thing to grieve her. Shall I not forever be careful not to grieve my Saviour?

"*November 25th.* Have had no music (in our morning prayers) on the melodeon since my precious wife died. We will have it this morning, and sing with it—

" ' *C*ome, let us join our cheerful songs
 With angels round the throne,
For thousand thousand are their tongues,
 But all their joys are one.

" ' Worthy the Lamb that died, they cry,
 To be exalted thus;
Worthy the Lamb, our lips reply,
 For he was slain for us.

" ' Jesus is worthy to receive
 Honor and power divine;
And blessings more than we can give,
 Be, Lord, forever thine.

" 'Let all who dwell above the sky,
    And air, and earth, and seas,
Conspire to lift Thy glories high,
    And speak Thine endless praise.

" 'The whole creation join in one
    To bless the sacred name
Of Him who sits upon the throne,
    And to adore the Lamb.'

"My precious wife has her lyre in her hand, whatever this lyre may be, and is singing unto him that loved me and washed me from my sins in his own blood. To him be glory and dominion forever and ever. Why should we not use our lyres also?

"This is the first Sabbath my dear companion is spending in heaven.

"*November 26th.* It will be one week to-night since my dear companion entered into her rest. Yonder she is, with that great company, who are singing the victory over sin and death, through the blood of the Lamb. Now she is clothed with the righteousness of her Redeemer, and will shine in all its brightness forever and ever. No more sin, no more sorrow, no more pain, no more doubts and fears of her interest in her Beloved. God has wiped away all her tears. Jesus, having gone to prepare a place for her, and having prepared it, has received her to himself. His prayer to his Father in her behalf has been answered. 'Father, I will that they also whom thou hast given me be with me, where I am, that they may behold my glory.' Oh that I may often take a tour, in my imagination, to the place where she is! My precious companion, shall I meet you there? Yes, yes; through sovereign grace I shall meet you there, and unite with you forever in singing the praises of our

Redeemer together. Thou hast gone before me. Soon, at longest, I shall follow.

"To-day (one week ago) my precious wife passed through her death-struggle. She died on her couch while I was sitting at her head. Oh, can I ever be light again in my conduct! How can I ever smile again! Oh that I may hereafter have more grace to act for Christ, and to speak for Christ, and to think for Christ, that I may the more sweetly die in Christ, and go to enjoy Christ, the more on this account, forever! Precious Saviour, my prayer to Thee this day is, that I may be filled full of Thee—full of Thy love.

"*November 26th.* It is now between seven and eight o'clock at night. It was between these hours, last week, that my dear wife died. Nearly one week has she been in heaven, with that precious Saviour whose character is so fully drawn out in Hawker's Poor Man's Morning Portion, 'Because of the savor of thy good ointments, thy name is as ointment poured forth.'

"Why, my precious Redeemer, is Thy name so truly blessed but because Thou hast so endeared it to thy redeemed by every tie which can gain the affections? Didst Thou, even before I had being, enter into suretyship engagements for me that Thou wouldst redeem me when fallen? that Thou wouldst take my nature, live for me, die for me, become a sacrifice for me, shed Thy blood for me, wash me in Thy blood, clothe me with Thy righteousness, justify me before God and Thy Father, become my advocate, high-priest, intercessor—betroth me to Thyself here in grace, and everlastingly unite me to thyself in glory hereafter? Didst Thou do all this, and art Thou still doing it, making my cause thine own, and following

me with love, and grace, and mercy every day, and wilt
Thou never leave me nor forsake me? And must not
Thy name be as ointment poured forth? Can there be
a savor so sweet, so fragrant, so full of odor as the name
of Jesus? Precious ointments, it is true, have a smell in
them very grateful; but what savor can be like that
which, to the spiritual senses, manifests Jesus in his person, love, grace, and mercy? in whom there is every thing
desirable, and nothing but what is lovely—all beauty,
power, wisdom, strength—an assemblage of graces more
full of odor than all the spices of the East! Precious
Lord Jesus, let thy name be written in my heart, and let
every thing but Jesus be forever obliterated there, that
nothing may arise from hence but what speaks of Thee!
that through life and in death, the first and last, and all
that drops from my lips even in the separation of soul
and body, Jesus may form, in the close of grace here and
in the first opening of glory to follow, the one only blessed, precious name, as ointment poured forth!

"I will now go and spend the season at the side of the
couch on which my dear wife breathed her last breath
near this time last week, and may my meditation be
profitable.

"*November 27th.* It is of the utmost importance that
in my conduct and conversation I should so treat my fel-
low-men that I shall not be ashamed to converse with
them immediately afterward on their souls' concerns, or
to pray with them. I could not do this without being
ashamed if I had spoken or conducted myself unbecom-
ingly.

"*November 28th.* It will be one week to-night since
we carried away the remains of my dear wife to the

house appointed for all the living. Her spirit, however, dwells in no such a gloomy habitation, but has entered into the New Jerusalem, of which the Lord God Al. mighty and the Lamb are the temple, and which the glory of God and the Lamb doth lighten. That, through the infinite grace of my Redeemer, is my home. This grace, which brought my dear wife there will by-and-by bring me thither also.

> " 'In yonder realms, where Jesus dwells,
>   Is my eternal home;
> Why should I any longer, then,
>   Through this wide desert roam?
>
> " 'My int'rests once were here below,
>   When Jesus was unsought;
> His love, which pitied me when lost,
>   Was then without a thought.
>
> " 'But now, how changed is all the scene!
>   My int'rests are above;
> There my affections too are placed,
>   There all my joy and love.'
>
> " 'Bless'd Jesus, what is all this world—
>   What are its joys to me?
> Fain would I bid them all farewell
>   To go and be with Thee.'

"*November 29th.* Yesterday evening Harriet, Louisa, and myself went again to visit the dear departed one. She has been an inhabitant of the grave for a little more than a week. Her sorrows, her last struggles, are all over. The latter she felt to be so severe that she prayed to her heavenly Father to make her dying bed easy. She said that the grasshopper was a burden.

"*December 2d.* This is the second Sabbath my dear companion is spending in heaven. Now, oh my precious Redeemer, as Thou hast taken this beloved one to Thyself, grant that my affections may more and more be placed upon Thee—oh yes, more and more placed upon Thee, whom my soul loveth!"

SEEKING FOR JESUS.

"This, my soul, should be thy constant employment. Wherever thou art, however engaged in going in or out, at rising up or lying down, whether in public or private, in the church or market-place, the closet, the family, the garden, the field, the house, the question ever arising in the heart should be, 'Where is Jesus?' Blessed Spirit, Thou glorifier of my Lord, wilt Thou constantly excite this seeking for Jesus in my heart! Wilt Thou, Lord, give me every moment a sense of need; then a view of His fullness, suitableness, readiness to impart; then bring Him whom my soul loveth and me together; and then open a communication in leading me forth in desire, and giving me faith to receive from the infinite fullness of my Lord, and grace for grace! Lord Jesus, I would desire grace to seek Thee as for hidden treasure. I would seek Thee, and Thee only, O my God! I would separate myself from all other things. It is Jesus my soul chooseth, my soul needs. I would trust in nothing beside. No duties, no works—neither prayers nor repentance—no, nor faith itself, considered as an act of my soul, shall be my comfort; but Jesus alone I would make my centre, and every thought, and every affection, and every desire, like so many streams meeting in one, should all pour themselves as rivers into the ocean of Thy bosom. And the nearer as a stream that draws near the sea is propelled to fall into it, so the more forcible and vehement let my soul be in desires after Thee as my soul draweth near the hour of seeing Thee. O Lamb of

God, give me to be seeking after Thee through life, pressing after Thee from one ordinance to another; and when
ordinances cease, and all outward comforts fail, then,
Lord, may I gather up (as the dying patriarch did his
feet in the bed) all my strength, and pour my whole soul
into Thine arms, crying out, '*I have waited for Thy salvation, O Lord!*'

"*December* 5*th*. Yesterday Harriet, Louisa, and myself
went again to visit the spot where our dear departed one
sleeps. There her remains will rest until the last trumpet shall sound and until the dead shall be raised. Now
her body lies in the *dark* grave, but her spirit is in the
enjoyment of all the *light* of heaven. When on earth
she saw through a glass darkly, but now face to face.
In her last hours she referred to that hymn in Dobell's
Collection entitled 'Unknown World.'

> " ' Oh, by what glimm'ring light we view
>   That unknown world we're hast'ning to!
>   God hath lock'd up the mystic page,
>   And curtain'd darkness round the stage.
>
> " ' We talk of heaven, we talk of hell,
>   But what they mean no tongue can tell.
>   Heaven is the realm where angels are,
>   And hell the chaos of despair.
>
> " ' But what these awful words imply,
>   None of us know before we die;
>   Whether we will or not, we must
>   Take the succeeding world on trust.
>
> " ' Swift flies the soul—perhaps 'tis gone
>   Ten thousand leagues beyond the sun,
>   Or twice ten thousand more thrice told,
>   Ere the forsaken clay is cold.
>
> " ' But ah! no notices they give,
>   Nor tell us where or how they live,
>   Though conscious, while with us below,
>   How much themselves desired to know,

    " ' As if bound up by solemn fate
      To keep this secret of their state,
      To tell their joys or pains to none,
      That man may live by faith alone.

    " ' Well, let our Sovereign, if He please,
      Lock up His marvelous decrees;
      Why should we wish Him to reveal
      What He thinks proper to conceal?

    " ' It is enough that we believe
      Heaven's brighter far than we conceive;
      And oh, may God our souls prepare,
      To meet, and bless, and praise Him there!'

"My dear companion has no more to complain of the glimmering light by which to view that happy world to which she but a few days ago was hastening. Having reached it, she has had all its realities opened to her view. And oh, what must have been her transport—what must have been her ecstasy when, after having gone to sleep on a bed of suffering and of death, she awaked and found herself in the possession of all its joys—found herself in the presence of that Saviour who had redeemed her to God by His blood, and who welcomed her—a once lost, but now found child—to His bosom. Oh, if that blessed song, 'Hallelujah to the Lamb,' ever burst from her lips, with what an elevated voice must she have proclaimed it then! 'And I heard a voice from heaven saying unto me, Write, blessed are the dead which die in the Lord from henceforth: yea, saith the Spirit, that they may rest from their labors; and their works do follow them.'

"*December 7th.* On Sabbath evening last the funeral sermon of my dear companion was preached in the kirk by Brother Winslow. He took his text from the seventh chapter of Revelations, 14th and 15th verses—' These are they which came out of great tribulation, and have

washed their robes, and made them white in the blood
of the Lamb, therefore are they before the throne of
God.'

> " ' The Saviour!   Oh, what endless charms
>   Dwell in the blissful sound ;
> Its influence every fear disarms,
>   And spreads sweet peace around.

> " ' Here pardon, life, and joys divine
>   In rich effusion flow,
> For guilty rebels lost in sin,
>   And doom'd to endless woe.

> " ' Oh the rich depths of love divine !
>   Of bliss a boundless store ;
> Dear Saviour, let me call Thee mine,
>   I can not wish for more.

> " ' On Thee alone my hope relics,
>   Beneath Thy cross I fall,
> My lord, my life, my sacrifice,
>   My Saviour and my all.'

"In the blood of this precious Saviour have the robes
of my dear wife been washed and made white, therefore is she before the throne of God.   Now is she singing in much more exalted strains than when upon earth,
'Worthy is the Lamb that was slain to receive power, and
riches, and wisdom, and strength, and honor, and glory,
and blessing.'   No alloy is now mixed with this song.

"*December 8th.* Oh, what a stroke was it to my *pride*
when my dear wife lay a corpse in her coffin!   How
anxious is corrupt nature to guard every avenue that its
pride be not wounded.   When I am willing to be abased
in the sight of others, and to yield points which come in
contact with this pride with a *quiet* spirit, and without
any anxiety to give reasons (whereby self may be exalted) for such submission; and when I am willing to hear
remarks which also wound this pride without any desire

to *retaliate*, then will it appear that I have something of a humble spirit.

"In my 'Hawker's Poor Man's Morning Portion' I find the following insertion: '*December* 8, 1848. Heard of the death of my dear brother Judson, of Milan, Ohio. He has overcome through the blood of the Lamb. Precious blood! He died August 20th, 1848.'

"*December 9th.* This is the third Sabbath my dear wife has spent in heaven.

"*December 10th.* This time three weeks ago my dear companion was dying. My tears for thee this day, my beloved wife, have shown that I have not forgotten thee. Received a note from Brother Little, of which the following is an extract: 'My beloved wife was early taken from me, blasting fondly-cherished hopes. Yours was called away after a long and happy union. I know not which situation is most full of sorrow. But you, in addition to the consolations from the assurance that our friends have died in Christ, may reasonably cherish the hope that very soon you may join your beloved in her glorious service and joys. It is, indeed, pleasant to live, but how much more pleasant to be permitted to leave this body of sin and death, and go to the place of perfect holiness. It must afford you much satisfaction to feel that very soon, at the longest, you will follow the departed.'

"*December 14th.* Whenever I am tempted to be angry, then let me be careful to speak *slowly*, and with a *low* voice. Blessed Spirit, graciously be pleased to grant me thy assistance in this thing.

"*December 16th.* This is the fourth Sabbath my dear wife is spending in heaven. I would go and be where she is—go and be free from sin and imperfection—go and praise my Jesus, without any of that alloy which now mixes with all my attempts to glorify him.

"*December* 17*th.* This night four weeks ago my dear wife died. It is a night long to be remembered.

"*December* 19*th.* It will be one month to-night since my dear wife died. We visited her grave again last night, as we did also on Saturday evening. Nearly one month ago she heard the voice of her Saviour saying unto her, 'Come up, thou blessed of my Father—come up and take possession of the mansions which I have prepared for you!' and she has gone and taken possession of them. Yonder she is, feasting on the everlasting smiles of this all-glorious Saviour, while I am spending my days in sighs, and tears, and groans; in meeting rebuffs from the world and Satan; in contending often with a hard heart, a dull and stupid frame, and with feelings of lamentation and woe that I love my Jesus so little. Oh, how would I rejoice could I hear the voice of my Saviour saying unto me also, 'Come up higher!' How would I rejoice to have my fettered soul released! How would I rejoice to have the prison doors opened, that the captive might go free! Again would I say—

> " 'Bless'd Jesus, what is all this world—
> What are its joys to me?
> Fain would I bid them all farewell
> To go and be with Thee.'

"*December* 20*th.* Went to the examination of the female schools of the Free Scotch Church by invitation. Returned between two and three o'clock, and was distressed when thinking of my precious wife. It will, perhaps, be most profitable for me, instead of thinking too

much of past scenes and events, and dwelling upon my
loss, to think more of my beloved one as a happy spirit
above, free from all pain and suffering, and in no need
of my friendship, or any thing that I can do to make
her joys complete. It will also be for my comfort to
think that my separation from her will only be for a short
season; to think that to-morrow, as it were, I shall meet
her again, and have all my loss made up.

"*December* 21*st*. It is one month to-day since we committed the remains of our dear departed one to the earth.
In her dying hour she referred to a letter which she had
been writing to her son Silas. I have found a copy of a
part of this letter in one of her drawers. It is as follows:

"'My very dear Son Silas,—This is your birthday,
if the Lord has spared your life. You are now sixteen
years old. Your image has been before me most of the
time since I arose this morning. A part of this day I
have shut myself up in a little room to seek for God's
blessing upon my absent child. Silas, my beloved son,
my heart has yearned over you. I have thought of you
as one afflicted in body, and I have grieved over your
sufferings, and asked the Lord, if consistent with his
will, to remove the disease which has been so long upon
you; but I have been more concerned this day for your
soul's welfare. My prayers and tears have been poured
out before the mercy-seat that the Lord will change your
heart. So deeply have I felt for you that I could almost
believe the Lord would hear and answer my supplications. I am assured that God is a prayer-hearing and a
prayer-answering God, and this encourages me to plead
that he will have mercy upon those of my dear children

who are yet out of Christ. It has been my privilege this day to bring *you*, Silas, with dear *John* and *Louisa*, and lay you down at the foot of the Cross, and by faith to look up to that dear Saviour who was nailed *there*, and *there* bled and died for poor sinners. I have again and again asked my heavenly Father, for the sake of a bleed. ing, dying Saviour, to have mercy upon each of you. Will a mother's prayers and tears prevail? Will the Lord bring my children into his kingdom? Silas, are you still rebelling against a gracious God? Are you yet withholding that heart from Jesus, who says to you, "My son, give me thine heart?" Jesus also says, "Come unto me, all ye who are weary and heavy laden, and I will give you rest." Oh, dear son, Jesus will be a better friend than any earthly one—far better than father, mother, brother, or sister. Go, then, and give your heart to him. He can and will comfort you and bless you when in pain and sorrow. He is a refuge in every time of need. Choose him for your portion, and it will send gladness into the hearts of your parents. The angels in heaven, too, will rejoice if you become a follower of the Lamb. I feel that I must stop here, and go away to my closet, and on my knees entreat God's mercy for *you*. Will the Spirit help me in my supplications—' Here the letter stops.

"*December 23d.* The great business of a renewed soul in this world is but dressing itself for the divine-presence —a preparation for that state wherein we are forever to be with the Lord. Would I not be most careful not to go into the presence of an earthly monarch with a spot upon my garments, and ought I not so to live that the garment of the Redeemer's righteousness wherewith I am clothed shall not appear spotted in that day when I shall be summoned to appear before Him, as well as throughout that eternity which, through His grace, I shall spend with Him? Dear Saviour, grant—oh, do grant that I may hereafter live in such a manner that I shall not defile this all-glorious garment.

"*December* 24*th*. Are we more sensible of the external calamities which befall us than of inward spiritual distempers? Do I so cry and bemoan myself because of the body of sin and death, as I do when I have lost my friend, my husband, my wife, my child, my house, my estate, my pleasant delectable things in this world? In such cases we cry out as undone persons. We mourn and refuse to be comforted. But I have an earthly, vain heart—a heart that will not be brought to live in love and communion with God; unapt to prayer, to meditation, to spiritual commerce with heaven. Do we so sensibly complain upon these accounts, I say, as men are apt to do under the sharp and acute sense of external evils?'

"*January* 1*st*, 1850. I congratulate you, my dear wife, on account of your happy new-year in heaven. O that I could go and be there also!

"*January* 19*th*, 1850. It is two months to-night since my dear wife died. Blessed Saviour, may I not hope that, through Thy precious merits, I am two months nearer Thy kingdom? To-morrow I expect to sit down at Thy table at this place. How much sweeter would it be to sit down at Thy table above! There my companion is enjoying her communion seasons without any of that alloy which is mixed with all my communion seasons here below. To-morrow, dear Saviour, oh, do grant that my soul may be made like the chariots of Amminadab.

"*20th.* Have this day been at the table of my divine Lord and Master. In times that have gone by I made the following minute: 'I am tired with earthly Sabbaths and ordinances, for I find but half a Jesus in the best of them. Oh, for the Sabbaths and ordinances above!'"

WOES CLUSTER.

How little thought this aged mourner that a beloved son had anticipated the mother, and entered "the pearly gates" ~~three~~ days in advance of her! And if spirits recognize, how joyous the surprise to find her loved one new robed and ready to welcome her!

Samuel D. Scudder was a young man of great promise. Highly gifted in mind—having no superior among his fellow-students—and with a disposition of such magnetic power that none could know him but to love him, he shone still more brightly as a consistent and growing Christian. But "Death loves a shining mark," and the fatal arrow struck down, in this case, as brilliant a one for his years as ordinarily can be found. There was great lamentation at his death. But I will leave the father to paint, in colors both dark and bright, the affecting dispensation.

"*31st.* Another of my beloved ones is in heaven. Received letters from America to-day informing me that my dear Samuel had entered into his rest—that he had safely passed over Jordan. And can I do otherwise than say, 'Bless the Lord, O my soul, and all that is within me, bless His holy name?' Joseph, another of my sons,

writes as follows: 'I send you glad tidings of great joy.
The glad tidings is a message from your beloved son
Samuel, in his own words: "Tell my dear parents that
their dear boy is in heaven." That he is there; that he
is now a member of the great family of the redeemed,
joining in the choir that are ceaselessly singing, "Unto
Him that loved us, and washed us from our sins in His
own blood, and has made us kings and priests unto God
and his Father, to Him be glory and dominion forever
and ever;" that he is now free from pains and doubts,
those who have known him through life, in sickness and
at the near approach of death, feel confident. I scarcely left him from the time that he was confined to his
bed. Three nights I attended to him, and then was
obliged to call on friends; and oh! what friends we have
had! 'No mother, no father could have done more. He
was flighty toward the last, but knew me as long as he
could speak—as long as he had his eyes open. A few
nights before his death he asked me to read the twenty-
third Psalm. I did so, and prayed with him. The next
day I left a student at his side while I went down to
dinner. He was a pious student. When I came up, he
called me to his bedside and said, "Joe, I have just been
expressing my views to Mr. Elmendorf, and I will now
express them to you. I may die in agony, and then you
will know nothing. I have had many doubts and fears
in my life, but they are all gone. I suffer more than
mortal man can describe; but my Saviour is precious.
He has made me happy, very happy!" I was overcome,
and told him he must not have the idea that he was going to die. I hoped that he had long to live yet. His
youth and strength would enable him to stand this shock.

"It is of no use;" and this he said from the beginning, "I must die." I asked him if he did not wish to live. He said, "In some respects it was hard to die young, but that he was perfectly resigned to the will of the Lord." I then said, "If you should express a wish to live, with what views would you make the wish?" He answered, "You know that I have dedicated myself to the work of the ministry, and if I should wish to live, it would be to bend my energies to the work of the ministry—to my Master's service." He then said, "Tell my dear parents that their dear boy is in heaven. Tell them how much .I love them." When the doctor first told me that the symptoms were alarming, I went to his bed. He was perfectly calm at the time. He raised himself, threw his arms around my neck, and said, "You have been a dear, good brother to me. You must forgive me for all that I have done wrong." I told him that I had nothing to forgive; that he must forgive me. He said repeatedly I had not done wrong. The same evening I got on the bed by his side. He then had a lucid interval. I asked him his views in regard to sin. "It was horrible in the sight of God; but Christ had removed all his sins, and that He was all and in all precious to him." I told him then to pray, and he prayed most fervently that his Saviour would take him home to himself.'

"His aunt Sophia writes: 'Mr. Voorhees told him I had come, and asked him if he wished to see me. He said, "Oh yes." I went up to his room with as much composure as I could. He put his arms around my neck and wept. I said, "Samuel, dear, you are better." "Oh no, aunt, I shall not recover. The doctor does not know my feelings as well as I do myself." I then asked him

M

how he felt in prospect of death. "Happy, very happy. I am not afraid to die. When I look at myself, I am all sin; but when I look to Jesus, he is all glorious; and he can forgive and pardon all. He is all my hope and trust." I then asked him if he had enjoyment in looking to Christ. "Yes," said he; "such happiness I have had on this bed as I can not describe." Such is, as nearly as I can remember, my conversation with him. I then found he was much exhausted, and would suffer him to speak no more. Mr. Mandeville, Mr. Floyd, Mr. Voorhees, and myself sat by him through the night.'

"My sister Jane writes: 'To one who asked if he did not wish to live, he replied, "It is rather hard for one so young to die;" and, referring to his having devoted himself to the missionary work, continued, "If the Lord pleases to give me a crown without permitting me to labor in his vineyard, it is all the better." And this crown has been awarded, and a harp, upon which he has hymned celestial music, has been put in his possession. Hark! it is the song of salvation.'

"My dear son died while a member of the Theological Seminary in New Brunswick, New Jersey. Perhaps he would have joined me in my missionary work year after next; but God has no need of his services here. All is well. It is enough for me that he is at rest with his Saviour.

"The following account of his funeral is taken from two of the publications which have reached me:

"'Perhaps it has never been the lot of New Brunswick to witness such a season of solemnity as that of Friday, the 16th instant, on the occasion of the funeral rites of our much-lamented young friend, Samuel D. Scudder.

Scarcely could it be possible to give a more unanimous utterance to the sad conviction that an estimable young man, in whom the Church had centred large expectations, had been taken away by the wise yet inscrutable providence of God. The students of the College and those of the Theological Seminary on the day previous held separate meetings to give suitable expression to their sorrowing sympathy, with which their hearts were overflowing full; and, in the impatience of grief, unable to wait the usual time, accompanied by their respective professors, they paid a visit to gaze upon the amiable features, sweet even in death, of their deceased companion. At half past eleven o'clock A.M. on Friday, the students of both the Literary and Theological Colleges, preceded by the faculties of both institutions, left the college grounds to unite with the friends of the deceased in the funeral train. As they slowly proceeded down the Campus, where the deceased had once walked with the glad accompaniment of festive music on the occasion of his graduating with the highest honor of his class, the college bell tolled a mournful requiem. The body, followed by a long train of sorrowing friends, was taken to the Second Dutch Church, and exposed to view immediately before the pulpit.

"'The funeral discourse was delivered by the Reverend Professor Alexander McClelland, D.D., from the sentiment in Ecclesiastes vii., 1—"The day of death is better than the day of one's birth." And such a sermon! The tears streaming from "eyes unused to weep" afforded its best eulogy. The preacher spoke of the superior knowledge which the soul enjoyed in the spirit land, and then, pointing to the placid face of the deceased, and

with a voice subdued by intensity of emotion, exclaimed,
" Yes, my dear young pupil, could thy now enlightened
spirit be permitted to inhabit its house, I would gladly
sit at thy feet and learn of thee wisdom." The effect
was electric; all wept—the professors and their students.
None were ashamed to let the pearl-drops flow from the
fount of feeling. "Once, by a coincidence sometimes
permitted by an inscrutable Providence," said the preacher, "a young man of large promise and buoyant hopes
stood before me. On his arm leaned a beautiful young
maiden in all the confidence of her sex. I united them
in marriage. This union was wonderfully blessed. Since
then, over thirty years have rolled away; and now, at this
moment, by the incomprehensible will of God, I am deliv-
ering a funeral discourse over the remains of their son."
It would be impossible rightly to depict the effect of this
simple but well-timed announcement.

"'After permitting the audience once more, one by
one, to gaze upon the deceased, the procession again
formed, and took up its line of march for the grave-yard.
As an indication of the pervading grief, it was observable that a very large portion of the ladies of the congregation joined the rear of the procession. For numbers
and depth of sorrow, this place has not seen its like before.

"'Samuel Scudder was taken away without being suffered to enter the great vineyard of missionary labor,
but his last testimony was a sermon of great power.
His resignation and Christian serenity proved how much
better was the day of his death than that of his birth.
And who but God knows the effect of his departure?
An awakening has evidently begun in the college, and

who will not pray that God may make his people willing in the day of his power ?'

"*April* 26*th*. 'Let no corrupt communication proceed out of your mouth; but that which is good to the use of edifying, that it may administer grace unto the hearers.'

"29*th*. We have received a letter from one of our connections, Miss Mary M. Pohlman, in which she gives a quotation from one of my sons (Samuel's) letters to them. He says, 'Within the last few days circumstances have occurred which make me feel it to be my duty to return to New Brunswick and resume my studies. I hear the voice of my father and brothers calling me from my native land, "Come over and help us," and I must hasten to obey.'

"*November* 19*th*, 1851. It will be two years to-night since my dear wife entered into her rest.

"21*st*. This day, two years ago, my dear wife lay a corpse in the room where I now am.

"*Cape of Good Hope, November* 21*st*, 1854. This day, five years ago, I buried my beloved wife."

THE EFFECT OF THESE BEREAVEMENTS.

On so sensitive a mind as Dr. Scudder's, these terrible strokes fell with crushing power. His own health failing—his day-star having set, no more to pour her mild radiance on his path—his promising son having gone on the higher mission—the mission angelic—no wonder that his spirit bowed in sadness, and his submission was mingled with the plaint of bruised affections.

From this date onward the old warrior thought of the day so near when he should exchange the spiritual pan-

oply for the crown immortal. The trumpet-note of
Providence warned him that the last enemy was advanc-
ing, and that he must enter upon one more struggle, and
then, with the shout of victory, pass to his reward.

But his zeal, unquenched, strove to stay up his mortal
frame - work, and every day saw him on the field, bat-
tling against heathenish errors, and striving to lead the
poor pagan " out of darkness into God's marvelous light."

His friends saw, however, that he was hastening an
event which they prayed might be postponed for many
years. They advised, and he at length consented to try
the effect of a sea voyage, and cessation from missionary
labors. He always said, "I wish to die in India." "There
I would be buried, side by side with my beloved wife."
He was not willing to make a second voyage to America,
so it was determined that he should go to the Cape of
Good Hope, accompanied by his son Joseph, and try the
effect of that salubrious region.

ONE LABOR MORE INDULGE.

Dr. Scudder and his son reached the Cape of Good
Hope November, 1854. He was much benefited by the
voyage, and commenced at once, with his usual earnestness, to preach Christ to the residents, and especially to
the children. Crowds flocked to hear him. He held
two, and sometimes even three services on the Sabbath.
It seemed as if Providence was about to give him a new
lease of life, and his spirits rose with his renewed ability
to labor. But it was a flame leaping from the socket.
" The golden bowl was about to be broken." The waters of the Jordan were heard lashing its shores. The
preparation for crossing had been made, and it only re-

mained for the celestial voyager to say to the angels inviting him from the opposite bank, " Lo, I come."

Tired with official labor, he laid himself down, as usual, to recruit a little before he entered upon a service which had been announced for him. He sank into a sweet sleep, which gradually became deeper and deeper, until, when the servant announced something unusual, and the affectionate son hastened to his bedside, the spirit was just taking its flight from earth to heaven. As we stand, in thought, over that sublime scene, we can not but exclaim,

> " Servant of God, well done!
> Thy glorious warfare's past;
> The battle's fought, the race is run,
> And thou art crowned at last."

This sketch of the life and labors of a distinguished missionary, however imperfect, is of some importance as to its influence on those who read it, whether professed Christians or professed worldlings. It may stimulate the one class in their aims at a higher degree of spirituality, and convince the other that religion is not a mere theory, but a system of practical holiness and self-denial.

Here is a man of high culture and refined taste—the result of an education in our best colleges, both academical and medical—offering himself, with all his attainments, to a work which requires expatriation, and the endurance of great labors and sufferings, with no reward but the consciousness of discharged duty. He leaves a lucrative profession for a bare subsistence. He goes from a home adorned with all the attractions of social and religious comfort to a dwelling among brutal and disgusting heathenism. How is this to be accounted for? None of the ordinary principles which sway our common humanity are sufficient to explain it. It must be that his heart was touched by a *higher* principle—one in accordance with that which led Him, " who was rich, for our sakes to become poor, that we, through his poverty, might be rich." The existence of true piety alone can account for it.

The spirit of benevolence and self-sacrifice was the more marked in this case, inasmuch as it was exercised in the view of a life-long exile. When missionaries left their native land *then*, it was expected by them and by the Churches who sent them that they were to live and die among the heathen. It was a farewell to home— final and forever. Dr. Scudder's face was never turned toward his native land but once, and then with great reluctance; and so soon as the possibility of return was evident, he cheerfully and with ardent longing set sail again for the field of his labors. He had his desire—a desire often expressed—that he might make his grave in India.

The record of such a life and of such labors, if lost to the Church and to the world, would, it seems to us, be a *great loss*. We need the stimulating effect of such examples. They rouse us from the self-indulgence to which we are so naturally inclined. They show us the possibility of high endeavor, and make us feel that if one Christian can exercise so much of the spirit of the Master, and tread so closely in his footsteps, why can not another—why can not we *all?*

If Luke had not traveled with St. Paul, sharing his

toils and trials—if he had not been inspired to make and transmit the record of that heroic servant of Christ, what a loss would it have been to all succeeding ages of the Church! Those writings have animated and sustained Christians in all their conflicts with their enemies, both human and Satanic. And, though we do not pretend to compare the life and labors of our humble missionary with the great apostle of the Gentiles, yet would the loss in the one case be as *real*, though by no means as great as in the other.

As one generation passes away to be succeeded by the influx of successive ones, obliterating, like incoming waves, the landmarks which had stood as signals of hope or of danger, so the coming ranks of later Christians will have forgotten the heavenly examples which had preceded them, unless we are at some pains to give them perpetuity. Patriots and warriors have their statues of bronze or marble. Science, by the same means, secures for her votaries the homage of posterity. Why should not they who have fought so manfully the fight of faith, and set so illustrious an example of victories achieved by grace over the allurements of the world, have also their memorial, more enduring than brass or marble? They, indeed, "rest from their labors, but their works do follow them." Their name is stamped not only on the records of Christian civilization, but still deeper on souls " brought out of darkness into God's marvelous light."

Few are now living who saw Dr. Scudder at the time when he made the sublime consecration of his all to the work of missions, and those who have come on to the stage since have but a vague and shadowy idea of this devoted man, so that if, by this sketch of his life and labors, we may fix his image on the minds of present and coming generations, we shall have done a service for which some, at least, will give us thanks. We shall save from oblivion an example not often seen even among those who profess the same faith and acknowledge the same obligations. What he was he was by the grace of God. By the same grace others may attain to a like spiritual elevation. Nay, they may reach beyond, and in their luminous flight get so near to the perfection of angels as shall lead us to cry out, with Dr. Young,

" Which is the seraph—which the child of clay ?"

REMINISCENCES

OF THE

Rev. JOHN SCUDDER, M.D.,

MISSIONARY TO INDIA.

BY

B. P. AYDELOTT. D.D., AND HENRY M. SCUDDER, D.D.

REMINISCENCES.

"I FIRST met with that eminent missionary of Christ, the late Dr. John Scudder, in the year 1813, when we came together, in company with many others, to attend medical lectures in the city of New York.

"He had finished his preparatory education in Princeton College, New Jersey, his native state, and we both found ourselves the private pupils of Dr. David Hosack, then the distinguished Professor of the Theory and Practice of Medicine in the College of Physicians and Surgeons of the University of the State of New York. We were therefore thrown together nearly all the time of our pupilage, instead of occasionally meeting in a crowded lecture-room during the winter months of each year.

"I know not why it was that Dr. Scudder at this period cultivated a closer intimacy with me than with our fellow-students generally under Professor Hosack's charge. Though morally correct, I made no profession of religion, and was not at all pious. But I have reason to thank Him who has all hearts in his hands that he inclined his servant to be specially friendly to me. I can trace many of my blessings to our intercourse all along from this early period to the last year of his devoted life.

"To any young man, attendance upon lectures in a large city, away from home influences, is a very dangerous trial. Multitudes of promising youth have thus been ruined. Even to a pious student it is full of peril, and always must be a painful ordeal.

"I can very distinctly call up Dr. Scudder's career as a medical student, and often reflect upon it as one of singular wisdom and firmness, and yet so softened and sweetened by Christian courtesy as to win for him the kindly regards even of the most thoughtless and worldly-minded of his fellow-students. Amid the tempting scenes and trials of patience in which he was placed at this time, I never witnessed in him the slightest departure from the purity, the rectitude, the amiability, or the calm dignity of the Christian character. This was so remarkable as to be universally felt, and to secure for him the respect of all. His presence among us had at least a powerful moral influence; and I can not but hope that, in the case of not a few, a still richer blessing flowed from it. I have continued reason to thank God for our early friendship.

"In May, 1815, Dr. Scudder was admitted to the degree of Doctor of Medicine. He decided to embark in the practice of his profession in the city of New York. I introduced him to the amiable family of the late excellent Mrs. Ruth Waterbury, into which he was at once admitted as an inmate. About a year afterward he was married to Harriet, the third daughter of Mrs. Waterbury. She was a young lady of rare personal beauty and winning manners, united with strong common sense, a soundness of judgment, a uniform cheerfulness of disposition, and a depth of piety which admirably qualified her for the wife of the future missionary. They knew not then, however, their high destiny, with its great trials and still greater usefulness. But He who knoweth the end from the beginning had doubtless fitted them for each other, and for the honorable and arduous work to which he subsequently called them.

"Here it may be well to remark that Dr. Scudder's mind and personal habits were eminently adapted to the medical profession. He was a close, accurate observer at the bedside, overlooking nothing, however small, that might throw light upon the case, and weighing every thing so calmly and judiciously as rarely to fail of a right decision; and when decided, none more energetic in carrying out his decision. It soon, therefore, became quite a general sentiment that, if professional knowledge, unwearied industry, soundness of judgment, and a most zealous, conscientious interest in whatever case he undertook were in the physician a sure ground of trust to the patient, Dr. Scudder's success was certain, and could not be long delayed. Accordingly, he very quickly found himself in the possession of a large and growing practice. Considering that he had no old-established practitioner to take him by the hand, or to make way for him, but had, single-handed, to build up his own fortunes, Dr. Scudder's success was without a parallel. The fifty-four years that have since elapsed have not supplied me with one other such example of rapid and sound professional advancement. His course was not that of the meteor, suddenly flashing upon us and soon extinguished, but like the steady growing light of the sun, in which all confide and rejoice.

"The particular incident which called Dr. Scudder's attention to the subject of foreign missions as a personal matter, and led him to give himself to the work, he related to me just after its occurrence. It was as follows. Upon visiting a patient, he took up a tract entitled 'THE CLAIMS OF SIX HUNDRED MILLIONS,' and carefully read it at the bedside. The Spirit of God thus brought the subject to his mind and heart in all its grandeur and the solemn weight of its responsibilities. 'What am I doing?' he thought; 'thousands may be found to seek wealth and reputation in the practice of medicine, but how few are willing to go and preach the Gospel! God helping me, I will, if my dear wife sympathizes with me. I will give up all, and go at once to the very ends of the earth, if need be, and preach Christ to perishing heathen.' After much communing upon the subject, and fasting, and much prayer, they both resolved, calmly, solemnly, immovably, *to live and die for Christ upon missionary ground.*

"It was in the year 1819 that Dr. Scudder made known the intention of himself and wife to go as missionaries to the island of Ceylon, under the auspices of the American Board. His announcement made a strong impression. The worldly stood amazed, not knowing what could induce a man who had realized so much, and whose prospects were so brilliant, to throw all these away, and embrace a life of toil, privation, and danger, among an ignorant, degraded people on the other side of the globe, there to wear out and die far off from home, and friends, and country. Some solved the difficulty at once; they pronounced him 'mad.' Even Christians were startled, it had been so uncommon at that day for an eminent professional man to give up every thing and go out as a poor missionary.

"But a large circle of Christian friends soon rallied

about him with increased affection, endeavoring to hold up his hands and those of his faithful partner, and to de- rive to their own souls also those rich blessings of grace which so rare an opportunity, and one that might never be enjoyed again, was calculated to impart. 'They glo- rified God in him.' A series of meetings for prayer and conference was held at his house and in those of Chris- tian friends. Well does the writer remember '*the feast of fat things*' which it was his privilege to enjoy on these occasions at that period with this dear servant of Christ and his beloved companion.

"A considerable company attended the departing mis- sionaries to the steam-boat, and there we took our leave, supposing that we should meet no more on earth. He went to the heathen to proclaim the 'unsearchable riches of Christ,' and I—not worthy of that high honor—staid at home to preach the Gospel as a pastor, or to labor here in some way to extend the Redeemer's kingdom.

"From the day that Dr. Scudder declared his inten- tion to go to India till the time of his leaving New York was a season of deep excitement. But he and his com- panion were calm throughout. 'What mean ye to weep and to break mine heart? for I am ready not to be bound only, but also to die at Jerusalem for the name of the Lord Jesus.' This was their spirit—not a stoical insen- sibility, but a holy composure, springing from a confi- dence in the Lord — solemn, joyful, and immovable. They entered into the spirit of the meetings held with them, manifested the liveliest sympathy with weeping friends, but were wonderfully supported themselves.

"The labors, trials, sufferings, and successes of Dr. Scudder and his devoted companion in Ceylon and other parts of India to which the Lord called them I pass over. The Missionary Herald, and his letters to the Board and Christian friends, will furnish his biographer with abundant materials for his public life abroad.

"After an absence of about twenty-six years, his health became so impaired by his toils and exposure in the climate of India as to make it necessary for him to try the effect of a temporary sojourn in his native land. Accordingly, he and Mrs. S. embarked for the United States, and here spent two or three years, during which his health seemed to be firmly re-established. In the meanwhile he was ' in labors more abundant,' visiting all the most important points in the land, addressing ecclesiastical bodies, lecturing to congregations, and especially endeavoring to excite an interest in the minds of children in behalf of missions.

"For the latter work few men ever exhibited so happy a talent. Every church in which he addressed children was crowded with them up to the very platform of the pulpit. He could hold them in breathless attention between one and two hours, and when he closed all seemed reluctant to depart. They crowded around him, each one striving to get his notice. Very many visited him at his lodgings, and none such were suffered to go away without much impressive counsel, and a present of some little book on missions. After his return to India he used to write most interesting letters to many of our Sunday-schools, and to some families in behalf of whose children a special interest had been awakened in his bosom. In these letters each little one was sure to be affectionately remembered. I feel very confident that multitudes of children in all the places where Dr. Scud-

REMINISCENCES. 283

der visited will be found to ascribe their first serious impressions to his influence. Very many such have doubtless already come to the Saviour; and many, won by his
counsels and example, have solemnly devoted themselves
to the missionary work. The Church at home and missionary stations abroad have yet to gather an abundant harvest from those labors of our beloved, departed
brother.

"During a large part of their stay in Cincinnati, Dr.
and Mrs. Scudder were pleased to make my house their
home. This I felt an indescribably precious privilege,
and I can see, every day since, that it is likely to be a
rich blessing even to the youngest of my children. It
has been greatly the means of drawing their attention to
the subject of Christian missions. All their pennies they
save up for this cause; and nothing is so interesting to
them as the publications of the Board, and especially
those private letters which Dr. Scudder was in the habit
of writing to me till the time of his decease. I trust
that this influence will never cease to operate till it
brings some of them also into the missionary field.

"Although we had been separated for upward of a
quarter of a century, yet I knew Dr. Scudder as soon as
he approached my house, though I had not been aware
of his arrival at the city.

"When he first went to India he was tall, very slender, of a fair complexion, and light hair; but upon his
return to the United States he was quite muscular and
portly, though his complexion and hair were unchanged.
Mrs. Scudder informed me, on that occasion, that when
the doctor left India he was feeble and reduced in flesh,
having passed through several attacks of jungle fever,

that it was hardly thought he would live to reach the
United States. In a few weeks, however, the sea air restored him to health, and rendered him, what he had
never been before—a stout, large man.

"Having been favored with the friendship of Dr.
Scudder, and knowing him so intimately from the period of our youthful studies, through 'all his walk with
God,' till he was not, for 'God took him,' I may be expected here to say something about the peculiar traits of
his character as a man, a Christian, and a missionary, and
of the influence he exerted. It would seem, however,
that little is needed here, for the larger part of his life
having been public, all who feel an interest in the Redeemer's kingdom must already know much of him.
But, in truth, they who know most of him are the very
persons who will desire to know more. Every scrap of
information that could be communicated concerning so
lovely a Christian, and so faithful a missionary of the
Cross, will be eagerly seized upon as suggestive of precious thoughts and profitable lessons.

"Let me here premise with a very brief notice of the
particulars of his death, as these were given in the peri-
odicals of the day. About six or seven years after his
return to India, and two or three years after the death
of Mrs. Scudder, he again became so enfeebled by his
indefatigable labors and attacks of disease that it was
thought advisable for him to take a voyage to the Cape
of Good Hope. Accordingly, he embarked for this purpose, accompanied by one of his sons. At the Cape he
was received very courteously, and especially by his
brethren of the Reformed Dutch Church. He immediately became much engaged in endeavoring to promote

the cause of missions. Just before the time appointed
for a public meeting for this purpose, in which Dr. Scudder had been announced to take a part, he retired to get
a few moments' rest. He was found lying apparently in
a placid sleep, but really in an apoplectic state, out of
which he speedily passed from his labors on earth to the
'rest which remaineth to the people of God.' 'Devout
men carried him to his burial, and made great lamentation over him.'

"1st. Dr. Scudder was pre-eminently a *wise and holy
man.* To this he owed his remarkable intellectual power and moral influence, which shone out not only in his
general course of conduct, but in whatever he said or did.

"The late Rev. Dr. J. L. Wilson, pastor of the First
Presbyterian Church of this city, observed to me, after
hearing one of Dr. Scudder's missionary lectures, that it
was one of the ablest and most interesting to which he
had ever listened. But it was just such, in point of ability and instructiveness, as were the many others delivered
in the different churches of our city. There was, indeed,
a striking uniformity in his efforts—I mean, uniformity
of power and interest. He seemed never to fall below
himself. This I know, for I presided at all these meetings.

"The same traits characterized his social and more
private intercourse. His conversation was always rich
in instruction and interest. You felt yourself in the
company of a *Christian gentleman*—remarkably such,
because *pre-eminently a wise and holy man.*

"In this respect Dr. Scudder was a striking example
of the power of the Gospel to invigorate, elevate, and re-
fine whatever is excellent in human nature. I had known

him from his youth; and frequently, in listening to his
public performances in Cincinnati, and while conversing
with him alone in the family or in my study, the thought
of him as a fellow-student in years gone by, and what he
now was, would often present itself to my mind. It was
manifest to me that the ordinary conventional Christianity of Christian lands never could have made Dr. Scudder what he was. In spirit, and wisdom, and tone of piety he was far above us all. Gladly have I sat at his
feet for hours, and felt myself richly profited. . Those
lofty views of Christian charity and obligation which we
pride ourselves for having at last barely arrived at, he
seemed to discern at once by a spiritual intuition, and not
only so, but spontaneously to act upon them. . To treat
all his brethren, of whatever name, who showed that they
loved the Lord Jesus Christ, was in him no special effort
of charity. He appeared incapable of doing otherwise;
and what we usually feel as privations, sacrifices, and con-
descension to the infirmities of others, never seemed such
to him. He manifestly stood on an eminence far above
us, and breathed a purer atmosphere, and could look over
and beyond those mists of pride, passions, and prejudice
that involve us. In looking *up* to him, I often asked
myself, Could any college course ever have given such
pre-eminent power and clearness to a mind not naturally
of great strength or brilliancy? I was confident it could
not. Would such wisdom and holiness be likely to grow
up under our systems of Christian training? I feared
not. The churches at home—the *common schools* of
Christianity—do not seem to have advanced so far in the
work of spiritual education. Only God's great *University*, the field of foreign missions, could form such a char-

acter as Dr. Scudder's. There, cut off from our chill-
ing expediencies, dwarfing precedents, and compromising conventionalities, and finding himself surrounded by
all the darkness, and abominations, and miseries of heathenism, in the midst of which Satan's throne towered
up and ruled supreme, he had no hope and help but in
the Word and Spirit of God. Free and untrammeled, he
came under the pure influences of the BIBLE—its glorious truths, its holy precepts, its precious promises, and its
only spotless *Exemplar.* By these was his mind trained,
and his whole character formed. Thus 'shut up to the
faith,' he came forth 'a perfect man.' No human system of education, not even our ordinary Christianity,
could have given him such strength, and wisdom, and elo-
quence. I have frequently remarked to friends that Dr.
Scudder was a living volume of the Evidences of Christianity far more convincing — especially to those who
knew him from the first—than even Butler's or Paley's
great argument. Nothing but the Bible could have lifted him to such an eminence of intellectual power and
moral influence.

"2d. Dr. Scudder united *extraordinary zeal with a
rare discretion and kindness.*

"True Christian zeal is an important grace; without it
little can be accomplished, but with it every other talent
becomes efficient for good. But our zeal may be so im-
prudently manifested as to make wise men afraid to co-
operate with us, or so unkindly put forth as to provoke
others into opposition, and thus may we not only fail of
accomplishing all the good we wish, but call out a large
amount of evil.

"And just in proportion to the intensity of zeal in the

bosom of any one is the danger of falling into the one
or the other, or both of these evils.   In such a character
great grace is the only safeguard; it alone can clothe
zeal with that discretion, and breathe into it that kindli-
ness of spirit which will be sure to command the confidence of the prudent, and make friends of all.

"Dr. Scudder was a striking example of the truth of
the foregoing remarks.   Though his zeal for Christ's
cause led him to say many things that could not but be
felt as strong rebuke by most Christians, and to propose
plans and methods of doing good which involved much
sacrifice, yet the pious every where gathered around him,
and readily fell into his plans and methods, and even the
worldly manifested no other than the kindliest feelings
toward him.   Hence, of all the returned missionaries that
ever left our shores, none, I am persuaded, went away
more beloved and respected among us; and yet his honest, glowing zeal impelled him to improve every occasion, private and public, to call sinners to repentance, to
rebuke the heartlessness and inconsistencies of professors,
and to point them to the loftiest standard of duty and
self-sacrifice.   But all this zeal was exhibited with a discretion and a kindness so rare that the most cautious
could find no reason for distrust, nor the most sensitive
any ground of offense.   And this trait of character leads
me to notice another.

"3d. His peculiar *talent for exciting others to effort.*

"His whole example, as a signally devoted servant of
Christ, had undoubtedly much influence here, and especially his ardent zeal, guided by prudence and tempered
by love; but it seemed also a specific power in him.   He
had the talent in a remarkable degree of inducing others

to co-operate with him, and of exciting others to do what he himself could not, or what it might not be proper for him to attempt. The working of this power within seemed to give him no rest. He was continually suggesting something to be done, some plan of usefulness, some new field of Christian enterprise. David says, 'He that telleth lies shall not tarry in my sight.' Dr. Scudder would have no idlers about him.

"4th. *Simplicity and disinterestedness* were prominent traits in Dr. Scudder's character. He had no concealment, and was incapable of art. His object, whatever it was, shone out, and he went openly and directly to it. Perfectly honest himself, it was difficult for him to suspect others of ill intention.

"He manifestly lived for the cause of Christ, and how any particular measure to promote this cause would affect his own interests never appeared to enter his thoughts. He was always ready to be any thing or nothing, as would most advance the divine glory. Believing himself called of God to the work of foreign missions, he cast himself unreservedly on his providence. He made no provision for infirmity, early death, or old age. If at the end of the year any thing was left of his salary, it was returned to the Board. And as he cast his care upon the Lord, so the Lord remarkably cared for him in providing for him a helpmate not only of devoted piety, but of uninterrupted health and active habits. Prudence, economy, and a thorough knowledge of domestic affairs in her left him free and unembarrassed to give up his whole time and strength to the duties of his ministry. And both he and she were spared till their numerous children could do without a parent's care.

N

" I have mentioned *devoted piety* as a characteristic of Mrs. Scudder. None but such a wife could have been suitable for him, however great her other excellencies. Dr. Scudder seemed deeply sensible of this; for while he valued those other excellencies and saw their importance, her piety was that which most endeared her to him, and called out his most grateful ascriptions to the Giver of every good and perfect gift. In a letter to me announcing the death of his wife, he dwells mainly on her character and labors as a Christian mother. '*She literally prayed her children into the kingdom*' was a part of his testimony on that occasion.

" 5th. Dr. Scudder was a *happy Christian.*

" That his sanguine temperament contributed much to his natural cheerfulness of disposition there can be no doubt; but such cheerfulness is a poor support in the trials of a missionary's life, and he who embarks in these with nothing but that to depend upon will assuredly fail. He must either sink under the burden or retire from the field.

" But Dr. Scudder was a happy Christian, not because his temperament was sanguine and his natural disposition cheerful, but because he habitually walked in the light of the Lord's countenance. Hence his spirit never yielded under the burden and heat of the day; and when bodily disease and infirmities drove him from the field, his heart was set upon a speedy return.

" He had long settled the great question that he was a child of God, and was engaged in his Father's work. Hence he gave himself no anxious thought for the morrow; all was bright and hopeful before him. He remarked to me, in a very interesting and instructive conversation during his stay at my house, that 'the thoughts of death seldom came across his mind; that they never troubled him; that he believed he had yet much work to do for the Lord, and that time would be given him for it.

"It would be easy and very pleasant to add to these reminiscences, but I must close—just now at least; and my age, with its increasing infirmities, renders much future effort of the kind quite doubtful. Indeed, one who knows my beloved, departed brother so well as you do can have little need of my communications—perhaps none at all—and yet I could not refuse your request."

To the Rev. Dr. Campbell.

"Vellore, October 26, 1855.

"MY DEAR BROTHER,—A few days since I wrote you a note from a bungalow while on a tour. I now sit down to redeem the promise then made that I would write you about my dear father. I knew him not only as a father, but also as a missionary, having labored for years by his side in the same mission. I shall try to sketch simply and briefly the main outlines of his character. I shall write freely, but be assured the portrait shall be a truthful one.

"1. *His physical frame was strong, tall, and well proportioned.* In his youth he was thin and sinewy, but in later life grew stout and portly. He had a sound, firm constitution, latterly much shaken and shattered by severe labors and exposures. His prominent and striking features, his erect bearing and commanding appearance, certified you, at a single glance, that he was a man.

"2. *He had a strong mind.* It chiefly resembled the

rugged, outstanding mountain, and yet it had characteristics which reminded you likewise of the gentle stream
flowing sweetly through the valley below. There were
great natural forces in his intellect. He investigated
those subjects which lay within the sphere of his work.
On them he concentrated his power, caring little for such
as lay beyond. He was a vigorous, able thinker. He
thought out his conclusions in straight lines of his own,
knowing nothing of circuitous approaches. Minor positions he left for others, himself content to seize upon
each important citadel until he became master of the
country. Whenever he took part in a discussion or treated a subject, all, no matter who might be present, were
constrained to feel the native strength and acknowledge
the majestic stride of his mind. Many excelled him in
length and breadth of information, and in acquaintance
with the writings of others, but few could gainsay or
withstand his plain, straightforward logic. If he moved
in a narrower circle than some others, it was like the
tread of a giant athlete within his own chosen arena,
compared with the gazing children who had come from
their sports over a wide plain.

"3. *He had decision of character.* This was manifest
to any one at first sight. His outward countenance was
the truthful index of the inward mental structure. There
was nothing facile in him. Every part of his composition was remote from such weakness. He could be de-
pended upon in any emergency. Convicted of an error,
none would be more ready than he to confess and aban-
don it; but where he had conscientiously taken up his
ground, earth and hell could not move him. He climbed
up to the hills and sought for light, and from that eleva-

tion he gazed and gazed till he saw the path of duty, opening out before him, and then, girding his loins, de_ scended to enter it without hesitation, whatever it might be. Hinderances were not heeded, nor consequences con_ templated. Having once heard the Word saying 'This is the way, walk you in it,' his soul summoned all its powers into one glowing response—'I WILL.' His thought and expression were of a peculiarly decisive cast where evil was concerned. A man who had been imposed upon by a counterfeit bank-note remarked to him that he could not pass it again, as that would be wrong. He replied, 'Wrong—yes, indeed! I would not do it to save my soul.'

"4. *He was endowed with perseverance.* Whatever he undertook he steadily pursued. He never relaxed his hold upon an object, nor retreated from a course which he believed to be right. Days, and months, and years might pass over him, but they found him still cleaving to his purpose. Harassing trials might encompass him, but they could not drive him from his design. So marked was this trait of his character, that, in thinking of it, I am reminded of the man who, when two hostile frigates were about to board each other, sprang toward the antagonist vessel, and seized the bulwarks with his hands. A cutlass blow divided both arms, but he hung on with his teeth. My father's perseverance was forcibly exhibited in his unremitted labors as a street-preacher. Apathy, ridicule, scorn, abuse, blasphemy, blows, stonings, physical languor, the natural shrinking of the spirit, and many other causes combined, could not force him to succumb in a single instance. That was his Lord's work, and must be accomplished statedly and perseveringly.

I well recollect that on one occasion he and I returned from a tour late at night. I went weary to bed before he retired. When I awoke in the morning, I found that he had gone out to preach in the streets. He would not rest even for that one day.

" 5. *He was capable of endurance, and willing to suffer.* He seldom spoke of pain, however severe. He had power to bear it. Fixedness of feature alone revealed it. Pain came in the course of a kind Father's providence, and was therefore to be borne with quietness. Many years ago a cancer appeared in his foot. Without telling Mrs. Scudder what he was about to do, he shut himself up in a room with a servant, and dissected out the malignant growth. It was a very painful operation, and he said that he just made out to get through it. Nevertheless, he did it without flinching. I feel sure that if a bed of fire had lain between him and his duty, he would have walked over it with the same composure as if it had been a bed of roses. Christ's sufferings were much in his mind. He was pleased to suffer for Christ's sake. Before God called him to the heathen, he was a physician just stepping into a profitable practice in New York City. Those who then began life with him in the same profession afterward became wealthy. So he might have become. After twenty years spent in India, he returned to his native land with a constitution racked by jungle fever. One night I was with him. He lay very ill upon a bed. There were but few of the comforts of this life around him. Languidly he opened his eyes, and, fixing his gaze upon me, alluded to the fact that he might have been rich, and that he had given up all worldly prospects for Jesus' sake, and expressed his satisfaction in having done so.

"6. *He was both stern and tender.* Wherever principles were at stake, he was rigid and unyielding. Men whose views were unsound, and whose practice was censurable, no doubt thought him severe. Did not the Pharisees think the same of Jesus?

"If there were less of compromising with evil, and more of open, manly, thorough resistance to it, would not the line of demarkation between the Church and the world be more plain, and the lives of professors be more pertinent and effective? Though he was thus stern in matters of right and wrong, he had a warm, kind heart, possessing deep fountains of tenderness and overflowing affection. He loved with the full energy of his spirit. Though a strict disciplinarian in his family, yet his children, if they wished a favor, would often seek it of him even sooner than of a fond mother. His eyes, from which personal suffering could extort no moisture, often ran with tears when Jesus' dying love was the theme of thought and conversation. At sacramental seasons his whole soul seemed to melt away at the foot of the Cross. Severity and tenderness are not incompatible. God is severe, and God is tender. Why may not regenerated humanity exhibit a miniature image of the divine heart, even as a drop of pellucid water may reflect, in perfect, though minute proportions, the sun which shines down upon it?

"7. *He was courageous.* Hell had once been his fear. That dread was now gone, and he feared nothing. It is dangerous for a missionary to enter the great temples in Southern India during their festival days. They can claim no protection from government there. Nevertheless, he went into one, and became involved in the throng which fills, on such occasions, those vast edifices. He could not find the way out again, and was obliged to wait till midnight, when he followed the procession which at that time left the temple. Any one there might have killed him with a single stroke, and the murderer never have been known. On one of his tours, an immense crowd being collected, a band of fierce Mussulmen demanded books of the bandy-man who was employed by my father to transport tracts, and when refused, one of them advanced brandishing a club, with which he, supported by his angry coadjutors, would no doubt have killed the bandy-man and my father also. With admirable self-possession, my father ran up to him, and, stroking his beard, exclaimed 'My brother! my brother!' This token of Oriental obeisance appeased his wrath, and quiet was restored. My father said that the danger was so imminent that the saliva in his mouth dried up instantly, leaving it parched as though by long thirst.

" 8. *The simple way in which his mind was determined to the missionary field is worthy of notice.* As I mentioned before, he entered life a physician; but there came a time when the wants and the woes of the heathen were brought clearly before him. It was thus. In professional attendance upon a lady, while in the anteroom, he took up a tract on which was inscribed the title 'The Conversion of the World, or the Claims of Six Hundred Millions, and the Ability and Duty of the Churches respecting them.' That tract brought him to India. The very copy through which God thus spake to him that night in that lady's parlor now lies on the table before me. Precious tract, written thirty-seven years ago, how wide and wonderful are the influences which have issued

from between thy humble covers! Under God, it is by
thee that I sit here writing these lines in this far-off land.
It is by thee that four of my brothers are missionaries
with me. Do I not recognize upon thy worn leaves the
impress of a divine hand?

" 9. *Before he was thus called he had been severely disciplined.* The Lord had caused him to pass through
spiritual conflicts of no ordinary kind. I will here record, in few words, the vivid impressions I retain of the
hints dropped by him concerning that awful period.
After he had found salvation in Jesus, and had united
with the Church, he was led out into a howling wilderness to be tempted. Satan was let loose upon his naked,
shivering soul. Faith and its foundations seemed gone
forever. He was in an agony to believe, but could not.
He doubted of all things—yea, even of his own existence.
Hope died within him, and Despair spread her pall over
him.. Every star went out in his sky. Satan and his legions assailed him on every side. He felt the flap of
their demon wings, and was poisoned by their blasphemous breath. Horrid thoughts, which could never be
uttered to mortal man, crowded thick and fast upon him.
His heart was like a sepulchre full of spectres. The terrors of hell rolled like quickly succeeding billows over
him, and he scarce got breath between. For many
months he ventured not to the communion table. Yet,
in the war and darkness of that fearful tempest, above
that wild ocean of anguish, there stood an unseen form,
the Holy One, the Crucified, who caused that gasping
soul, in all its blind struggles, to come nearer and nearer
to himself. He had once seen the Cross; he had once
been near it, and experienced its pardoning and sancti-

fying power, and it was still the magnet of his soul. He
kept his eyes on that point of the spiritual horizon where
he had seen it fade from view, and he never turned them
elsewhere. When God had sufficiently shown him Satan's power and his own weakness; when he had bruised,
and broken, and humbled him, then again he flooded his
sky with the light of the Sun of Righteousness. Satan
slunk away. Peace spread out her wings over his weary
heart, and the foretaste of hell's agonies was changed
into an antepast of heaven. While the storm raged, God
fastened him to the Rock of Ages as he never had been
fastened to it before. As the surge was sweeping him
away, grace guided it near the Cross of which he had
lost sight, and he got a death-grip of it, which nothing
ever after could loosen. He came out of these conflicts
like gold out of the fire. He began with calm joy to
climb the Delectable Mountains, and he from that time
dwelt mostly on their happy summits. These trials eminently fitted him to encounter the difficulties of the missionary work. He was to meet none so great as those
he had already overcome, and he was thrust forth a well-
equipped and experienced warrior, to carry the battle
with an intrepid spirit into the heart of Satan's territo-
ries—even to the grim, frowning walls of one of his oldest and strongest fortresses, Hindoostan. God had thus
prepared him, and then he called him to the mission
field.

"10. *My father was a Calvinist in his theological
views.* The doctrines of grace which he had experienced he found to be none other than those which Cal-
vin had experienced and stated. Though attached to
these doctrines, and to the Dutch Church as a sound ex-

positor of them, he was a man of most liberal spirit. All who owned and truly loved the Lord Jesus as the divine Redeemer from sin, he hailed as brethren beloved, and with them he was ready to work in the Lord's vineyard. He had not an iota of bigotry in him. His love was too real and comprehensive to allow it any footroom in his heart. While he, with Christian frankness and firmness, would maintain his own views if occasion required, he desired that others should enjoy the same liberty of thought which he claimed for himself. All things which affected not the essentialities of the faith once delivered to the saints were accounted by him as of minor importance, and not to be exalted into a position subversive of charity and fellowship.

"11. *He was entirely devoted to Christ.* I verily believe his *only* aim on earth was the glory of Jesus. Every thing was subordinated to this—was literally swallowed up in it. His eye was single. All the strong feelings of his strong nature were concentred in the holy passion of love to Christ. He loved the Saviour profoundly, tenderly, wholly. His was no half consecration. Jesus was the beginning, the middle, and the end of his life. It gives me true joy to look back and think how beautifully evident was the union of his soul with Jesus. The parable of the vine and the branch was in him sensibly demonstrated to us. I shall never forget the reply he made when I asked him to admire some flowers: 'Yes, my son, they are pleasant to me when I think that the Babe of Bethlehem made them.'

"12. *He took pains to maintain communion with Jesus.* It was one of the axioms of his spiritual life that if one would have fellowship with Christ, he must use the means for it. An hour and a half at early morn, and an hour at night, were always sacred to reading the Bible, meditation, prayer, and praise. In these seasons of morning and evening devotions, he chose some portion of Scripture, which he read and carefully pondered in connection with the marginal references. At noon he read the Bible regularly in course. Every Friday until midday was set apart as a special season for fasting and prayer. In latter years physical debility made it necessary for him to eat a little. His worship of God was not, however, confined to these appointed hours. These were never omitted, while others were often added. His heart was a shrine on the front of which 'JEHOVAH JESUS' was written, and from it a cloud of incense was always going up. He walked constantly with Jesus, and spake unto the Lord his Master by night and by day as he had opportunity. Prayer was no task, but the irrepressible instinct of his new-born nature. He told me that he wished to be one of the inner circle around Jesus in heaven. That was his ambition, and he lived near here, that he might also be near there. Living thus, he reaped fruits for his soul. His religion had no spasms. For years he had no doubt of his salvation. His soul was like one of our rich Oriental gardens, in which the numerous intersecting channels pervade every foot of the soil with full tides of water. Perfect assurance, like a river of God, rolled its calm, fertilizing volume along the course of every thought and passion. He was very fond of sacred music, both vocal and instrumental. To praise God was his delight. He said that was the employment of heaven, and he wished to enjoy as much of it on earth as he could. He spent much time in singing to the Redeemer, sometimes in hymns which he had learned, and sometimes in extempore composition. How often in the morning have I heard his voice soaring before the lark up to the gates of the New Jerusalem!

"13. *He was a Bible Christian.* Other books were comparatively nothing to him. He scarcely read any other. He never read a novel except the Vicar of Wakefield. God had become an author, and that was the book for him. Here, in the company of patriarchs, prophets, and apostles, with Jesus at the head as Lord of all, he strengthened his intellect and refreshed his heart amidst the toils and trials of a missionary's life. Next to Christ, Paul was the character he most admired. He sympathized more with Paul than with any other mere human being. While Jesus is the Sun of the Scriptures, is not the planetary world of Old Testament sages and New Testament saints prominently introduced because we have some grounds of sympathy with such beings as Paul, which we can not have even with our Lord? My father laid great stress on meditation. This he felt to be the food of the soul, and much of his devotions consisted in prayerful musing upon the divine Word. The Bible was his counselor. Man was in no sense his teacher. His mind was not constituted to bow to uninspired men, but before the Bible he bowed like a little child. I am persuaded that few men read the Bible so much, and meditated on it so deeply and persistently as did my father. This attachment to the Bible was one of the most observable facts of his life. When about to set forth to preach or perform some other duty, frequently the last act before leaving the house was to open the Bible, and catch some precious promise or stirring exhortation.

Thus he girded his loins. I need not add that he was a happy man. How could it be otherwise? He loved the innocent pleasantries of social life, and would mingle cheerfully in them when he had time.

"14. *He was a zealous Christian.* His zeal was no flickering flame—no smoking wick. It was a lustrous beam from the throne of God, shining through him upon the earth. It never grew dim and doubtful. He need-ed no preparation for a time of revival. God's work seemed always revived within him. He felt himself to be a soldier of Christ, so he did not unbuckle his armor nor sleep at his post. Jesus was his watchword. He wrote it on the banner which he carried high before him with a strong arm. When he went from India to Amer-ica in quest of health, he felt himself called to labor dili-gently among children, that he might make impressions in favor of a world's evangelization upon their tender hearts. A gentleman, remonstrating with him, told him he ought to consult his conscience lest he should over-work himself; to which he replied that he had 'quashed conscience *of that sort* long ago.'

"15. *He was faithful to impenitent sinners.* It was his resolve and constant practice to converse about their souls with all who came into contact with him. Be he cooly, hawker, servant, stranger, or friend—be he black or white, child or adult, poor or rich, he spake to all of Jesus and the great salvation. Even those who were on their guard against him could seldom outwit him, or foil him in his design. An English lady, high in rank and influence, called on him, and her daughter, having heard of Dr. Scudder's habits, determined not to see him, and remained in the carriage; but he managed, with politeness and kindness, to have a brief interview with her, and tell her the way of life. It was also his custom to have one or more unconverted persons as objects of special, continued prayer. To such persons he would sometimes write earnestly and solemnly, beseeching them to turn to the Lord, and declaring his intention to pray daily for them until a certain date, after which he should cease from such particular effort. God made him the means of many conversions. Among his tracts, the one entitled 'Knocking at the Door' has been much blessed. There are those both in heaven and upon earth who ascribe their union with the Saviour to his instrumentality.

"16. *He had the true spirit of a reformer.* What he saw to be wrong he struck at with no uncertain blow. Nothing could abash or intimidate him. Derision, threats, and the et cætera of opposition, whether individual or organized, fell like snowflakes upon his iron armor. When he came to India, missionaries drank wine. He drank it himself. All then believed it to be right. But as soon as the trumpet-clang of teetotalism smote, across the ocean, upon his ears, he stopped, examined the subject, decided that total abstinence was the only rational and righteous course, and he dashed the wine-cup from his table forever. He was obliged to encounter a determined hostility, but he wavered not, and rested not, till he established teetotalism in his mission. When he was sent to form, with another missionary, the Madras Mission, he assailed the whole community with his teetotal enginery. He was immediately made the object of virulent attacks from every quarter. Professing Christians and worldlings joined in the hue and cry. A caricature, purporting to be a description of his death and funeral obsequies, appeared in one of the English newspapers. Some persons even threatened to tar and feather, and ride him on a rail. Here also he steadily persevered. In a journal which he had established, he gave his adversaries harder knocks than they bestowed upon him, turned the tables upon them, routed them from their refuges of lies, and founded a flourishing teetotal society. Again, when the question of caste in the Christian Church was mooted, he studied it thoroughly, and put his hand vigorously to the extirpation of caste, root and branch. He was then a member of the Madura Mission. Led by him, they threw off this enemy which was feeding upon their very vitals, and from that day the course of that mission has been upward and prosperous. Thus he always acted. He never inquired whether there were many or few to attend him in any measure. Having satisfied himself as to the rectitude of his course, he marched on in it as though the whole world flowed with him.

" 17. *He was never disheartened.* He was asked in America, 'What are the discouragements in the missionary work?' He answered, 'I do not know the word; I long ago erased it from my vocabulary.' Nothing could cast him down. His obedience and hopes, being based upon the command and promise of the Lord, did not fluctuate with the changes of exterior events. Here was the command, 'Preach the Gospel to every creature.' Here likewise was the promise, 'My Word shall not return unto me void.' These furnished him with immovable foundations. Upon them he stood, and no opposition, however malignant and protracted; no exhibition of the human heart, however appalling; no obstacles,

however formidable; no reverses, however heart-rending, could dismay him. His work was simply to glorify
Christ by going forth bearing precious seed, with weeping and prayer, and then all the rest was the Master's
work, which he would accomplish in his own time.

"18. *He laid aside a tenth of his annual income for
the Lord's use.* He used to say that he wished Christians would cease talking about self-denial, and each one
give a tithe of his substance from year to year, and the
Lord's treasury would never want. He strove to induce
other Christians to conform to this standard. In his will
he directed that from the sale of his effects the first pay-
ment should be two hundred dollars to the American
Board, and if any thing more should be realized, each
son was to have twenty-five, and each of the two daughters fifty dollars.

"19. *He sought not the praise of men.* I feel quite
sure that it never entered into his mind, in any shape or
degree, as a motive of action. Obloquy could not de-
press, nor applause elate him. The esteem and love of
men were not desirable to him, if conditioned upon even
the slightest concession of principle or practice on his
part. Such concessions he never made. The Saviour's
approval was his aim. Beyond that he seemed not to
have a thought.

"20. *He was a pioneer in Indian missions*—a John
the Baptist appearing in this wilderness to herald the
coming kingdom of the Son of God among these wretched Hindoos. Almost every large town in this part of
India has heard his voice proclaiming salvation by Jesus. He made many extensive tours, distributing portions of Scriptures and tracts. While on one of these

journeys, he once stood laboring eleven consecutive hours
without moving from his post. He did not even stop to
eat, but had coffee brought to him. It was his habit,
when thus standing, to lean upon his left arm, and it was
supposed by his medical advisers that this was the cause
of its becoming paralyzed. When he left India to visit
America, it hung motionless by his side. He recovered
its use on the voyage. For some years before he died,
being physically unable to make long excursions into the
interior, he was accustomed to preach twice daily in the
city of Madras, except on Friday mornings, which, as I
before mentioned, were sacred hours. Thus he used to
preach thirteen times each week. When he heard that
his son Samuel, whom he expected would soon join him
as a missionary, was dead, he resolved that he would,
since so few came as missionaries to India, endeavor to
make up Samuel's loss by extra work on his own part.
So he commenced preaching thrice daily. Though I ex-
postulated with him, he thought he could endure it. He
soon broke down, and his first serious illness after I was
associated with him had its origin in this excessive labor.
I thought he would die, but, by God's mercy, he slowly
recovered. He subsequently preached twice daily, but
this was too much; and he gradually failed in health
until he was removed, in a very critical state, to the Cape.
There he seemed to rally, but it was the sudden upshoot-
ing of a flame just before it expires. He is gone, but
will never be forgotten. On the records of our Indian
Zion his name stands registered as a faithful evangelist,
an energetic pioneer. In the sky of India's night I see
his name shining forth like a lustrous star, not lone and
solitary, but associated with kindred luminaries, such as

Zeigenbalg, Schwartz, Rhenius, and Poor. He has left behind him a memory more valuable than thousands of gold and silver. He was a great man and a good man. May our gracious Lord raise up many like him in faith, and zeal, and labors, until every strong-hold of Satan in this land shall be laid low in the dust, and the temple of Immanuel shall be erected in such spacious proportions and attractive glory that the tribes of India shall be gathered as devout and happy worshipers within its solemn aisles!

"I hope, my dear brother, that this brief account may be of use to you in the work which you have so kindly undertaken. I have written very hastily, in the midst of many labors and cares. Please excuse all imperfections.

"I am very sincerely yours,

"HENRY M. SCUDDER."

The interest awakened among the children in Dr. Scudder, by his labors for their spiritual benefit, induced them, after his death, to erect a cenotaph to his memory. This beautiful marble monument, a representation of which is given on the following page, was placed by the General Synod in their Seminary grounds at New Brunswick, N. J.

THE END.

THE FIELD IS THE WORLD

REV. JOHN SCUDDER
BORN SEPT 3 1793 DIED JAN 13 1856

VALUABLE STANDARD WORKS

FOR PUBLIC AND PRIVATE LIBRARIES,

PUBLISHED BY HARPER & BROTHERS, NEW YORK.

For a full List of Books suitable for Libraries, see HARPER & BROTHERS'
TRADE-LIST *and* CATALOGUE, *which may be had gratuitously on application to the Publishers personally, or by letter enclosing Five Cents.*

HARPER & BROTHERS *will send any of the following works by mail, postage prepaid, to any part of the United States, on receipt of the price.*

MOTLEY'S DUTCH REPUBLIC. The Rise of the Dutch Republic. A History. By JOHN LOTHROP MOTLEY, LL.D., D.C.L. With a Portrait of William of Orange. 3 vols., 8vo, Cloth, $10 50.

MOTLEY'S UNITED NETHERLANDS. History of the United Netherlands: from the Death of William the Silent to the Twelve Years' Truce —1609. With a full View of the English-Dutch Struggle against Spain, and of the Origin and Destruction of the Spanish Armada. By JOHN LOTHROP MOTLEY, LL.D., D.C.L., Author of "The Rise of the Dutch Republic." Portraits. 4 vols., 8vo, Cloth, $14 00.

ABBOTT'S LIFE OF CHRIST. Jesus of Nazareth : his Life and Teachings; Founded on the Four Gospels, and Illustrated by Reference to the Manners, Customs, Religious Beliefs, and Political Institutions of his Times. By LYMAN ABBOTT. With Designs by Doré, De Laroche, Fenn, and others. Crown 8vo, Cloth, Beveled Edges, $3 50.

NAPOLEON'S LIFE OF CÆSAR. The History of Julius Cæsar. By His Imperial Majesty NAPOLEON III. Volumes I. and II. now ready. Library Edition, 8vo, Cloth, $3 50 per vol.

Maps to Vols. I. and II. sold separately. Price $1 50 each, NET.

HENRY WARD BEECHER'S SERMONS. Sermons by HENRY WARD BEECHER, Plymouth Church, Brooklyn. Selected from Published and Unpublished Discourses, and Revised by their Author. With Steel Portrait by Halpin. Complete in Two Vols., 8vo, Cloth, $5 00.

LYMAN BEECHER'S AUTOBIOGRAPHY, &c. Autobiography, Correspondence, &c., of Lyman Beecher, D.D. Edited by his Son, CHARLES BEECHER. With Three Steel Portraits, and Engravings on Wood. In Two Vols., 12mo, Cloth, $5 00.

BALDWIN'S PRE-HISTORIC NATIONS. Pre-Historic Nations; or, Inquiries concerning some of the Great Peoples and Civilizations of Antiquity, and their Probable Relation to a still Older Civilization of the Ethiopians or Cushites of Arabia. By JOHN D. BALDWIN, Member of the American Oriental Society. 12mo, Cloth, $1 75.

WHYMPER'S ALASKA. Travel and Adventure in the Territory of Alaska, formerly Russian America—now Ceded to the United States—and in various other parts of the North Pacific. By FREDERICK WHYMPER. With Map and Illustrations. Crown 8vo, Cloth, $2 50.

DILKE'S GREATER BRITAIN. Greater Britain: a Record of Travel in English-speaking Countries during 1866 and 1867. By CHARLES WENTWORTH DILKE. With Maps and Illustrations. 12mo, Cloth, $1 00.

LOSSING'S FIELD-BOOK OF THE WAR OF 1812. Pictorial Field-Book of the War of 1812; or, Illustrations, by Pen and Pencil, of the History, Biography, Scenery, Relics, and Traditions of the Last War for American Independence. By BENSON J. LOSSING. With several hundred Engravings on Wood, by Lossing and Barritt, chiefly from Original Sketches by the Author. 1088 pages, 8vo, Cloth, $7 00.

LOSSING'S FIELD-BOOK OF THE REVOLUTION. Pictorial Field-Book of the Revolution; or, Illustrations, by Pen and Pencil, of the History, Biography, Scenery, Relics, and Traditions of the War for Independence. By BENSON J. LOSSING. 2 vols., 8vo, Cloth, $14 00; Sheep, $15 00; Half Calf, $18 00; Full Turkey Morocco, $22 00.

SMILES'S SELF-HELP. Self-Help; with Illustrations of Character and Conduct. By SAMUEL SMILES. 12mo, Cloth, $1 25.

SMILES'S HISTORY OF THE HUGUENOTS. The Huguenots: their Settlements, Churches, and Industries in England and Ireland. By SAMUEL SMILES, Author of "Self-Help," &c. With an Appendix relating to the Huguenots in America. Crown 8vo, Cloth, Beveled, $1 75.

WHITE'S MASSACRE OF ST. BARTHOLOMEW. The Massacre of St. Bartholomew: Preceded by a History of the Religious Wars in the Reign of Charles IX. By HENRY WHITE, M.A. With Illustrations. 8vo, Cloth, $1 75.

ABBOTT'S HISTORY OF THE FRENCH REVOLUTION. The French Revolution of 1789, as viewed in the Light of Republican Institutions. By JOHN S. C. ABBOTT. With 100 Engravings. 8vo, Cloth, $5 00.

ABBOTT'S NAPOLEON BONAPARTE. The History of Napoleon Bonaparte. By JOHN S. C. ABBOTT. With Maps, Woodcuts, and Portraits on Steel. 2 vols., 8vo, Cloth, $10 00.

ABBOTT'S NAPOLEON AT ST. HELENA; or, Interesting Anecdotes and Remarkable Conversations of the Emperor during the Five and a Half Years of his Captivity. Collected from the Memorials of Las Casas, O'Meara, Montholon, Antommarchi, and others. By JOHN S. C. ABBOTT. With Illustrations. 8vo, Cloth, $5 00.

ADDISON'S COMPLETE WORKS. The Works of Joseph Addison, embracing the whole of the "Spectator." Complete in 3 vols., 8vo, Cloth, $6 00.

ALCOCK'S JAPAN. The Capital of the Tycoon: a Narrative of a Three Years' Residence in Japan. By Sir RUTHERFORD ALCOCK, K.C.B., Her Majesty's Envoy Extraordinary and Minister Plenipotentiary in Japan. With Maps and Engravings. 2 vols., 12mo, Cloth, $3 50.

ALFORD'S GREEK TESTAMENT. The Greek Testament: with a critically-revised Text; a Digest of Various Readings; Marginal References to Verbal and Idiomatic Usage; Prolegomena; and a Critical and Exegetical Commentary. For the Use of Theological Students and Ministers. By HENRY ALFORD, D.D., Dean of Canterbury. Vol. I., containing the Four Gospels. 944 pages, 8vo, Cloth, $6 00; Sheep, $6 50.

ALISON'S HISTORY OF EUROPE. FIRST SERIES: From the Commencement of the French Revolution, in 1789, to the Restoration of the Bourbons, in 1815. [In addition to the Notes on Chapter LXXVI., which correct the errors of the original work concerning the United States, a copious Analytical Index has been appended to this American edition.] SECOND SERIES: From the Fall of Napoleon, in 1815, to the Accession of Louis Napoleon, in 1852. 8 vols., 8vo, Cloth, $16 00.

BANCROFT'S MISCELLANIES. Literary and Historical Miscellanies. By GEORGE BANCROFT. 8vo, Cloth, $3 00.

DRAPER'S CIVIL WAR. History of the American Civil War. By JOHN W. DRAPER, M.D., LL.D., Professor of Chemistry and Physiology in the University of New York. In Three Vols. *Vol. II. just published.* 8vo, Cloth, $3 50 per vol.

DRAPER'S INTELLECTUAL DEVELOPMENT OF EUROPE. A History of the Intellectual Development of Europe. By JOHN W. DRAPER, M.D., LL.D., Professor of Chemistry and Physiology in the University of New York. 8vo, Cloth, $5 00.

DRAPER'S AMERICAN CIVIL POLICY. Thoughts on the Future Civil Policy of America. By JOHN W. DRAPER, M.D., LL.D., Professor of Chemistry and Physiology in the University of New York, Author of a "Treatise on Human Physiology," "A History of the Intellectual Development of Europe," &c. Crown 8vo, Cloth, $2 50.

BARTH'S NORTH AND CENTRAL AFRICA. Travels and Discoveries in North and Central Africa: being a Journal of an Expedition undertaken under the Auspices of H.B.M.'s Government, in the Years 1849–1855. By HENRY BARTH, Ph.D., D.C.L. Illustrated. Complete in Three Vols., 8vo, Cloth, $12 00.

BELLOWS'S OLD WORLD. The Old World in its New Face: Impressions of Europe in 1867–1868. By HENRY W. BELLOWS. 2 vols., 12mo, Cloth, $3 50.

BOSWELL'S JOHNSON. The Life of Samuel Johnson, LL.D. Including a Journey to the Hebrides. By JAMES BOSWELL, Esq. A New Edition, with numerous Additions and Notes. By JOHN WILSON CROKER, LL.D., F.R.S. Portrait of Boswell. 2 vols., 8vo, Cloth, $4 00.

BRODHEAD'S HISTORY OF NEW YORK. History of the State of New York. By JOHN ROMEYN BRODHEAD. First Period, 1609–1664. 8vo, Cloth, $3 00.

BULWER'S PROSE WORKS. Miscellaneous Prose Works of Edward Bulwer, Lord Lytton. In Two Vols. 12mo, Cloth, $3 50.

BURNS'S LIFE AND WORKS. The Life and Works of Robert Burns. Edited by ROBERT CHAMBERS. 4 vols., 12mo, Cloth, $6 00.

CARLYLE'S FREDERICK THE GREAT. History of Friedrich II., called Frederick the Great. By THOMAS CARLYLE. Portraits, Maps, Plans, &c. 6 vols., 12mo, Cloth, $12 00.

CARLYLE'S FRENCH REVOLUTION. History of the French Revolution. Newly Revised by the Author, with Index, &c. 2 vols., 12mo, Cloth, $3 50.

CARLYLE'S OLIVER CROMWELL. Letters and Speeches of Oliver Cromwell. With Elucidations and Connecting Narrative. 2 vols., 12mo, Cloth, $3 50.

CHALMERS'S POSTHUMOUS WORKS. The Posthumous Works of Dr. Chalmers. Edited by his Son-in-Law, Rev. WILLIAM HANNA, LL.D. Complete in Nine Vols., 12mo, Cloth, $13 50.

CLAYTON'S QUEENS OF SONG. Queens of Song: being Memoirs of some of the most celebrated Female Vocalists who have performed on the Lyric Stage from the Earliest Days of Opera to the Present Time. To which is added a Chronological List of all the Operas that have been performed in Europe. By ELLEN CREATHORNE CLAYTON. With Portraits. 8vo, Cloth, $3 00.

COLERIDGE'S COMPLETE WORKS. The Complete Works of Samuel Taylor Coleridge. With an Introductory Essay upon his Philosophical and Theological Opinions. Edited by Professor SHEDD. Complete in Seven Vols. With a fine Portrait. Small 8vo, Cloth, $10 50.

DU CHAILLU'S AFRICA. Explorations and Adventures in Equatorial Africa: with Accounts of the Manners and Customs of the People, and of the Chase of the Gorilla, the Crocodile, Leopard, Elephant, Hippopotamus, and other Animals. By PAUL B. DU CHAILLU, Corresponding Member of the American Ethnological Society; of the Geographical and Statistical Society of New York; and of the Boston Society of Natural History. With numerous Illustrations. 8vo, Cloth, $5 00.

DU CHAILLU'S ASHANGO LAND. A Journey to Ashango Land: and Further Penetration into Equatorial Africa. By PAUL B. DU CHAILLU, Author of "Discoveries in Equatorial Africa," &c. New Edition. Handsomely Illustrated. 8vo, Cloth, $5 00.

CURTIS'S HISTORY OF THE CONSTITUTION. History of the Origin, Formation, and Adoption of the Constitution of the United States. By GEORGE TICKNOR CURTIS. Complete in Two large and handsome Octavo Volumes. Cloth, $6 00.

DAVIS'S CARTHAGE. Carthage and her Remains: being an Account of the Excavations and Researches on the Site of the Phœnician Metropolis in Africa and other adjacent Places. Conducted under the Auspices of Her Majesty's Government. By Dr. DAVIS, F.R.G.S. Profusely Illustrated with Maps, Woodcuts, Chromo-Lithographs, &c. 8vo, Cloth, $4 00.

DOOLITTLE'S CHINA. Social Life of the Chinese: with some Account of their Religious, Governmental, Educational, and Business Customs and Opinions. With special but not exclusive Reference to Fuhchau. By Rev. JUSTUS DOOLITTLE, Fourteen Years Member of the Fuhchau Mission of the American Board. Illustrated with more than 150 characteristic Engravings on Wood. 2 vols., 12mo, Cloth, $5 00.

EDGEWORTH'S (MISS) NOVELS. With Engravings. 10 vols., 12mo, Cloth, $15 00.

GIBBON'S ROME. History of the Decline and Fall of the Roman Empire. By EDWARD GIBBON. With Notes by Rev. H. H. MILMAN and M. GUIZOT. A new cheap Edition. To which is added a complete Index of the whole Work, and a Portrait of the Author. 6 vols., 12mo (uniform with Hume), Cloth, $9 00.

GROTE'S HISTORY OF GREECE. 12 vols., 12mo, Cloth, $18 00.

HALE'S (MRS.) WOMAN'S RECORD. Woman's Record; or, Biographical Sketches of all Distinguished Women, from the Creation to the Present Time. Arranged in Four Eras, with Selections from Female Writers of each Era. By Mrs. SARAH JOSEPHA HALE. Illustrated with more than 200 Portraits. 8vo, Cloth, $5 00.

HALL'S ARCTIC RESEARCHES. Arctic Researches and Life among the Esquimaux: being the Narrative of an Expedition in Search of Sir John Franklin, in the Years 1860, 1861, and 1862. By CHARLES FRANCIS HALL. With Maps and 100 Illustrations. The Illustrations are from Original Drawings by Charles Parsons, Henry L. Stephens, Solomon Eytinge, W. S. L. Jewett, and Granville Perkins, after Sketches by Captain Hall. A New Edition. 8vo, Cloth, Beveled Edges, $5 00.

HALLAM'S CONSTITUTIONAL HISTORY OF ENGLAND, from the Accession of Henry VII. to the Death of George II. 8vo, Cloth, $2 00.

HALLAM'S LITERATURE. Introduction to the Literature of Europe during the Fifteenth, Sixteenth, and Seventeenth Centuries. By HENRY HALLAM. 2 vols., 8vo, Cloth, $4 00.

HALLAM'S MIDDLE AGES. State of Europe during the Middle Ages. By HENRY HALLAM. 8vo, Cloth, $2 00.

Romanism (Portuguese) Catholicism in the [...] in Churches, desertions: 66

Catechetical preaching: p. 77.

Revivals: 107-15, 118,

Differences of worship in various temples

Cholera: superstition, connected with.

Colleges, Scudder's interest in: 131. [...]

Superstitiousness of the people, & terror caused by it: 133.

Catechetical form of preaching: 77

Health, means necessary for preservation

Worshipping a book: 145.

Protestants of old churches: 159

Officials & English gentlemen, Dr Scudder's infl[...]

Mt. Holyoke Sem. Sem: interest in missions, able contributions to for. mis. ($1,000 a year).

Distribution & sale of small books:
    The Harvest Perishing
    Letter to S.S. Ch'n
    " on Juv. Mis. Soc's in S.Schools
    " To Little Girls: [...]
    Appeals to Bishops: [...]
Mis. Conventions: 93.

Professors in colleges, & teachers, responsib[...]

JLA

Form :

CPSIA information can be obtained
at www.ICGtesting.com
Printed in the USA
BVHW04s1804021018
529065BV00018B/157/P